THEOLOGY AND ETHICS OF OPPRESSED AND MARGINALIZED PEOPLES

THEOLOGY AND ETHICS OF OPPRESSED AND MARGINALIZED PEOPLES

Social Ethics and Agency in World Christianity

Edited by
NIMI WARIBOKO
and
RAIMUNDO C. BARRETO

PICKWICK Publications · Eugene, Oregon

THEOLOGY AND ETHICS OF OPPRESSED AND MARGINALIZED PEOPLES
Social Ethics and Agency in World Christianity

Copyright © 2025 Wipf and Stock Publishers. All rights reserved. Except for brief quotations in critical publications or reviews, no part of this book may be reproduced in any manner without prior written permission from the publisher. Write: Permissions, Wipf and Stock Publishers, 199 W. 8th Ave., Suite 3, Eugene, OR 97401.

Pickwick Publications
An Imprint of Wipf and Stock Publishers
199 W. 8th Ave., Suite 3
Eugene, OR 97401

www.wipfandstock.com

PAPERBACK ISBN: 979-8-3852-2648-1
HARDCOVER ISBN: 979-8-3852-2649-8
EBOOK ISBN: 979-8-3852-2650-4

Cataloguing-in-Publication data:

Names: Wariboko, Nimi, 1962–, editor. | Barreto, Raimundo, editor.

Title: Theology and ethics of oppressed and marginalized peoples : social ethics and agency in world Christianity / edited by Nimi Wariboko and Raimundo C. Barreto.

Description: Eugene, OR : Pickwick Publications, 2025 | Includes bibliographical references and index.

Identifiers: ISBN 979-8-3852-2648-1 (paperback) | ISBN 979-8-3852-2649-8 (hardcover) | ISBN 979-8-3852-2650-4 (ebook)

Subjects: LCSH: Social justice—Religious aspects. | Church and social problems. | Christianity and justice. | Church and the world.

Classification: BR115.W6 .T54 2025 (paperback) | BR115.W6 (ebook)

VERSION NUMBER 090225

Scripture quotations marked NRSV are from New Revised Standard Version Bible, copyright © 1989 National Council of the Churches of Christ in the United States of America. Used by permission. All rights reserved worldwide.

Dedication:
Adrienne Paris

Contents

Acknowledgments | ix
Contributors | xi

Introduction: World Christianity and Social Ethics | 1
　—Raimundo C. Barreto and Nimi Wariboko

Chapter 1
The Evasion of Ethics: Peter Paris Feels the Spirituals | 10
　—Nimi Wariboko

Chapter 2
Traveling Black Bodies: *The Spirituality of African Peoples* **and the Importance of Embodiment** | 34
　—Anthony B. Pinn

Chapter 3
Two Congolese Christians Epitomize Self-Initiation Principle in Their Quest for Justice and Fullness of Life | 53
　—Nyambura J. Njoroge

Chapter 4
Environmental Racism, Global Warming, and Human Flourishing | 74
　—Rubén Rosario Rodríguez

Chapter 5
The Impact of Afro-Brazilian Spirituality on Brazilian Culture and Christianity | 90
　—Raimundo C. Barreto

Chapter 6
Strengthening the Ties That Bind: Examining Peter J. Paris's Search for a Common Moral Discourse Among African Peoples and Its Implications for World Christianity | 119
　—Moses O. Biney

Chapter 7
Mapping African Christianities Within Religious Maps of the Universe | 135
— Afe Adogame

Chapter 8
Friendship, Love, and Justice as a Path to Christian Social Responsibility | 173
— Luiz Nascimento

Chapter 9
A Tribute to Peter Paris: Colleague, Teacher, Academic Statesman, Friend | 189
— Max Lynn Stackhouse

Chapter 10
Interview with Peter Paris: Roots and Routes of an African American Scholar | 202
— Nimi Wariboko

Index | 219

Acknowledgments

We would like to thank all the contributors to this volume, who stayed with us as the project suffered one delay after another. The project started in 2021, and we had planned that it would be released in either late 2022 or early 2023. Neither of us would have done this work without the contributors and their infinite patience and support.

Thanks to Stephen R. Di Trolio, a doctoral student at Princeton Theological Seminary, Princeton, and advisee of Raimundo, who did the copyediting, reformatting the chapters to conform to the publisher's demands (including each chapter's bibliography), and making sure the entire manuscript is in accordance to the publisher's style guidelines.

Our conversations with Wipf and Stock started early 2023, and Michael Thomson, George Callihan, and Matthew Wimer encouraged us, and their support made this publication possible. We are grateful for their support. Finally, we owe a debt of gratitude to Professor Peter Paris, whose excellent scholarship, masterful career, and virtues inspired this project.

Contributors

Raimundo C. Barreto, Associate Professor of World Christianity at Princeton Theological Seminary, Princeton.

Nimi Wariboko, Walter G. Muelder Professor of Social Ethics at Boston University, Boston.

Anthony B. Pinn, Agnes Cullen Arnold Distinguished Professor of Humanities and Religion at Rice University, Houston.

Nyambura J. Njoroge, Kenyan Presbyterian Theologian and Ecumenical Leader in Nairobi.

Rubén Rosario Rodríguez, Clarence Louis and Helen Steber Professor of Theological Studies at Saint Louis University, St. Louis.

Moses O. Biney, Professor of Religion and Society and African Diaspora Studies at New York Theological Seminary, New York.

Afe Adogame, Maxwell M. Upson Professor of Religion and Society at Princeton Theological Seminary, Princeton.

Luiz Nascimento, Dean and Professor of Religion and Society at Seminário Teológico Batista do Nordeste (STBNE), Feira de Santana.

Max Lynn Stackhouse, Rimmer and Ruth de Vries Professor of Reformed Theology and Public Life Emeritus at Princeton Theological Seminary, Princeton.

Introduction
World Christianity and Social Ethics

Raimundo C. Barreto and Nimi Wariboko

INTRODUCTION

During a consultation on the status of world Christianity scholarship at Emory University in the fall of 2018, a conversation erupted about areas and approaches still underdeveloped in this burgeoning field of studies.[1] One of those underdeveloped or even neglected areas identified in that conversation was social ethics. Although world Christianity studies are trans- and interdisciplinary, most scholars involved in this conversation come from history, mission, sociology, anthropology, and theology disciplinary backgrounds. Theologians are a minority. Very few scholars trained in social ethics are part of the guild.

In addition to that, despite its multiple origins, most of the initial developments in this burgeoning field came from historians and theologians whose work focused for the most part on the unprecedented demographic boom in African Christianities vis-à-vis the apparent numerical decline of Christians in the North Atlantic. The initial language in the rise of world Christianity as a field thus emphasized the demographic shift in world Christianity from the North to the Global South, especially to sub-Saharan Africa. Methodological concerns regarding the need to retell the Christian story from non-Eurocentric perspectives abounded. One of the pioneers in that kind of literature was British historian of missions, Andrew F. Walls,

---

1. While the editors of this volume see world Christianity as a field of study, and that seems to be an increasingly dominant view, other scholars see it as an approach to or as a subfield in Christian or religious studies.

who challenged missionary-centered historiographies of Christianity focused on transmission, which nurtured the self-proclaimed myth that held Europe and its US colonies as Christian lands and the non-Western world as the territory of missions, proposing, instead, an incarnational historical narrative, which emphasized the cross-cultural dimension in the writing of Christian history, paying particular attention to Indigenous-led processes of translation and conversion.[2] Lamin Sanneh took the translatability principle a step further by emphasizing the interpretation of Christianity from culture to culture and affirming the necessity of Christian diversity. In other words, he contrasted the normative universality of European culture with the translatable character of the gospel, showing how the latter helps Christianity break free from absolutizing cultural frames.[3]

Whereas the emphasis on indigeneity and vernacularity in early world Christianity writings have ethical implications, since they underscore Indigenous agency, very little is derived from that discussion to address asymmetrical power structures and the struggle for other dimensions of liberation beyond the cultural dependency. The work of Dana Robert pointing to the centrality of women's agency in the world Christian movement added concerns with gender and religious agency in world Christianity, which also have social ethical implications.[4] Yet, as Deanna Womack and Raimundo Barreto have shown, despite this initial progress toward the acknowledgment of women's agency, the field of world Christianity lacks any consistent engagement, for instance, of theological contributions from women, seldom engaging "feminist, womanist, mujerista, and other scholarly contributions from Global South women, including that produced by the Circle of Women Theologians in Sub-Saharan Africa."[5] The same can be said about other theological responses from minoritized, oppressed, marginalized, and discriminated groups. Such an engagement of justice concerns is important not only to fill significant gaps in the agenda of the field but also to interrogate world Christianity discourse itself, as for the extent to which it "may still perpetuate colonial mentalities and hegemonic norms or fail to recognize the diversity of Christian life expressions around the globe."[6]

This book addresses those demands not only by focusing on social ethical concerns and discourses but also by engaging Peter J. Paris's work as a critical conversation partner. Although not a self-identifying world

---

2. Walls, *Cross-Cultural Process in Christian History*, 29.
3. Sanneh, *Translating the Message*, 50.
4. Robert, "World Christianity as a Women's Movement," 180–88.
5. Womack and Barreto, *Alterity and the Evasion of Justice*, 8.
6. Womack and Barreto, *Alterity and the Evasion of Justice*, 8.

Christianity scholar, his work reflects an understanding of African spirituality and virtues which travels and can be retrieved and retooled in the Americas, which might be helpful for the development of approaches to social ethical concerns among world Christianity scholars.[7] The Pan-African and transatlantic approach to poverty seen in the reflections coming out of the network of scholars from the African continent and diaspora point to methodological tools which combine world Christianity concerns with Indigenous agency and comparative approaches to enable "the poor" to voice their "own understanding of their situation and lot in life under various historical and social situations," interrogating in conversation with one another "economic and social poverty and subhuman living conditions generated by the transatlantic and trans-Saharan slave trades, colonialism, postcolonial democracy, or military rule by African[s] themselves."[8]

Such an interaction not only enriches the toolkits in both world Christianity and social ethics scholarship but also pioneers conversations between two fields, which, although significant to each other, are still to interact more consistently and meaningfully, especially when issues such as poverty, global warming, and other challenges, while global in nature, also need to take particular agency and responses into consideration based on localized understandings of oppression and marginalization.

OVERVIEW OF BOOK

More specifically, this book focuses on both historical and theological developments in social ethics, and world Christianity and social ethics, especially ethical challenges and opportunities that face minorities, oppressed, marginalized, and discriminated groups in any country or region of the world. It addresses the issues of methods and practices in social ethics, culture and morality in Christian communities and theological discourse, and the virtues of Christian friendship in philosophical and practical terms. All these engagements are geared toward deepening our knowledge about the ethical dimensions of world Christianity. The authors of the ten chapters of the manuscript took as their point of departure the scholarship of the eminent African American Christian social ethicist Peter Paris, but by no means limited themselves to his work. Each chapter clearly relates to the broad theme of the ethics and agency of a specific group of marginalized and oppressed people in the world, even as they also reasonably or critically

---

7. Although focusing mostly on North America, Paris is fully aware of the extension of the African diaspora in Latin America and the Caribbean.

8. Paris, *Religion and Poverty*, xi.

engage with Paris's work and scholarship. Thus, the final product of the sum of their efforts is a collective searing critique of the ethical failures of world Christianity and contemporary global efforts at building just societies.

This book is a book on the subject of theology and ethics of oppressed and marginalized people anywhere in the world through the critical lenses of historical, theological, and social developments.

ORGANIZATION OF CHAPTERS

The book of ten chapters is divided into three parts. The first part (three chapters) deals with methodological issues in the study of social ethics and religion and society. In the next part (four chapters), we focus on the relationship between culture and morality at various sites and issues of world Christianity. Our authors explore key ethical concerns in Africa, Brazil, African Christianity, and the environmental crisis in the United States. The final part (three chapters) deals with the nature and character of Christian friendship. The authors cover the philosophical, theological, and empirical dimensions of the virtue of friendship. Two of the three chapters here focus on the virtue of friendship as exemplified in Paris's life.

"The Evasion of Ethics: Peter Paris Feels the Spirituals" is the opening chapter, and in it Nimi Wariboko explicitly interprets Peter Paris's work from the perspective of the elimination of racism in the United States as necessary for good human functioning of all persons. Paris reveals the relevance of the particular African American narrative context and the experience of racism in the study of ethics in the United States. Chapter 1 shows students how the commitment of African Americans to the eradication of racism nudges many of them to "evade" the establishment's definition of the subject matter of and approach to social ethics in the academy. Peter Paris is an exemplary scholar in this regard.

This chapter provides not only a systematic account of Peter Paris's theology and ethics but also a critical interpretation of his thought. Racism is identified as the major problem that has engaged Paris's academic career and at the same time the theological-ethical methodology he has developed to understand and explain it. He has been able to do all of this in ways that *evade* and challenge the American theological enterprise.

The primary theme of Paris's work is evading epistemology-centered ethics, exposing racism and injustice, and accenting the transformation of the structures of domination and subordination in the light of an ethical ideal, which is usually the thwarting of evil or actualization of human potentialities. In doing this, he converts ethics into a positive science of social critique and a cultural investigation of the social crises of the United States.

The importance of this chapter goes beyond interpreting Paris's thought, as it will be useful to scholars teaching ethics in general and African American ethics in particular. Paris's evasion of ethics is rooted in the Black religious tradition of ethical critique of American society in order to expose its moral limits and remind it of its blindness. The chapter, in also locating the thought of Paris in the deep ethos that informed the *spirituals*, reveals another major dimension of the African American ethical scholarship. Most importantly, by carefully discussing the ethical methodology of Paris in particular, this chapter clarifies that of African American ethicists in general.

Anthony Pinn continues the discussion of Paris's methodology, this time focusing on a neglected or poorly studied dimension of it: embodiment. In chapter 2, "Traveling Black Bodies: The Spirituality of African Peoples and the Importance of Embodiment," Pinn examines the epistemological linkage between Africa and the African diaspora animated through various processes and performances of religiosity. This attention to processes and performance is rooted in the theological and ethical importance of the Black (embodied) body and the manner in which Black bodies retain and transmit information. He then explores the sense of shared moral insight ethicists and theologians might gain when they highlight the significance of Black bodies in making the Western world. The high point of Pinn's essay is his provocative search for the meaning of embodied religious-theological memory for the Black theological tradition as an embodied discourse.

Nyambura J. Njoroge takes up the issue of the body and the body being in pain; bodies violated, and dehumanized, bodies made to endure perpetual poverty. She goes on to narrate how such bodies and selves have taken the initiative to protect themselves and create an environment that will enable them to thrive, if not flourish, by forging a communal ethics rooted in Christianity. In chapter 3, "Two Congolese Christians Epitomize Self-Initiation Principle in Their Quest for Justice and Fullness of Life," she discusses the principle of self-initiation as a method for the ethical study of means of eliminating poverty in marginalized and oppressed communities. In this chapter, she situates the "self-initiation principle" and its theological and ethical implications in the life and ministry of some Congolese Christians (Presbyterians and Pentecostals). She explores how Congolese Christians have made a covenant with life in the deeply entrenched institutionalized violence and inhumanity of the postcolonial Democratic Republic of Congo's greed and terror.

Institutionalized violence and dehumanization are not the only concerns of Christian ethics or world Christianity. The environmental crisis has long risen to the top of the agenda of the two fields. Rubén Rosario Rodríguez in chapter 4, "Environmental Racism, Global Warming, and Human Flourishing," the opening essay of part 2 of the book, carefully dissects how climate change disproportionately affects the poor, reflecting generations of colonialism, racism, and political marginalization. Environmental racism, a systemic problem whereby communities of color suffer from policies and practices that force them to live in proximity to sources of toxic waste such as sewage works, mines, landfills, power stations, major roads, and other emitters of airborne particulate matter, has become a global problem. The COVID-19 pandemic further exposed existing racial and economic disparities, heightening the need for a theological response that seeks to transcend *political* emancipation in favor of *human* emancipation focused on preserving the basic dignity of every human life. Rodríguez, in this chapter, describes the type of theological response that accents the basic dignity of the oppressed and marginalized peoples. This response is exemplified by African and African American moral tradition. Drawing his conclusion from the scholarship of Peter Paris, Rodríguez maintains that

> The truest form of the African and African American moral tradition is distinguished by its commitment to liberating the oppressed. Accordingly, a black ecological ethics is not in competition with a black theology of liberation. Rather, it is a manifestation of black liberation given the intersection of racist oppression and environmental exploitation under the stranglehold of white supremacy. In solidarity with their black and brown brothers and sisters around the world, black voices—like those in Flint, Michigan—need to prophesy against the corruption and ungodliness of modern capitalism and cultural imperialism.

Raimundo C. Barreto deepens our comprehension of the challenges facing world Christianity in a country like Brazil, where Black Brazilians endure dehumanizing inequality and discrimination, even as they have significantly contributed to Brazilian Christianity. Barreto provides us with a fascinating account of the interplay between skin-color discrimination and the cultural creativity of Black Brazilians as veritable insight into the indestructible agency of oppressed and marginalized peoples. In chapter 5, "The Impact of Afro-Brazilian Spirituality on Brazilian Culture and Christianity," Barreto discusses the impact of Afro-Brazilian spirituality upon Brazilian Christianity, shedding light on Afro-Brazilian contributions to the formation of the Brazilian cultural and religious mosaic. It highlights the agency of Afro-Brazilians as social, religious, and cultural actors who have not only resisted colonial and neocolonial efforts to whiten Brazilian culture but have also positively contributed to the formation of Brazilian identities through a dynamic relation with their African roots. Despite centuries of discrimination, persecution, and suppression, Afro-Brazilian spirituality has survived in different forms and must be considered an important shaper of the religious landscape in Brazil, more specifically of Brazilian Christianity.

We have come to chapter 6, "Strengthening the Ties That Bind: Examining Peter J. Paris's Search for a Common Moral Discourse Among African Peoples and Its Implications for World Christianity." Here, Moses Biney seeks to do three interconnected things. Biney examines Peter J. Paris's contributions to the fields of theology and ethics and in addition to exploring and interrogating his vision of unity and ethical discourse among African peoples. Finally, he outlines broader implications for the study of world Christianity, particularly among African peoples in a diverse and interconnected world driven by migration and transnationalism. Biney demonstrates that Paris's emphasis on community-centric ethics provides world Christianity with a robust paradigm for cultivating a sense of shared responsibility and interconnectedness. Biney argues that Paris's work serves as a clarion call for Christian communities to immerse themselves in dialogue and learning across various cultural and theological traditions. Such engagement is vital in navigating the plurality within the Christian faith, allowing for a deeper appreciation and respect for the diversity that characterizes the global Christian community.

Afe Adogame in chapter 7, "Mapping African Christianities Within Religious Maps of the Universe" expatiates on the history, dynamism, spirituality, and theological issues of African Christianity that Biney pointed out in chapter 6.

Adogame narrates the story of African Christianity as one of faith in motion. Taking a *longue durée* view of the history of Christianity on the continent, he provides insights into its dynamism and innovation, creativity, and relevance. He identifies certain academic narratives that have, in his view, hampered proper study of Christianity in Africa. As he puts it:

> Such hegemonic discourses obscure the rich flavor and flowerings of Christianity just as it reifies its homogeneity as opposed to its heterogeneity. Such power dynamics seem to caricature the dynamic nature of Christianity as a faith that transcends geographical, racial, social, ethnic, cultural, class dichotomies; a

faith that can germinate and survive in both conducive and unfavorable conditions; one that responds to both local and global stimuli; one that has the potential to speak all languages either mundane or esoteric. It is also a faith that can survive in oral and written cultures; one that is resilient but transforms and changes in historical perspectives.

The final part of the book opens with Luiz Nascimento's chapter 8, "Friendship, Love, and Justice as a Path to Christian Social Responsibility." Returning to the task of addressing the plight of poverty in world Christianity, Nascimento explores how the virtue of friendship might help social ethicists and students of world Christianity to reconstruct social existence that gives preferential option to the poor. Most theological ethicists believe that poverty is a social barrier that impedes the movement of the oppressed and marginalized peoples toward the realization of their potentialities, thus causing their suffering. Luiz Nascimento uses the Christian notion of friendship and responsible self to ground liberationist "preferential option for the poor," a sound manifestation of Christian love in pursuing the common good. He demonstrates that friendship (seeking the human flourishing of others) toward the poor reduces the disenfranchisement of minorities in the social order. This kind of friendship needs to be deliberately constructed. As he puts it, "If moral virtues and a well-lived life are the result of a cultivated experience in life, then it needs to be understood as a communal construction, as something that is learned in contact, interaction, and shared experience with others. Friendship constitutes a crucial element in the cultivation of virtue."

Max Lynn Stackhouse, who died before this book could come to fruition, continues the focus on the construction of social ethics to address the plight of oppressed and marginalized people. Drawing from his decades of friendship with Peter Paris and careful attention to his scholarship over the same period, he offers in chapter 9, "A Tribute to Peter Paris: Colleague, Teacher, Academic Statesman, Friend," a chapter that offers a rare perspective on the intersection of friendship, scholarship, and fervent commitment to social justice in Christian living. In addition, he deploys the academic work and social life of Paris to illustrate how scholars operating from a minoritized position construct social ethics to move their societies toward equity and justice, "to form and maintain an inclusive and equitable community grounded in a common ethic."

The book concludes with a sit-down section with Peter Paris, "Interview with Peter Paris: Roots and Routes of an African American Scholar." Nimi Wariboko, a former student of Professor Peter Paris, conducted an interview with him to explore his early experiences in Nigeria. After graduating from seminary, he visited Nigeria twice to serve the Student Christian Movement. His visits to Nigeria greatly influenced what he later became both as man and as scholar. Paris's sojourns in the 1950s and sixties in Nigeria were made possible by the commitment to world Christianity and trans-regional Christian friendship by him and those who supported and mentored him.

BIBLIOGRAPHY

Paris, Peter J., ed. *Religion and Poverty: Pan-African Perspectives*. Durham: Duke University Press, 2009.

Robert, Dana L. "World Christianity as a Women's Movement." *International Bulletin of Mission Research* 30.4 (2006) 180–88.

Sanneh, Lamin O. *Translating the Message: The Missionary Impact on Culture*. 2nd ed., rev. and exp. Maryknoll, NY: Orbis, 2009.

Walls, Andrew F. *The Cross-Cultural Process in Christian History: Studies in the Transmission and Appropriation of Faith*. Maryknoll, NY: Orbis, 2001.

Womack, Deanna Ferree, and Raimundo C. Barreto, eds. *Alterity and the Evasion of Justice: Explorations of the "Other" in World Christianity*. Vol. 5. Minneapolis: Fortress, 2023.

Chapter 1

The Evasion of Ethics
Peter Paris Feels the Spirituals

Nimi Wariboko

OPENING WORD

THIS CHAPTER CRITICALLY AND constructively reflects on the methodology, style, and goal of the ethical analysis of Peter Paris, an eminent African American ethicist. His approach is to start from the lived experiences of African Americans, putting this ahead of normative reflection, authoritative teachings, or divine revelation. Yet, a theoretical or methodological framework and assumptions organize the discourse. Part of my task in this chapter is to unveil the skeleton of the framework for students to see or appropriate for their own scholarship.

This unveiling will also offer practical wisdom on the connections between analysis practices, a habituated and embodied sense of engagement with the present situation, and a theoretical model of analysis. In this way, the students are led to engage with the varieties and nuances of ethical analyses as they develop their own voices or styles of ethical evaluation.

This chapter shows Paris's work as a model of ethical discourse or "reasoned speech." I want the reader to also pay attention to how the discussion of Paris's ethical methodology plays into ethical reasoning or presentation. His work is analyzed according to a three-pronged format: (a) a statement of the ethical problem that threatens the moral fabric of the American society,

(b) the sources of theology and philosophy he brings to bear or shed light on the problem, and (c) solution. His goal is to eliminate racism in the United States. The "ethical window" he opens for us to see an alternative to the current situation in the United States is clearly highlighted.

CHAPTER INTRODUCTION

The thesis of this chapter is that Peter Paris evades ethics, meaning he disregards and transcends the dominant ethical theories of the late twentieth and early twenty-first centuries. He refused to discuss dominant ethical theories and ethical questions abstractly, seeking universally valid principles. Rather, he transitioned from abstract, epistemology-centered ethics to the more contextual approach of comparative and social-problem focused ethics. This inclination in his thought is due to the one all-pervasive evil of racism that casts a shadow on American society and his native Canada. This evasion of ethics has an affinity with Latin American liberation theology, the dominant theological-ethical paradigm at the time he came of academic age in the 1970s and 1980s. While for liberation theologians the one all-pervasive evil was the capitalist system, for him it was the contempt and discrimination suffered by Black people in the United States and Canada.

The vexing problem that engaged Peter Paris's academic career is racism. In the corpus of his work he has tried to understand and explain the experience of racism and at the same time develop a theological-ethical methodology that is adequate for his subject matter. The aim of the methodology is to unconceal the experience of racism and the responses to it in Black religious practices in ways that evade and challenge the American theological enterprise.[1]

---

1. Paris is conscious of the need to develop a methodology for and to express the meaning of his work for Black theology. He criticizes James Cone for failing to do this in his work:

> Cone does not discuss the implication of this study [*Martin and Malcolm*] for theological methodology. . . . One does not expect a major systematic theologian to write such an important work as this and make virtually no explicit reference to constructive theology. Cone's decision not to explicate the meaning of this book for black theology is very troublesome. (Paris, "Review of 'Martin and Malcolm,'" 87–90, quote p. 90.)

What Paris means by Cone's failure to explicate the meaning of the book for Black theology is not very clear. So I sent an email to him to shed more light on his critique. He responded:

> My criticism of Cone is that his book is a fine comparative analysis of Malcolm and King; but there is no indication in the book that it is being

This chapter not only shows how Paris evades ethics but also highlights the creative role of feeling in his work. He is in solidarity with suffering Black people, and his anguish has profoundly nourished his intellectual work. His feelings are anchored to the history of slavery, discrimination, and suffering of Blacks in North America and are grounded in a vision of love, hope, equality, and justice.

At their best, his essays exude the rueful lamentation of a "motherless child" mingled with the hope of escape from the misery of alienation and degradation to *heaven*.[2] Like the old spirituals, Paris's ethical analyses are conversations with America about Blacks' experience of pain and suffering, struggle and striving, and the unity of protest and hope in their religious thought—all carried out in plaintive tones and sad rhythms.[3] With the simplicity of his prose, precision and clarity of thought, and the evocative power of his analytical descriptions, his essays have a mournful beauty to them.

In doing all this Paris avoided being driven and tossed by the winds of flavor-of-the-period philosophies and theories, especially those from Europe that easily beset and beguiled lesser self-controlled and self-confident ethicists in the four decades that he actively thought, researched, and wrote. Not so moved, he endured in his task of rendering in concrete (never abstract and highfalutin) terms the experience of racism. For Paris, ethics is about identifying concrete problems that threaten the moral fabric of a community and seeking to address them with the best of theological, philosophical, and social scientific resources. And the goal of good ethical reasoning is to advance human flourishing. As he puts it in the introductory lecture of his 2008 Harvard University course on the "Ethics and Politics in Black America":

---

done by a black theologian. As I read the book I kept waiting to see how these two men related to Cone's black theology project. What do they exemplify in that context? Since neither of them appears to be exemplars of black theology, why does a black theologian choose to write a book about them? Is it that they represent the ambiguity that African American identity entails and which black theology addresses? In any case, Cone does not provide any answers to such questions. Thus I was disappointed with the book because I think he should have told his readers how these men related to his central project which is the construction of black theology. (Paris, e-mail message to author, April 14, 2010.)

2. For his understanding of heaven or rather the notion of heaven in the spirituals as a principle of social criticism, see Paris, "When Feeling Like a Motherless Child," 113; Paris, "Linguistic Inculturation," 80–81, 89–90; Paris, "Problem of Evil," 304.

3. I have adapted Paris's words from "When Feeling Like a Motherless Child," 115–16, for my purposes here.

> In my perspective, ethics always takes as its point of departure some concrete actions, deeds, practices performed by persons or groups of persons. In this sense, ethics is always empirical and its aim is to discern the nature of the good or the right or the appropriate inherent in some actual occasion and to describe its limits and possibilities; i.e., what values are sacrificed or not allowed to see the light of day and the difference it would make were things to be otherwise.[4]

The primary concrete problems of the United States are lingering racism and poverty, and ethicists must endeavor to inform thinking on them. In the twentieth century the color line, in the language of W. E. B. Du Bois, was the problem. In the twenty-first century it is still here, but Paris adds to it "poverty both at home and abroad."[5] Social ethicists of the twenty-first century must aim at expanding and enhancing moral community by eliminating all obstacles to life, eradicating policies, institutions, and patterns of behavior that thwart flourishing life.

In thinking about racism and poverty, several questions preoccupied Paris for nearly half a century. How can the moral problems of racism and poverty be solved? How can the social structures that sustain them be changed for the good of the oppressed, marginalized, and poor persons? What have been the thoughtful public responses of African Americans to these problems? Did the responses arise from how American citizens (both Black and white) deliberately and intentionally worked to reorder human relations so as to include those excluded from participating at the bounteous table of this great nation? For him, social ethics begins when the citizens of a country start reasoned discourses about the quality of the human relations, actions, and practices that sustain the problems that threaten their society's moral fabric, with a view to reordering society for the better. His publications have captured some of the most reasoned discourses of African American leaders on racism and poverty. In this Parisian way of approaching the social problems faced by African Americans, ethics and politics are inseparable.

Though trained in major philosophical and theological discourses of the twentieth century, as well as ancient Greek thought (especially that of Aristotle), much of Paris's creative thinking has drawn strength and direction from the struggle for freedom and justice in his African American heritage. The primary aspects of this heritage that inform his work are its politics and ethics. The politics of African Americans is the ethical critique

---

4. Paris, "Ethics and Politics," 4.
5. Paris, "African-American Religion," 487.

of the American society in order to create a flourishing life for Blacks in this country, not only for them but for all Americans. Du Bois stated this clearly in *The Souls of Black Folk* by stating that one of the three important gifts of Blacks to the United States is an ethical critique of the society to expose its moral limits, to remind it of its blindnesses and silences in white America's reflections on the nation's problems, and to enhance its morality.[6]

According to Paris, "African American political leaders have been forced by the nature of their primary concerns to keep the moral problem of racism clearly visible on the political agenda. And that has constituted their unique contribution to the nation's moral life."[7] Paris's work has therefore focused on making visible to the world the oppression of Blacks that has been systematically and carefully concealed from the public, but more importantly, the gallant ways Blacks have responded to their oppression with virtues of love, forgiveness, and redemption or reconciliation.

With this sort of cultural investigation or academic approach to America's social crises, some scholars may be led to argue that Paris has not done ethics, but evaded it. He avoids ontological abstractions, metaphysical language, or philosophic speculation, but always looks carefully into areas of human experience in which resistance to injustice and passion for actualization of creative potentials are central. For instance, while others may write tomes on how racism is socially constructed and historically constituted, he will prefer to expose the structures of oppression and profile Blacks' experience of it and their responses to alter their situation.

Paris converts ethics into a positive science of social critique. He insists both in his classroom lectures and academic publications that such a critique must be specific and particular. For him the nature of such critique—and for that matter, ethics—is to discern the nature and dynamics of the threats to human flourishing in every particular sociality. And this it can only do in direct confrontation with concrete, present threats to the moral fabric of the sociality, and never as abstract analysis or argument, never in advance or once and for all.

For him, this commitment to ethics as defeasible and incompletable—as social critique—means that one cannot set down a definitive method for doing ethics or replicating any major work of ethics. Paris does not want to convert concrete criticism into a philosophy of social science (humanities) or a paradigmatic methodology. For him, neither social criticism nor the

---

6. Du Bois, *Souls of Black Folk*, 205, 214–16. See also West, *American Evasion of Philosophy*, 143.

7. Paris, "Ethics and Politics," 5.

process of gathering facts and assessing values about a particular configuration of social relations can or need be totalized.

My interpretation of Paris's work as an evasion of ethics demands a more sustained argument, as this will enable me to show the prophetic dimension of his scholarship, which is a key to understanding his commitment to ethics as social critique. I am using the word *prophetic* in the special sense given by Cornel West: "The basic contribution of prophetic Christianity, despite the countless calamities perpetrated by Christian churches, is that every individual regardless of class, country, caste, race, or sex should have the opportunity to fulfill his or her potentialities."[8]

THE EVASION OF ETHICS

There are ethicists who do ethics and there is Paris who does ethics by evading ethics. Those in the first group engage in the following kinds of ethics. There is epistemology-centered ethics; that is meta-ethical views of cognitivism and noncognitivism. These involve inquiry into or debate about the basis of objective moral knowledge. There is theory-centered ethics, in which scholars fiercely debate whether ethics is truly about duty (obedience to law) or telos to be achieved (or aimed at). Yet others debate the merits and demerits of general theories or proper definitions of words like *good*, *right*, or *virtues*. There are also ethicists who are committed to the bifurcation of the "ought" and the "is" and see its violation as accenting to the "vulgar systems of morality." There are still others who work from facts or common knowledge and from such derive some ultimate principle. Finally, there are scholars working to provide a full, systematic method of doing ethics. The most common thread of these approaches to ethics is that they are removed from the practical, urgent problems of society. Their advocates pride themselves in transcending the quotidian human struggles for identity, dignity, freedom, and survival.

Peter Paris evades all these by turning away from the wispy cloud of theories floating as a halo over the earth to stand firm on the terra firma of actual moral problems. He aims to illuminate practical problems by forcing theories to touch the ground. As most of his former doctoral students will attest, Paris will listen patiently to a brilliant presentation, wearing a smile of approval, only to ask with the intense concentration of an Olympic gymnast on a slim iron bar, "Where do all these touch the ground?"[9] An ethical work touches the ground when it is on the side of human freedom and affirms

---

8. West, *Prophesy Deliverance*, 16.
9. I was a doctoral student of Paris's at Princeton Theological Seminary, Princeton.

human flourishing in its broadest sense. It can only do so when it starts by focusing on concrete problems and finding ways to liberate the agents trapped in them. Thus he declares:

> An inquiry in social ethics should begin with some actual, concrete problems arising among human beings in their public actions. That is to say, such an investigation should begin with some conflicting views about the good that humans can and should do. . . . The result of such an investigation should be some resolution of the problem or a restatement of the problem in order to liberate the agents and their activities and to establish thereby the conditions for more creative enterprise.[10]

The primary theme of Paris's work is evading epistemology-centered ethics (conscience-centered, fundamentals-centered, revelation-centered, or philosophic/biblical absolutism), exposing racism and injustice, and accenting the transformation of the structures of domination and subordination in the light of an ethical ideal, which is usually the thwarting of evil or actualization of human potentialities.[11] The far-reaching appeal of his thought lies in its commitment to social and cultural criticism, moral emphasis, and vitality for transformation. For Paris social ethics is a form of cultural criticism, cultural investigation of injustice, and the clarification of its solutions in the light of a religious and/or ethical ideal.

His preoccupation with evading ethics determines his methodology of ethical analysis or argumentation. His ethical analysis starts with a definition of the problem or a description of the ethical concern. Once the problem is adequately identified and laid out, he will undertake a social scientific examination of it and then provide a theological-ethical interpretation. Next, he will point his readers to likely solutions to the problem that is threatening the moral fabric of the given community. The accent of the solution is always political, on reordering of the human relations in the community.

He sees every solution, whether suggested by him or inherited, as ultimately subject to the law of transformation in history. In this light every institution and tradition—especially the ones that buoy up racism, injustice, and poverty—are dissolvable by the power of this law that holds them fluid, protean, and dynamic. Human relations may be perfect for a historical moment but are never complete. All social practices or ordering of human relations are revisable and contingent. He argues that "societies are not natural constructs. They were designed and built by humans and each one could

---

10. Paris, *Black Religious Leaders*, 31–32.

11. This way of interpreting Paris's work was fueled by intellectual stimulus I got from West, *American Evasion of Philosophy*.

have been different than it is. They are not controlled by the laws of nature even though they are subject to certain natural conditions that place some limits on their aspirations."[12]

Paris took the path that swerves from mainline ethics not because he wanted to be different but because he only wanted to be faithful to the concerns of his Black community and its understanding of ethics. His evasion of ethics is, therefore, seen as an embrace of an African American tradition that stridently resists white racism, a life-threatening situation:

> Suffice it to say that ethics in the black community has racism as its subject matter; i.e., human action that views race as a significant condition for preserving and enhancing privileges for one group and the corresponding denial of such privileges to the excluded group. . . . Ethics in the black community has not been a speculative enterprise. Rather, it has been concrete, experiential, practical and deeply rooted in the realities of racial conflict.[13]

He believes not only that racism is the subject matter of Black ethics but that it should have been the main subject matter of the American theological enterprise in the last century. Thus, when asked to evaluate the first hundred years of Catholic social teaching in America, he began his response by saying, "Since racial injustice has been the paramount reality for African-American existence for over four centuries, no adequate evaluation of the Christian churches in general, or the Catholic Church in particular, can be undertaken apart from this fact."[14]

Accordingly, the celebrated Christian theologians and ethicists of the twentieth century who avoided the race question cannot be deemed the greatest of American theologians. He boldly nominates Martin Luther King Jr. and James Cone as the worthiest of all American theologians in the twentieth century:

> In my judgment, Martin Luther King, Jr., and James H. Cone are the two major American theologians of the twentieth century, black or white. The most significant similarity between the two is their respective understandings of the relationship of the Christian gospel to the struggle for racial justice in the United States. . . . Clearly, neither King nor Cone engaged in speculative theology concerning the nature of God nor did they participate in much academic discourse about classical doctrines of faith. Rather, their theologies served the practical purpose of

12. Paris, "Ethics and Politics," 3.
13. Paris, "Ethics and Politics," 6.
14. Paris, "Catholic Social Teaching," 299.

effecting racial justice. Each believed that the truth of the gospel is evidenced in its capacity to restore wholeness to a broken community. Hence, it was imperative for them that theology be integrally related to the concrete issues of social injustice in general and to the pursuit of racial justice in particular. Each viewed theology as prophetic because Jesus was a prophet.[15]

Anyone who has read Paris's book *The Spirituality of African Peoples*, which deals with the virtues of African Americans, might contend that in it he was not successful in completely evading virtue ethics in particular. The virtue school of ethics derives from Plato and Aristotle and it is a bastion of mainline ethics. In anticipation of this kind of criticism, Paris flagged his credentials of evasion by cutting a swath of difference first between him and modern virtue ethicists, then between him and Aristotle, whose inductive method of inquiry characterizes aspects of his book.

Paris states that "many modern virtue ethicists have much in common with the Platonic and Augustinian tradition. My approach, however, differs from theirs in being more closely related to the Aristotelian tradition."[16] What he evades is Plato's notion of virtues that are ideal forms and the Augustinian view of "moral life as faith in Jesus Christ and obedience to the dictates of God."[17] For him, the virtues of this approach are in wispy clouds, far above the struggles of human beings. He wants to bring them back to the ground. "By identifying God with the true end of human action, ethics becomes deductive inquiry that begins with the being of God rather that the strivings of humans. From this line of Platonic thinking the Christian virtues were understood as supernatural and transcendental of human strivings."[18]

In the case of Aristotle, he maintains that there are only a small number of methodological similarities between the ethics of African Americans and that of the great philosopher. Yet he admits that an Aristotelian shadow haunts many parts of his text. This is only because Aristotle's theory of moral virtue has an enormous influence on the development of moral theories. Nonetheless, he tells us that he tried very hard to swerve from the path Aristotle carved out for mainline ethics: "I have made every effort to stay within the thought forms of the latter [Africans and African Americans] throughout this study. In my judgment, any structural similarities between Aristotle's ethical thought and that of Africans and African Americans

---

15. Paris, "Comparing the Public Theologies," 220–21.
16. Paris, *Spirituality of African Peoples*, 183n7.
17. Paris, *Spirituality of African Peoples*, 182n7.
18. Paris, *Spirituality of African Peoples*, 182n7.

should not be viewed as another instance of Western epistemological imperialism since the content of the African and African-American ethic is decidedly culturally specific."[19]

His commitment to evading ethics as it was understood or executed by the leading ethicist of the past five decades also colored his understanding of political power. Since he viewed theology and ethics as practical sciences in the service of one's community's well-being—academic enterprises pursued for the sake of revealing practical solutions for everyday problems—he regarded them as "intrinsically political." This view flows from his understanding of the Black church tradition:

> The Black churches have always had profound concern for the bitter and painful realities of black existence in America as a well as for a bright and radiant future (eschaton) free from any form of racial injustice. The latter designates the locus of ultimate value where all people are in harmony with the transcendent, holy, and supreme God of the Judeo-Christian faith. Traditionally, the Black churches have interpreted human life, including all its suffering and pain, in accordance with that ultimate goal in which they have never lost faith. The convergence of that sacred principle with their efforts for improved temporal conditions reveals the integral relationship of religion and politics in the Black churches.[20]

He thus rejects the ethics of Stanley Hauerwas whose work explicitly rejects "direct responsibility for political engagement."[21]

In conclusion, Paris evades twentieth-century ethics, first by rejecting epistemology-centered, knowledge-focus problematic of modern ethics. For him, ethical problems are linked to social crises and quotidian human struggles for selfhood, identity, and power in specific communities. He does not see theological ethics as a form of knowledge or a means of acquiring knowledge, but as efforts to address and ameliorate social problems. Second, he avoids the quest for philosophical respectability and theological sophistication, preferring to apply theological ethics to the historical interpretation of race relations. Third, he skillfully refuses theology or philosophy's search for enduring, universal truths. He argues, "Morality pertains to the cultural ethos and, hence, is culturally specific. According to this perspective, there is a no universal morality as such, even though some common moral values are widespread among diverse cultural groups. Yet in my judgment morality

---

19. Paris, *Spirituality of African Peoples*, 183n8.
20. Paris, "Social World," 1–2; see 1–16.
21. Paris, *Spirituality of African Peoples*, 132, 182n6.

is univocal only within particular communities. That is to say, it is determined by the norms, values, and goals of particular communities."[22] And finally, he exposes Western theology's affiliation with whites' privileges and romance with structures of power.[23]

INTELLECTUAL ROOTS OF PARIS'S ETHICS

My effort to interpret Paris as evading ethics should neither imply parochialism nor suggest that his work is ahistorically *novum*. He is not a Melchizedek without a father or, mother or ancestors. Neither is he an Athena who burst forth from her father Zeus's forehead, fully mature. He drank deeply from some of the major intellectual fountainheads of twentieth-century theology, ethics, and philosophy. A close reading of his works easily reveals that their roots burrow into the minds of Aristotle, Paul Tillich, Reinhold and Richard Niebuhr, Ernst Troeltsch, and Hannah Arendt, to mention only a few.

In learning from and appropriating the thoughts of these great thinkers, he always put a question mark behind them. For him, these thinkers never dealt adequately with racism, with the death-dealing evil of structural marginalization and exclusion. In a discussion with him, he will accept the influences of these scholars on his thinking, but he is likely to evade any attempt to push him too closely to them. He thinks that the African American tradition of ethics and politics is the predominant influence on his thought. This much is clear to him, and he thinks this influence is predominant in the thoughts of even those African American theologians who do not explicitly reflect on the religious heritage of African Americans and its power on their creative thinking and acting. He will put Martin Luther King Jr. in this category, quoting the authority of Cone to buttress his point:

> Thus much of King's writings reflect theological and philosophical discourses that had little to do with his actual creative thinking and acting. The source of the latter is not Gandhi or Bostonian personalism, despite his implied claims to the contrary. King's creative thought and power in the struggle of freedom were found in his black heritage. This was the heritage that brought him face to face with agony and despair but also hope and joy that somewhere in the bosom of God's eternity, justice

---

22. Paris, *Spirituality of African Peoples*, 134. See also Paris, "Moral Development," 23.

23. On this see in particular his piece on Kuyper: Paris, "African and African-American Understanding," 263–80.

would become a reality "in the land of the free and the home of the brave." This was the source of King's dream and his anticipation that "trouble won't last always."[24]

In spite of all this demurring, we can still trace the powerful influences of other traditions on Paris's thought, including those of Aristotle, Tillich, Niebuhr, Troeltsch, Arendt, liberation theology, and social science method in his thought, even if these influences are only remote.

From Aristotle, he learned the craft of ethics as an inductive and empirical inquiry into the ethos of particular communities. The scholar starts with concrete problems—investigating what is actually happening in society, what is undermining the good—and ends with the creation of capabilities, virtues, and polis to ensure the good. Incidentally, Paris taught the *Nicomachean Ethics* and *Politics* of Aristotle as a doctoral seminar at Princeton Theological Seminary for decades.

If the empirical, inductive method comes from Aristotle, Paris's style of relating ethical analysis to concrete problems comes from his teacher, Paul Tillich, and his *correlation method*. A theological-ethical analysis must deal with the questions people are asking and address them with resources of the faith. Simply, the ethicist is to correlate problems and questions with resources, myths, and symbols of their faith to address them. Not only does he take this approach in his study, it also informs the way he treats his subjects. He presents them as expert in doing this. Take, for instance, his 1985 book, *The Social Teaching of the Black Churches*, where he uses the categories of ordinary folks (pastors and denominational leaders) outside the academe. He tried to weave a theology (more precisely, theological ethics/religious social ethics) from their actions and words in reaction to racism and other environmental conditions. The theology of the Black churches he constructed, therefore, is not supernatural, transcendental of human strivings. In this is the sense of his work: it does not stand above and outside of the collective praxis of Blacks. His strength is his capacity to relate theological ethics to the structured and unstructured social practices of Blacks in America over the past two hundred years—from when David George founded the first Black church in the United States to the present era.[25]

In this potent brew of theological ingredients, we need to add a dash of Niebuhr to give some flavor. Niebuhr once said that anyone answering questions that have not been asked is foolish. He also argues that we must pay attention to self-interest and power imbalance in our ethical analyses.

---

24. Cone, *God of the Oppressed*, 221–22, quoted in Paris, "Comparing the Public Theologies," 226. See also Noll, *God and Race*, 107–23.

25. For the story of David George see Paris, "David George," 2–9.

Paris in *Social Teaching* and in all of his other books always addresses the questions that Blacks in the United States are asking. Niebuhr's "realism" is also evident in his work. In *Social Teaching*, the reader will notice a succinct analysis of the imbalance of power and injustice, men and women in an immoral society, the self-interests of the dominant and oppressed groups, and occasional dialectics of argument in presenting the reaction of Blacks to racism. Paris not only taught courses on Niebuhr and his brother Richard for many years, but he has also been an active member of the Niebuhr Society right from its inception.[26] He calls himself "a Niebuhrian pragmatist," without necessarily accenting the aspects of Niebuhr's Christian realism that advised African Americans to be cautious and patient in their demand to eradicate racial injustice as they must endeavor to take into account all other factors.[27]

This revelation of his pragmatic bend is very important in understanding the direction his work has taken: ethical problems as linked to societal problems, conceptions of ethics as struggles over a societal ordering of human relations and cultural ways of life, and the rethinking of ethics as a form of cultural criticism for flourishing of human progress and moral enhancement of societies. As West has argued in *The American Evasion of Philosophy*, the evasion of epistemology-centered philosophy—in the thought of American thinkers such like James Dewey, Du Bois, Reinhold Niebuhr—

> Results in a conception of philosophy as a form of cultural criticism in which the meaning of America is put forward by intellectuals in response to distinct social and cultural crises. In this sense, American pragmatism is less a philosophical [ethical] tradition putting forward solutions to perennial problems in the Western philosophical conversation initiated by Plato and more a continuous commentary or set of interpretations that attempt to explain America to itself at a particular historical moment.[28]

Paris is Troeltschian in his execution of his project, especially in *The Social Teaching of the Black Churches*. "I think that the title of [this] book gives a strong preference for the spirit of Troeltsch because I wanted to emphasize the force of God's parenthood and human kinship as the primary counteracting force against the racist agenda of the nation at large and the white churches in particular. As such that principle constitutes the raison

---

26. Paris, "Response to Langdon Gilkey's," 475–79.

27. Paris, email message to author, February 26, 2009. See also Paris, "Moral Development," 24.

28. West, *American Evasion of Philosophy*, 5.

d'être of the black churches which represents its institutionalization."[29] Troeltsch, the German theologian of the late nineteenth and early twentieth century, presented in his influential book, *The Social Teaching of the Christian Churches*, the ethics of Christian churches as an investigation into how religious ideas and social interests are (become) congruent. His goal was to show how religious ideas agree with actual, material reality; what are the compromises (co-promising deals) that have been made to achieve the church's interest since religious ideals cannot be fully realized in society. This encounter of religious ideas and social reality is the realm of social teaching. Troeltsch developed three "ideal types" of religious organizations: church, sect, and mystic. The church is the only one of the three capable of adapting the original religious idea to hard material and social interest to produce a social teaching. It is capable of making compromises in the public realm.

Richard Niebuhr's *Christ and Culture* was influenced by Troeltsch's "ideal types" which in turn influenced Paris's use of the biblical leadership ideals of prophet, priest, and king in his first book, *Black Religious Leaders*. Also Niebuhr's book *The Responsible Self* influenced Paris's understanding of Blacks as agents who respond to God's initiative toward them. That response begins with interpreting the action that they confront before responding in accordance with God's purpose for humanity. Like Richard Niebuhr, Paris is also an ethicist engaged with hermeneutics, social science, theology, and history in doing Christian social ethics. All this is very evident in his *Black Religious Leaders* and *The Social Teaching of the Black Churches*.

In his analysis of the social teaching of the Black churches, Paris accented political actions as the originative, sustaining basis, and even the subject matter of social ethics.[30] This move to accent political action is not totally innocent or arbitrary. One sees the influence of Arendt, one of his favorite philosophers. In her influential 1958 book, *The Human Condition*, she shows that political actions, deeds, and speeches in the public realm have the function of disclosing and affirming identity of agents—who they are, not what they are. They reveal themselves as the unique individuals that they are. The political or the polis is the "space of appearance" where people appear to one another as they come together to undertake common projects. For her, power (not strength, force, or violence), the main instrument of the political realm, arises when persons act in concert for a common public-political purpose. Thus, both the polis as the space of appearance and power as an outcome of collective engagement are always potential

---

29. Paris, email message to author, February 26, 2009.
30. Paris, *Social Teaching*, 2–3.

and are actualized in actions and speeches of persons who act in concert for a common public project. In her view, the analysis of the political or social-ethical should be focused on the public space. This is again reflected in Paris's works as he has overwhelmingly focused on political leaders acting in the public realm.

There is another way Arendt influenced him. As we have already shown in the analysis of the nature and meaning of history in the Black churches, he limited himself to political actions. To my chagrin, as an economic ethicist, he ignores economic actions.[31] More correctly, he subsumes economics under politics. This preference reflects the subtle influence of Arendt on his thinking.[32] (Though she is not directly mentioned in the book, I know, as his former student, his love for her thought.) He appears to be working from her schema of *labor*, *work*, and *action*. In *labor* and *work*, people only show their talents, abilities, deficiencies, and shortcomings. What she calls labor is necessitated by the demands of biological survival. There is no room for uniqueness or distinction. We are all the same insofar as we are parts of the human species chained to natural necessities, the needs of the body. The products of *labor* do not last—they are very short-lived. Here, the criterion of judgment is the ability to sustain human life. In *work*, the situation is slightly different. We are able to show some individuality, our products bear some distinctive marks, but the maker is subordinated to the end product and the product will outlive him or her. The end product tells us very little about the maker except that he or she has certain skills and capabilities. The

---

31. When I queried him about this he responded in this way:

> I am sorry about the lack of any attention to the economic sphere. I thought a great deal about that and decided to leave it out because it seemed to me that the black churches did not pay much attention to it apart from beginning various micro businesses that displayed no thought that was different from the status quo of the day.
>
> Previously, I had worked closely with Jesse Jackson in the early days of his work in Chicago when his program Operation Breadbasket was the economic arm of Martin Luther King's SCLC. Apart from opposing the racism in the many big businesses that refused to employ blacks while readily taking their cash, neither King nor Jackson displayed any novel economic thought. When the book is revised I think that perhaps I now need to say something about this matter and would welcome your insights.
>
> You are certainly right in discerning that I view politics as prior to economics even though the state needs a material basis as a necessary condition. (Paris, email message to author, February 26, 2009.)

32. This tendency may also have been influenced by Aristotle, who viewed economics as a household responsibility and, hence, outside of the political realm. It is needless to say that Arendt also worked from Aristotelian ideas.

criterion of judgment is the ability to create a world fit for human existence. In *actions* relating and interacting with others, without intermediary matter or things, for a common purpose, persons disclose and affirm their unique identities and actualize their capacities for freedom. Actions have the potential to introduce the *novum* and the totally unexpected into the world. This potential cannot be actualized in isolation from others who are there to work in concert with us and/or to judge the quality of what is being stated and/or enacted. The criterion of judgment is the capacity to reveal unique identities and introduce the new, a novelty into the world, to expect the unexpected. Blacks needed to reach this level of living, which for Arendt is the *differentia specifica* of human life. In Paris's theology, political action is what will affirm their claim as being created in the image of God and what will differentiate them from the life of animals and objects of possession, which was their lot under white slave masters.

The affinity with Arendt's thought notwithstanding, Paris is quick to distance himself from aspects of her theory of power in the public realm:

> I love Hannah Arendt's understanding of the public realm even though I shun some of the elitism that attends it and see no reason why it could not be less elitist than it seems to be. I also am more a Niebuhrian pragmatist than she in seeing an important ethical role for power as a corrective to the wrong use of power. Also, I think Niebuhr's view of sin is more realistic than her seeming lack thereof even though her view of Totalitarianism fits very nicely with Niebuhr's view of sin.[33]

Liberation theology is another influence on his thought.[34] For him, practice is prior to thought in theological-ethical reflection. Even though it is less in vogue these days, he still holds onto one of its valuable insights: the purpose of theological or ethical analysis to liberate people from oppression. Though working within the liberation theology paradigm, Paris did not see it necessary to develop any systematic connection between racism and economic injustice in the United States in the ways that, for example, Cornel West has been able to do.

Finally, Paris uses a lot of social scientific data and archival research to analyze the history and distinctive identity of African Americans. As was related to this writer, the reliance on the social scientific method comes from his doctoral training at the University of Chicago Divinity School in the 1960s. He feels very strongly about the place of the social sciences in

---

33. Paris, email message to author, February 26, 2009.

34. See Paris, "Religious Social Ethics," 135–45; Paris, "Character of Liberation Ethics," 133–40; Paris, "Womanist Thought," 115–26.

theological education, even advocating that seminary students spend "as much as a year's study in university disciplines or programs considered relevant to [their] professional needs" in order to be adequately prepared for the people and the country they will serve.[35]

The value of social analysis in theology and ethics is deliberately keyed to his hermeneutics derived from his commitment to liberation theology. He is impatient with scholars who profess doing liberation theology while ignoring social analysis. This much is revealed in his review of Cone's 1991 book, *Martin and Malcolm and America: A Dream or a Nightmare*. Trenchantly, Paris criticizes his friend:

> Throughout his career Cone's work has been criticized for its lack of social analysis. The subject of this book could have provided an excellent opportunity for the possible correction of that deficit. Seemingly, Cone refused to accept the challenge. Rather, by employing a narrative approach he has analyzed a cultural phenomenon in such a way as to obscure the political dimension of the social problem. This is especially problematic for black theology, which has always claimed to be a political theology deeply rooted in the praxis of liberation. Cone does not tell us how this analysis helps in liberating blacks from their present condition.[36]

PARIS'S ETHICAL METHODOLOGY

The ethical methodology of Paris can be summarized as an intersection of eight key insights. First, the good of the public realm or social is measured by the full actualization of human potentialities.[37] According to him, "the purpose of ethics is to enhance the quality of human action by enabling people to actualize their full potentialities."[38] This concern with actualization of potentials is scattered all through his works.[39] Start from where he is analyzing forms and approaches to racism in the *Black Religious Leaders*, that is, the approach of Black religious leaders in adjusting the ideals of the Bible to American reality; move over to an account of their efforts to realize biblical ideals in America in the *Social Teaching*; then shift your gaze

---

35. Paris, "Overcoming Alienation," 194.
36. Paris, "Review of 'Martin and Malcolm,'" 90.
37. Paris, *Social Teaching*, 2, 58–59, 115–16.
38. Paris, "Is it Moral," 51.
39. For instance, see Paris, "Social World," 2; Paris, "Justice and Mercy," 222; Paris, "Bible and the Black Churches," 140.

to where he is looking at the spirituality of African peoples, and you will discover that his great concern (implicit and explicit—often implicit) has always been about what is blocking the unfolding of the potentialities of Blacks in America. How can they overcome obstacles to actualization of their potentialities, or how are (were) their traditional (African and African American) forms of sociality organized so that a Black person can be all that he or she can be—can experience full human flourishing?

Second, the focus of his ethical analysis is on finding out what is threatening the moral fabric of the society, especially in ways that inhibit the actualization of potentialities of persons and their community as a whole and then addressing it in ways that can remove the threats.[40] He examined the interplay between politics (the ordering of human relations in society) and the part of life we call spiritual or religious as lived—not as argued. The weight of his work always tilts toward empirical facts and observable social practices rather than theory. Take, for instance, his major academic concern with racism. He does not engage in theoretical debate about the nature or origin of racism, but he lets his subjects reveal their understanding of it and he then tries to capture their responses and resistance to it.

Third, there is a good mixture of social, scientific, and historical methods at work in his scholarly output. Most good ethicists employ social science methods and insights in their works, but very few resort to the craft of the historian to do ethics. Paris goes into archives to ferret out and interpret historical records. He is comfortable with employing research skills and the principles and methods of historical analysis. Especially in the *Social Teaching of the Black Churches*, the reader can easily notice the excellent use of primary and secondary sources in interpreting the theological responses of Black churches to racism.

Fourth, every person needs a community (*communal eros*) to become fully human and to fully actualize his or her potentialities as an American citizen. If this is denied a group of persons, they are bound to form a substitute one. The systematic and society-wide racism that African Americans experienced resulted in their loss of place and in becoming exiled within their own country. Racism also denied Blacks the process and opportunity for self-actualization. The church became a surrogate community. "Since it is necessary for persons to be nourished by a communal eros in order to become fully human, an imposed exile necessitates the formation of a substitute community, and, as we have seen, that has been one of the major functions of the black churches."[41] In another place, he states that:

---

40. Paris, *Black Religious Leaders*, 31–32.
41. Paris, *Social Teaching*, 59; see 59–61.

> A fundamental assumption underlying my understanding of social ethics is the dialectical relationship between person and community. That is to say, personhood is established only in the context of a community of persons that in turn constitutes both a limiting condition and a liberating resource for all thought and practice. Similarly, community is constituted when persons choose to come together to create, preserve, and enhance the conditions that make possible their common life.[42]

Fifth, ethics cannot be separated from politics. He states that "ethics and politics are integrally united. The aim of ethics is to help persons become morally good, and the aim of politics is the same."[43] And he would add that without the strong foundation and interplay between ethics and politics, neither the individual nor his or her community can actualize their full potentialities.

It is quite tempting to wholly attribute Paris's insistence on interweaving ethics and politics to his self-professed embrace of neo-Aristotelianism. Aristotle had theorized the close connection between ethics and politics. It might also be tempting to interpret Paris's inclination as solely arising from his location as an African American. After all, most white theologians and ethicists avoid writing about racism.[44] The better (additional) argument as far as his methodology is concerned is his focus on concrete problems. Many American theologians who are also neo-Aristotelian have not made racial injustice and the struggles against it the pivot of their scholarship and social activism. Early in his academic career, Paris set his eyes on focusing on concrete problems, the major problems that threaten the moral fabric of American society, the agency of Blacks in resisting them, and the Black churches' response to them.[45] He thus set race and politics as the key components of American ethical life and the pivot of his scholarship. By doing this Paris latched onto the most profound moral problem of this country. As the famed historian Mark A. Noll informs us in his 2008 book *God and Race in American Politics*:

> First, race has always been among the most influential elements in American political history, and in many periods absolutely the most influential. Second, religion has always been crucial for the workings of race in American politics. Together, race and religion make up, not only the nation's deepest and most

---

42. Paris, "Moral Development," 23–32.
43. Paris, "Moral Development," 25.
44. Cone, "Theology's Great Sin," 139–52.
45. See Paris, "David George."

enduring moral problem, but also its broadest and most enduring political influence.[46]

Sixth, there is always an indication in his work that it is done by a Black theologian. He consciously expresses the meaning of all his work for constructing Black theology. When he writes about personalities like Martin Luther King Jr., Malcolm X, Joseph H. Jackson, Adam Powell Jr., David George, and James Cone, or institutions like the Black churches, he endeavors to show how what they do exemplifies the Black religious tradition. He asks and answers this basic question of what they do represent in terms of the ambiguity that African American identity entails and that Black theology addresses.[47]

Seventh, Paris writes from the vantage point of the victims of American history. He is aware that he was not only thinking and writing about America's most enduring moral problem but also about the "strange experience of being a problem."[48] Paris turned Western theological tradition inside out by not simply legitimizing the capacity of its ethical reasoning to overcome the profound moral problem of America, but more importantly, by asking over and over again how it feels to be a problem[49]—a problem that America has ignored for too long, that its white theologians are reluctant to face squarely to develop "antiracist theologies that go beyond simply condemning racism because they engage the histories, cultures and theologies of people of color."[50] The aim of Paris's ethical discourse is to "convey and enact the 'strange experience' of 'being a problem'":[51] that is, being an ethicist of African descent in America and refusing to measure the Black experience by "the tape of a world that looks on in amused contempt and pity."[52] He is able to pull this off without having "double consciousness" in his professional identity and status.[53]

---

46. Noll, *God and Race*, 1.

47. See discussion in footnote 1 of this chapter for details.

48. Du Bois, *Souls of Black Folk*, 3–4.

49. This is a paraphrase of West's turn of phrase in *American Evasion of Philosophy*, 142.

50. Cone, "Theology's Great Sin," 139.

51. West, *American Evasion of Philosophy*, 142.

52. Du Bois, *Souls of Black Folk*, 5.

53. As a citizen he may have "double consciousness" insofar as he is an African American, but here I am talking about double consciousness in his work and identity as a Black scholar. He is not trying to locate his scholarship simultaneously in two worlds or let himself be measured by the tape of those who want to sweep racism under the academic rug or both evade and affirm the constricted Western theological enterprise.

Finally, it is important to mention that Paris does not only focus on African American as victims. More importantly, he has demonstrated in all his work that African Americans have been agents throughout their history and not merely victims. Victims are acted upon. They do not act. Agents respond and do something about their situation. Their agency reveals their subjectivity and, hence, their humanity. This is a fact, he believes, took American whites a long, long time to affirm.

CONCLUDING REMARKS

On the whole, the extensity and intensity of Paris's conception and method of ethics suggests that he is a scholar who evades modern theological ethics as we know it. This evasion is pursued to render, in my judgment, his academic work as a form of the *spirituals*. He wants his audience to feel the pathos and passion of centuries of oppression of Blacks in this country. To fully appreciate his work, the reader needs to feel the sorrow and the hope that are embedded in the descriptions and analyses of racial injustice and responses to it. For him, the capacity to feel (written by the one who feels them and hoping in turn to make his readers feel them as well) is more important than any display of erudition and obeisance to Western theological tradition. The eros for justice and political engagement in all concrete relational contexts requires some passion.

The evasion and the *feel* that characterize Paris's fierce ethical engagement with white racism and Western theological tradition are interwoven and jointly arise from his deep and profound understanding of the spirituals. He considers the spiritual as the "primary repository of African American theological thought."[54] These slave songs in their linguistic format of double entendre evaded the slave masters' theology, panoptic gaze, and intrusive ears only to unleash passions for everyday resistance and give courage to those who had the *hearts* to hear their concealed messages. Our master-teacher Paris, like the unnamed bards of the spirituals, countless great Black preachers, and brave Black activists, drew from the same ethos formed by a deep concern for oppression and liberation. This concern, according to our learned professor, is (should be) the central focus of the gospel and theological ethics. And it is what drives his commitment to ethics.

The first major weakness of Paris's ethical thought is his consistent and persistent focus on a single unifying category for American social ethics—racism—when ethics needs to be more comprehensive.[55] Has he reduced

54. Paris, "Linguistic Inculturation," 80.
55. I asked Paris to defend himself about this charge and this is what he had to say:

the specificity of Christian ethics to a particular material content? Second, what we have portrayed as a virtue in his published books and essays, that is the evasion of ethics, some may consider as a weakness in the sense that he failed to situate ethics as a theological enterprise well connected to Scripture, systematic theology, and philosophical conceptual framework.

He may be acquitted of these serious charges if we consider that at the heart of his work are the two central experiences of all human beings: love and suffering, as Margaret Farley informed us.[56] Add to this list the central goal of social ethics: justice as informed by concern for flourishing life for all human beings. Paris's work, building on the Black Christian tradition and the legacy of Martin Luther King Jr., has consistently shown how love (especially love for the neighbor as oneself) is both the appropriate response of those who have and continue to suffer racism and the antidote for poisoned hearts of the perpetrators of racism.[57] Paris's work as we have already noted

> I wonder why it should be a major weakness that I have focused my work on racism. I have done so because it is the primary ethical problem in the American situation since racism denies people their humanity. It is a frontal attack on their humanity; always a threat and its logic leads to genocide. Racism is virtually synonymous with violence against humans. Always and at the same time racism exudes psychological, social, economic, political and physical violence. I think it is altogether immoral that white theologians and ethicists have devoted so little attention to this paramount moral evil on which this society was built and sustained for centuries. My quarrel with social science is that it has a long history of focusing its attention on measuring the pathological effects of racism and very little on the responses African Americans made and continue to make to effect a better world for themselves and the nation. In fact, the actions of helping to rid the nation of its racism have benefited the moral lives of blacks and whites alike. In fact, blacks have been the primary agents in healing the nation of its greatest moral threat—racism, which Martin Luther King, Jr. said constituted a malignancy in the heart of the nation itself, which, if left unchecked, will destroy the nation.
>
> Most important, my normative criterion for my ethics is the "black Christian tradition," the parenthood of God and the kinship of all peoples. This is the Christian gospel that was institutionalized in the black churches and all societal well-being is judged by that ethical norm which is the heart of the gospel for which Jesus lived, proclaimed and died. Because I wanted to take this tradition seriously, I chose to study ethics in a Divinity School rather than a philosophy department. The latter had no concern for religion and religion is an integral part of the African American experience because it provided for them the theological and moral basis for love, justice, compassion, and life itself. (Paris, email message to author, May 12, 2010.)

56. See Keenan, *Catholic Moral Theology*, 197.

57. For example, see Paris, "Christian Way," 125–31, especially 129; Paris, *Social Teaching*, 115–17; Paris, "Meditation on Love," 1–4.

also points us to justice as giving everyone the real possibility to realize his or her potentialities and to justice as a social expression of love. Love, suffering, and justice are at the heart of the Christian moral life. And his work builds bridges between them.

BIBLIOGRAPHY

Cone, James H. *A Black Theology of Liberation*. Maryknoll: Orbis, 1986.
———. *God of the Oppressed*. New York: Seabury, 1975.
———. "Theology's Great Sin: Silence in the Face of White Supremacy." *Black Theology* 2.2 (2004) 139–52.
Du Bois, W. E. B. *The Souls of Black Folk*. New York: Penguin, 1996.
Keenan, James F. *A History of Catholic Moral Theology in the Twentieth Century: From Confessing Sins to Liberating Consciences*. New York: Continuum, 2010.
Noll, Mark A. *God and Race in American Politics: A Short History*. Princeton: Princeton University Press, 2008.
Paris, Peter J. "African-American Religion and Public Life." *Cross Currents* 58.3 (2004) 475–94.
———. "The African and African-American Understanding of Our Common Humanity: A Critique of Abraham Kuyper's Anthropology." In *Religion, Pluralism and Public Life: Abraham Kuyper's Legacy for the Twenty-First Century*, edited by Luis E. Lugo, 263–80. Grand Rapids: Eerdmans, 2000.
———. "The Bible and the Black Churches." In *The Bible and Social Reform*, edited by Ernest R. Sandeen, 133–54. Philadelphia: Fortress, 1982.
———. *Black Religious Leaders*. Louisville, KY: Westminster John Knox, 1991.
———. "Catholic Social Teaching and the African-American Struggle for Economic Justice." In *Catholic Social Thought and the New World Order: Building on One Hundred Years*, edited by Oliver F. Williams and John W. Houck, 299–307. Notre Dame, IN: University of Notre Dame Press, 1933.
———. "The Character of Liberation Ethics." In *Struggles for Solidarity: Liberation Theologies in Tension*, edited by Lorine M. Getz and Ruy O. Costa, 133–40. Minneapolis: Fortress, 1992.
———. "The Christian Way Through the Black Experience." *Word and World* 6.2 (Spring 1986) 125–31.
———. "Comparing the Public Theologies of James H. Cone and Martin Luther King, Jr." In *Black Faith and Public Talk: Critical Essays on James H. Cone's Black Theology and Black Power*, edited by Dwight N. Hopkins, 218–31. Maryknoll: Orbis, 1999.
———. "David George: Paramount Ancestor of the Black Churches in the United States, Canada and Sierra Leone." *Criterion: A Publication of the Divinity School of the University of Chicago* 35.1 (Winter 1996) 2–9.
———. "Ethics and Politics in Black America: An Introductory Lecture." Harvard Divinity School, Cambridge, MA, Fall 2008.
———. "From Womanist Thought to Womanist Action." *Journal of Feminist Studies in Religion* 9.2 (Spring/Fall 1993) 115–26.
———. "Is it Moral to Make 'Test-Tube Babies'? A Response." In *The Befuddled Stork: Helping Persons of Faith Debate Beginning-of-Life Issues*, edited by Sally B. Geis and Donald E. Messer, 50–56. Nashville: Abingdon, 2000.

———. "Justice and Mercy: The Relation of Societal Norms and Empathic Feeling." In *Doing Justice to Mercy: Religion, Law, and Criminal Justice*, edited by Jonathan Rothchild et al., 222–30. Charlottesville: University of Virginia Press, 2007.

———. "The Linguistic Inculturation of the Gospel: The Word of God in the Words of the People." In *Making Room at the Table: An Invitation to Multicultural Worship*, edited by Brian K. Blount and Leonora Tubbs Tisdale, 78–95. Louisville, KY: Westminster John Knox, 2001.

———. "A Meditation on Love." *Princeton Seminary Bulletin* 27.1 (2006) 1–4.

———. "Moral Development for African-American Leadership." In *The Stones That the Builders Rejected: The Development of Ethical Leadership from the Black Tradition*, edited by Walter Earl Fluker, 2–32. Harrisburg, PA: Trinity, 1998.

———. "Overcoming Alienation in Theological Education." In *Shifting Boundaries: Contextual Approaches to the Structure of Theological Education*, edited by Barbara G. Wheeler and Edward Farley, 181–200. Louisville, KY: Westminster John Knox, 1991.

———. "The Problem of Evil in Black Christian Perspective." In *Justice and the Holy: Essays in Honor of Walter Harrelson*, edited by Douglas A. Knight and Peter Paris, 297–309. Atlanta: Scholars, 1989.

———. "Response to Langdon Gilkey's Inaugural Address at the Niebuhr Society, 22 November 2003 in Atlanta." *Political Theology* 5.4 (2004) 475–79.

———. "Review of 'Martin and Malcolm and America: A Dream or a Nightmare' by James H. Cone." *Religious Studies Review* 20.2 (Apr. 1994) 87–90.

———. *The Social Teaching of the Black Churches*. Philadelphia: Fortress, 1985.

———. "The Social World of the Black Church." *Drew Gateway* 52.3 (1983) 1–16.

———. *The Spirituality of African Peoples: The Search for a Common Discourse*. Minneapolis: Fortress, 1995.

———. "The Task of Religious Social Ethics in Light of Black Theology." In *Liberation Ethics: Essays in Religious Social Ethics in Honor of Gibson Winter*, edited by Charles Amjad-Ali and W. Alvin Pitcher, 135–45. Chicago: Center for the Scientific Study of Religion, 1985.

———. "When Feeling Like a Motherless Child." In *Lament: Reclaiming Practices in Pulpit, Pew, and Public Square*, edited by Sally A. Brown and Patrick Miller, 111–20. Louisville, KY: Westminster John Knox, 2005.

West, Cornel. *The American Evasion of Philosophy: A Genealogy of Pragmatism*. Madison: University of Wisconsin Press, 1989.

———. *Prophesy Deliverance: An Afro-American Revolutionary Christianity*. Louisville, KY: Westminster John Knox, 1982.

Chapter 2

Traveling Black Bodies
The Spirituality of African Peoples and the Importance of Embodiment

Anthony B. Pinn

Reflection on the significance of Africa as either a cultural symbol or materiality has marked much scholarship within the study of Black religion over the past fifty years.[1] However, few have grounded their work in the "African-ness" of thought and experience as richly as Peter Paris. What I find most intriguing about Paris's approach is his attention to the epistemological linkage animated through various embodied processes and performances—serving to outline a set of ethical considerations that frame what it means to be of African descent.

    Paris and I disagree on the extent to which this Africa-based religiosity is always-theistic in orientation and geared toward the "good."[2] Yet, we share a sense of the importance of embodiment as the primary cartography of the religious. For Paris, issues of identity and personhood can't be detangled from the history of Black bodies within the Western world, and I have argued explicitly for Black religion as embodied thinking. However, much of what Paris gathers concerning the significance of embodiment is subtext within his work. Mindful of this, and by re-reading *The Spirituality*

---

1. For example, see Long, "What Is Africa to Me?," 247–59.
2. See, for example, Pinn, *End of God-Talk*; and Pinn, *African American Humanist*.

of African Peoples, I explore in these pages what one might gain concerning Paris's sense of shared moral insight if one highlights the significance of Black *embodied* bodies, and the manner in which these bodies retain and transmit information.

The Spirituality of African Peoples, along with so much of his professional life, is tied to the significance of "recovery." In addition, undergirding the text is an implied question: What of this recovered and rethought epistemological and aesthetic past could be used to think through and refine the religious base of life for so many of African descent in North America? As Black religious studies—particularly in the forms of history, theology, and biblical studies—pushed for description and analysis of African American religiosity from the vantage point of "Blackness," Paris called for a step further in this process. He called for mining African traditions for sensibilities and insights that might refine the moral and ethical reach and impact of Black religion.

As Paris indicates in the preface, he is tied to a people's movement to Canada (Nova Scotia, to be exact) in the eighteenth century—a people who, despite the hardships, suffering, and false promises of the British, "constitute[ed] the ancestral base for the enduring African Canadian population in that place."[3] For Paris, embodied reminders of these ancestors marked out in part through ongoing racial injustice urges a commitment to transformation through the wisdom and philosophies that shaped the self-understanding and practices of those early ancestors moving forward. As he notes, this commitment involved the physicality of African ways tied to epistemological traditions—all given significance through the political shifts and movements for independence that defined much of the mid-twentieth century.[4] "The primacy that these movements gave to the moral and political spheres of human relationships," Paris reflects, "was soon extended to all dimensions of the academic enterprise . . . they were motivated by the desire to produce useful knowledge that would contribute

---

3. Paris, *Spirituality of African Peoples*, viii.

4. The colonial project in Africa and white supremacy in North America involved epistemological perversion by means of which African-ness and Blackness were constituted as naming the problematic "Other"—not quite human, not exactly "animal-like"; that which constituted both a threat and a necessity. One might say Paris gets at this dimension of "contact" when speaking about the manner in which the colonial educational process (and higher education in the United States) were meant to hamper a robust sense of self. Yet, this work wasn't simply an abstraction—discourse layered unto—a systematic ripping away of what Hortense Spillers labels "flesh"; but instead, it also involved a hyper-visibility or a type of public reworking of bodies through modes of use, confinement, mutilation, and so on. See Spillers, "Mama's Baby, Papa's Maybe," 64–81.

not only to academic discourse but, more importantly, would enhance the quality of life in their respective communities of origin."[5] Reflecting back on these developments, Paris writes:

> The function of African traditions in all spheres of the newly independent nation was an overriding concern of students, teachers and clergy alike. It seemed that virtually every Nigerian wanted to participate in the task of historical retrieval and reappropriation as the first step in reconstructing their national purpose. Everyone wanted to help in determining the extent to which their ageless traditions could and should contribute necessary resources for nation-building in the twentieth century.[6]

VALUES AND RESISTANCE

Growing out of this history, there are for Paris elements of a "peculiar worldview of blacks" that warrant attention to the degree—as an ethicist—he sees embedded in them a broad moral vision undergirding deep religious thought and practice. Put differently, from this worldview, one gains the structuring of moral philosophy of significance both on the African continent and in the diaspora. Key in tracking this worldview is experience—an experience that is tied to an "ongoing connectedness with the religious and moral ethos of its African homeland."[7] But what can we know about that experience if embodied bodies don't serve as guide? Isn't the "African factor" (i.e., enduring morality and ethics) discussed by Paris tied to flesh and blood—borne out through movements, positioning, and activities of embodied peoples? He references Frantz Fanon early in the text, and isn't it Fanon who proclaims "Oh my body, make of me always a man who questions!"[8] This is a questioning that lives—that presses into the world, and that is tied to conditions of materiality and an effort to name and recast those conditions. Take that quotation for what you will. But in some way, it seeks to announce a linking of embodiment to reason/analysis-thought, and seeks to use this relationship (i.e., lived experience) to understand and move through the world.[9] How is the embodied shape of that experience named?

---

5. Paris, *Spirituality of African Peoples*, 2.
6. Paris, *Spirituality of African Peoples*, ix.
7. Paris, *Spirituality of African Peoples*, 20.
8. Fanon, *Black Skin, White Masks*, ch. 8.
9. See Fanon, *Black Skin, White Masks*.

Is there more that can be teased out regarding how that experience is "worn" or carried through time and space?

As I read Paris for the presence of embodied bodies at work, the importance of physicality in the crafting of religious sensibilities is at play. Moral and ethical considerations have to be experienced—felt and acted out. What is the point of a moral claim—whether related to the spirituality of Black people or larger claims of democratic possibility for the nation—if it isn't attached to the physicality of embodied beings active in the world? Rituals and rituals items that figure into theological conversation and analysis do not exist outside the physical labor of embodied bodies, and they do not exist—on a more fundamental level—outside of the existence of other "things" (e.g., trees, herbs, rivers) that impact and impinge upon our movement through the world.[10] In short, the "African factor" of concern to Paris is dependent on material expression shaped by interaction with embodied bodies in the world. But this connection to the physical isn't without its troubles—particularly for those despised and marginalized because of certain dimensions of their physicality and the socially sanctioned denigration of said "look."

Undergirding much of Paris's argument is concern with moral evil and suffering as enslaved Africans and their descendants wrestled with white supremacy and its dehumanizing intents. And this concern often took the form of an embodied theodicy not content simply with abstract principles of mutuality and destiny. Rather, it was a theodicy tested within the arena of lived meanings. It was guided by a need to respond to communal well-being as practices in the form of nurtured and nurturing relationships. For example, the spirituals have made famous notions of heaven; but Christian devotion also had its "horizontal" markers of purpose fulfilled, and these markers enabled something new within the sociality of embodied existence—e.g., access to public goods, and so on. And African-based traditions (such as Lucumi) are guided by an awareness of divine energy—*ashé*—lodged in the materiality of the world. Such is the case, at least in part, due to orientation within African and African American traditions privileging embodied horizontal dynamics of encounter: *nature, history,* and *spirit.*[11]

---

10. My reference to "things" here is meant to bring to mind the theorization of materials as impactful—related to humans as another mode of thing. See Brown, *Things*; and "Thing Theory," 1–22.

11. Paris, *Spirituality of African Peoples*, 47.

EMBODIMENT: WHERE VALUES ARE "FOUND"

All too often, significance of embodied has been lost on academic inquiry—even by those whose work speaks from a place of hyper-visibility and body-based disregard. In a word, the Black body was used within the context of colonialism and North American white supremacy as a material sign of a deeper difference often discussed theologically. Such is a white "lie": a suggestion that the religious response to the degrading and hyper-visibility of subjected bodies is to "hide" them—to obstruct attention to them. Nonetheless, the mechanisms of capitalized anti-Black racism mark and make the embodied body hyper-visible and loaded with socio-cultural codes that deform and, in a metaphysical sense, erase the meaning of the embodied body seen.[12] Perhaps this is what novelist Jason Mott is getting at when saying, "memory and death are countries that know no geography."[13] As Mott notes, there are ways in which our "story"—the history of our encounter with the processes of *othering*—"seeps into our skin. We bleed it even as we're covered by it."[14] And so, what is the role of embodiment, of the body, in the academic revising of moral and ethics over-against these frameworks of white supremacy and injustice?

In *The Spirituality of African Peoples*, the body often is assumed. It is for Paris a given that Blackness demands a body—and the effort to foster alternate moral-ethical ways of thinking and doing are performed through the body. It, the body, is both the source and content of religious experience without which theological and ethical claims have no grounding—hence no practical meaning. The "African factor" of such central concern for Paris involves a sense of connectedness that ties together past, present, and future through energetic modes of physically arranged meaningfulness not just mindfulness. To the degree the "African factor" requires embodiment to be "known," related theological claims must take the form of material expression. This, then, entails a push against tendencies in the "West" to theologize as an abstraction privileging distance from the "stuff" of materiality and physical encounter—seeking to privilege disciplined thinking before and beyond physicality, but the "African factor" de-normalizes such a theological stance by naming the embodied body. Theology and ethics, according to Paris, are "arts" rather than "sciences" to the degree they are concerned with "general rules and principles that can be practical guideposts for the

---

12. Related to this, for an intriguing discussion of colonialism and anti-Black racism, see Andrews, *New Age of Empire*.
13. Mott, *Hell of a Book*, 291.
14. Mott, *Hell of a Book*, 313.

enhancement of thought and action in specific contexts."[15] To say that "nature, history, and spirit are ontologically united and hence interdependent"[16] is to also say something about the physical placement of bodies in time and space. The nature of morality through the "African factor" is a matter of contact, of connection—pulling at and directing our materiality within the arena of sociality.[17]

In chapter 5, Paris makes most explicit (to the extent it's explicit) the embodied nature of the "African factor" as he reflects on the tangled nature of the individual in relationship to family and community. "One can," Paris remarks, "rightly claim that the African person is related to the family as the part of a living organism related to the whole."[18] "*A living organism*" . . . through this phrase, Paris highlights the materiality undergirding modes of relationship—or, the manner in which various bodied subjects interact; impinge upon each other; inform each other; and constitute through this interaction family and community as something more than their parts. Embodiment (i.e., materiality and physicality) isn't simply the conveyer of religious sensibilities, but rather in significant ways it is the content of these sensibilities in that they have to do not simply with how time and space are defined and divided but how time and space are occupied and engaged. Think, for example, of the way in which the gods are made materially manifest through possession or the way in which the birth of a child speaks to interaction with the gods or the ancestors.[19] Pre-body determinations that inform the "when," "where," and "why" of individual and collective existence are dependent upon materiality for expression. The structure of cosmological interplay is worked out in and through corporeality.

Paris moves between the significance of the body as a target of racialized terror and the imagination or mind as the "home" of religious response. "The basic struggle against the dehumanization process of slavery," Paris writes, "took place in the consciousness of the African slaves. In the midst of their suffering, they forged new structures of religious meaning, social

---

15. Paris, *Spirituality of African Peoples*, 21.

16. Paris, *Spirituality of African Peoples*, 21.

17. Paris, *Spirituality of African Peoples*, 162. Such is not to move in the direction of the "biologistic" reading cautioned against by Paris. I am not suggesting genetic determinations for these cultural forms and patterns of behavior. I am suggesting the physical body can't be downplayed in terms of the presentation and interpretation of the cultural forms of importance to Paris. This is not to suggest there is no abstraction involved in naming or articulating these virtues—but like within any discourse, ideas "matter": the practicality of those ideas requires bodies.

18. Paris, *Spirituality of African Peoples*, 101.

19. Paris, *Spirituality of African Peoples*, 103.

identity, cultural expression, and moral value."[20] Yet, there is a hint of the enactment only enabled through embodiment when Paris says, "A person of moral virtue is one who exercises good habits and, conversely, the exercise of good habits constitutes a person of moral virtue."[21] In a word, "the goal is not separate from the practice . . . . There can be no good people apart from the doing of good actions."[22] Still, something about this arrangement easily renders the body a phantom—a "dark" shape of activity. I wonder, are there dimensions of this animating power, or what Paris calls "African spirituality," that are better accessible when more is made of embodied bodies in a consistent fashion? Here is the key, as Paris himself writes, "African spirituality is never disembodied but always integrally connected with the dynamic movement of life."[23] One might extend Paris's assertion in such a way as to center the physicality of embodiment and in this way see the manner in which embodiment shapes perception, conditions "reality," and encompasses the "feel" of our existential realness.

Here, I am suggesting an exploration of what is available to us *if* Paris's religion/theology and morality/ethics are perceived not in relationship to the consequences of embodiment but rather as already-always *about* embodiment.[24] By extension, spirituality—as an animated structuring of meaning—is not without its materiality impinging upon the geography of sociality. How is this spirituality "felt," "located," and "transferred"? Community, which is the central concern within African spirituality, is embodied—formed and acted out as bodies come into relationship. Bodies anchor this spirituality to the "ground." And in this process, the embodied body is exposed through various qualities and capacities—its suppleness and communicative potential noted. Paris speaks of aesthetics as the effort to make life better;[25] yet, this focus on embodiment actually allows for a shift to a more concrete engagement with the body that marks out its beauty, its "wholeness," and other qualities expressed in/through its materiality in the world. This is not reducible to counting Africanisms or vague pronouncements of ritual stylizations as "muscle memory";[26] rather it is the mapping

---

20. Paris, *Spirituality of African Peoples*, 71.
21. Paris, *Spirituality of African Peoples*, 134.
22. Paris, *Spirituality of African Peoples*, 135.
23. Paris, *Spirituality of African Peoples*, 22.
24. I have in mind Susan Bordo's argument for the importance of bodies, which doesn't rule out the nature of bodies constructed through discourse but also recognizes the fundamental significance of physical bodies. See, for example, Bordo, "Bringing Body to Theory," 84–99; and Bordo, *Unbearable Weight*.
25. Paris, *Spirituality of African Peoples*, 147.
26. Over how many generations would similar attention to dance be accounted for

of religious experience through a rhythmic and embodied "darkening" of metaphysics.

The working of the embodied body within the religious experience of people of African descent, those of concern to Paris, doesn't render the body less visible. Instead, these embodied practices shift the intent of this visibility as well as the source of this visibility. The former—i.e., capitalized anti-Black racism—seeks a visibility that reifies as troubling "other," and the latter—i.e., religiously highlighted bodies—seeks visibility that produces the Glorified Ones who hold in tension the horizontal and vertical dimensions of theologized thought. Through the former is communicated a caution against pollution, and the latter is meant to suggest energy fueled possibility. The latter is meant to "break open" space, so to speak, whereas the former is meant to reify and fix space, rendering it unsuitable for embodied Black life to thrive. And so, to borrow an idea from Jacob Olupona, "matter matters . . . material practices are not a manipulation of the sacred, but the sacred itself."[27] The body is connective tissue between ideals and existential contexts of actualization. These bodies, in a word, re-member. The argument is noteworthy when made by Yolanda Covington-Ward and Jeanette S. Jouili, who write, "Religious communities and individuals of African descent have reacted to . . . stereotypes about Black bodies and embodiment and these proscriptions against certain embodied practices in various ways, whether in Chicago, Colombia, or Côte d'Ivoire."[28] The embodied body in motion—at "work"—can point religious attention to both the limits of its context (e.g., horizontal considerations) and the *More Than* it seeks to touch (e.g., vertical considerations).[29]

There is much to learn from the physicality of the body: What does the clothing worn on the embodied body say about religiosity and community—the expression of a theologized personhood? What does the movement of the embodied body say about the expressivity of belief? What is known only through the workings of the embodied body? And, what can

---

through muscle memory, over against explicit observance and instruction? Is muscle memory selective in that not all people of African descent are skilled dancers? Authors such as Jacqui Malone and Brenda Dixon Gottschild, at times, speak in terms of muscle memory as a way to connect artistic expression across the Middle Passage and diaspora. See Malone, *Steppin' on the Blues*; and Gottschild, *Black Dancing Body*.

27. Olupona, Foreword, xi.

28. Covington-Ward and Jouili, "Introduction," 5.

29. In making this and related comments, my aim isn't to suggest a reading of Paris through New Materialism. My work, including this essay, holds some relationship to the rethinking of "substance" posed by New Materialism, but in general I don't adhere to it. For my thinking on the materiality of religion in relationship to New Materialism, see Pinn, *Interplay of Things*, introduction, chs. 1–2.

be known when embodied bodies "connect" by sharing an orchestrated movement through a set aside time and space? The worlds—social and conceptual—are dependent on the touch of these bodies. Such is the intent of religious engagement—and this is even more the case for peoples whose history involves struggle against graphic and violent modes of anti-Blackness. To get at these questions and considerations, I want to employ some of the innovations in Black studies, along with certain dimensions of thing theory to reassess the nature of embodiment and the function of the embodied body by rethinking one of the activities Paris briefly associates with this diasporic tradition along the lines of its body dependency.[30] After all, as Jacqui Malone, reminds us, "Africans' strong attitudes toward music and dance—and of the vital links between them—set the stage for the dancing and music-making cultures to come in North and South America."[31] And, to the extent this is the case and is reflected on the micro-level in the performance of the "African factor," turning to dance serves to heighten perception of embodiment undergirding Paris's text.

TAKES A BODY TO DANCE

The Spirituality of African Peoples doesn't provide much description of the cultural forms that animate the "African factor" at work in community. However, intriguing for my purposes, there are numerous passing references to dance. For instance: "The way in which music, dancing, and singing are integrated into the activity of work," writes Paris, "contributes energy and beauty to the improvisational and cooperative spirit of the people involved."[32] Within this text dance is a mechanism of ritual connection—a binding of personhood to larger forces and obligations that mark inclusion in community. It can be a marker—a particular framing of time/space occupied—that speaks to embodied cooperation. Accordingly, dance relates to the transference of the "African factor" in at least these ways: (1) serving as a cultural creation tying together two African contexts and their horizontal-vertical dynamics; (2) constituting a source of social bonding essential

---

30. While Paris doesn't theorize the body and doesn't define what is meant by embodiment, my effort to unpack the implications of the physical body for his argument requires a more explicit definition. In this essay, I mean by *body* the conjunction of the discursively constructed form and the bio-medical, physical, reality. By *embodiment* I intend to point out the manner in which the more abstract presentation of the body is given physical depth of presentation. For a more detailed presentation of my thinking on the body, see Pinn, *Embodiment and the New Shape*; and Pinn, *End of God-Talk*.

31. Malone, *Steppin' on the Blues*, 22.

32. Paris, *Spirituality of African Peoples*, 146.

for the maintenance and nurturing of community; and, (3) demonstrating practices for restoration of balance that maintains proper relationship between horizontal and vertical dimensions of engagement.

While I don't have space adequate for a detailed discussion of dance within African American cultural history, it is important to provide some sense of what is meant by dance within the following pages. However, in providing this brief contextual material, I am less concerned with particular dimensions of African retention found in dance. (I want to assume such retentions—at least in light of Paris's argument for an "African factor.") Instead, I am more concerned with the role of the body in dance. Beyond contextual and theoretical discussion of dance in general, I limit my attention, for the most part, to dance in the form of particular religious engagements such as the ring shout briefly mentioned by Paris but of significant importance in discussions of early African American Christianity—yet marked by intriguing commonalities with dance/possession in other African based traditions in African American communities.[33] Perhaps something of this "African factor" names a standard process for Black people in anti-Black climates to maintain themselves "in spite of . . ." through the ritualization of life acted out as their embodied bodies move rhythmically through time and space?[34]

Black embodied bodies in motion defy Western logic and push Western socio-religious comfort. They sweat; they gyrate; they speak—which is to say that promote a type of "mad" agency and ecstatic presence the bondage of their ancestors and continued anti-Blackness were meant to tame, if not prevent.[35] Embodied bodies active in such a way confuse the social logic. They urge a re-evaluation of humanity so as to make it definable not strictly in terms of horizontal regulations (although it seeks to amend these), but rather through vertical claims and faith-fueled possibilities that seek to jettison regulations as "bending"—refusing to understand these regulations as making meaningful sense.[36] Some dance is meant to revive the embodied body—to connote value within its materiality. It is a reconstruction of the despised—e.g., the body targeted by the various practices of anti-Blackness—into an altered form through, in part, new placement

---

33. Paris, *Spirituality of African Peoples*, 119n35.

34. The idea of ritualization of life is borrowed from Jacqui Malone, who, in turn, references Albert Murray's attention to the manner in which Black people ritualize life. See Malone, *Steppin' on the Blues*, 27.

35. This sense of "madness" should be read in light of the conceptualization-theorization of madness offered by Bruce in *How to Go Mad Without Losing Your Mind*.

36. I say this in relationship to arguments made by Harney and Moten, *Undercommons*.

in time and space. By dance is generated, in this regard, an altered sense of embodiment that both captures (e.g., meaningfulness) and releases (e.g., signs of disregard).

The body in motion—as in dancing—is a complex conveyer. By this I mean something along the lines of what Dana Mills chronicles when saying, "dance is a sustained method of communication that includes grammatical structures and units, just like verbal language; at the same time, it is a method of intervention that brings new speaking beings into shared space. Dance has its own methods of interpreting values through symbolic structures."[37] Dance, then, can be said to constitute in this context of the "African factor" not simply meaningful awareness that gives time and space a particular charge, but rather a metaphysical claim not hamstrung by the limits of verbal communication. And such is the case whether dance is thought out in accordance with prescribed mechanics or done as a free-form and unstructured engagement. It serves as a means by which the embodied body is extended beyond itself—serving to connect the "what was" with the present, and the "not yet" lodged in the theological claims it enacts. Through theologized movement, experience is reconstituted and recast as composing both the need for and resolution to moral-ethical concerns. Within the context of religious ritual—i.e., meaning-*full* dance—activity takes on new connotations and assumed possibilities. It is an altered location, one that seeks to hold in tension vertical and horizontal timing and intent. Steps, for instance, are not simply the work needed to move from one place to another. They are in this ritual context an invitation to consider other vertical-horizontal dynamics of engagements and purpose. And so, one might capture the meaning here by arguing any ongoing presence of the "African factor" involves not a body *and* religion framework but rather the body *as/in* religion—embodiment as encountered (or living) theology, with theology understood as a "charged" and purposeful ordering of asserted metaphysical assumptions.

The religiously engaged and embodied body isn't simply the discursive body, the political body, the cultural body, in normative terms; rather, the embodied body *as/in* religious experience becomes something "different"—i.e., a conduit for encounters and possibilities best defined in terms of theological values and pronouncements. Or, if one borrows language from Brenda Dixon Gottschild, one might say the dancing embodied body advances the "African factor" through its presentation of "soul," which serves to "mediate between flesh and spirit." More to the point, "it has a sensual, visceral connotation of connectedness with the earth (and the

---

37. Mills, *Dance and Politics*, 2.

earth-centered religions that distinguish West and Central African cultures) and, concomitantly, a reaching for the spirit."[38] Which is to say, continuing with Gottschild, "soul is the nitty-gritty personification of the energy and force that it takes to be black and survive."[39] And, in this religious equation, "spirit is the reacher, extending our bodies beyond our pores and allowing us to mirror and reflect (to embody) the aura bodies of ancestral and cosmic entities in the housing of our own physical baggage."[40] To know something of the theological assumptions undergirding the rhythm of Black religiosity, watch embodied bodies as they "move" and in their moving affirm the "messy" nature of theological claims within a world that seeks to tame and manage bodies. In a social world marked by deceit and disregard, little can be relied on to advance Black moral vision other than the "protective" casing of embodied bodies in motion and "grounded."

This is not to speak of "revealed truths" as such, but rather to recognize and center the stories of life encased through embodiment—and activated by means of modalities of movement that give greater visibility to cultural stress points. Such is not dance as spectacle, for the advantage and benefit of status-quo cultural curiosity. No, it is, in fact, movement that short-circuits that curiosity by signifying it and by re-envisioning embodiment. Of course, there would be some continuity between "then" (i.e., configuration of a past marked by policy-driven anti-Blackness) and "now" (e.g., extra-policy and popular modalities of anti-Blackness contested but present nonetheless). And this continuity would be expressed through embodied bodies engaging the material and non-material dynamics of sociality. Would one expect less if, as Brenda Dixon Gottschild, notes, "dance, indeed, is a measure of society and a barometer of culture"?[41] Such is a reference to dance beyond the generic string of movements, but rather it pushes toward additional dynamics of embodiment: oppositional activities serving to transform the meaning/intent of activity. This draws the conversation back to what Gottschild references as the "soul" in *Black* movement.

The *soul* in *Black* movement . . . Early in the development of the Black church there is the ring shout, a rhythmic movement of the body that must have resembled the sway and jerk of bodies associated with trances and "ecstatic" behavior in traditional African religions. The shout involves a creative rejection of the dominant religious discourse and its replacement with a commitment to visibility, being, meaning. What takes place is

---

38. Gottschild, *Black Dancing Body*, 223.
39. Gottschild, *Black Dancing Body*, 223.
40. Gottschild, *Black Dancing Body*, 223.
41. Gottschild, Foreword, xii.

a metamorphosis of sorts, through which the despised gain a new understanding of and space within life, pushing through invisibility to a more complex form of subjectivity. It is a movement beyond what historian of religion Charles Long refers to as the "opaqueness of the condition" encountered by Africans as "others." In this sense it is the transformation of the despised into beings of beauty and worth through a signifying of their assumed static status.[42] Yet, there are dilemmas or problems associated with this embodied performance in that—while it might seek to name, position, and enhance (differently) embodied Black bodies—it is a liminal space that by its nature succumbs to the demands of the social world. That is to say, enactment of the "African factor" doesn't jettison the embodied body as both promise and problem; rather, through the arrangement of (alternate) time and space, the problem is amplified actually. It is this intersection, the place where the collision between vertical aspiration and horizontal condition is most forceful, Paris doesn't address. Instead, one could say *The Spirituality of African Peoples* turns away from the body as body and instead highlights the ephemeral theological values Paris seeks to foreground. However, what these values "say" about the "African factor" through this wrestling, I would suggest, is secondary: theory follows data.

If one reads carefully, one comes across markers for Paris's preference. For example, the actual activity of the body is mentioned briefly—e.g., in a passing reference to dance, a footnote suggesting a source, or the implications undergirding an announcement of what people of African descent do. The latter—the implications—entails the assumption that the "body" is the "concrete" outlining of values developed and implied. There are ways in which these values are meant to cover the body—not as in dressing the body, but as in hiding the body, i.e., to "pause" the hyper-visibility that tends toward a warping of their supple nature rendering them objects open for manipulation to safeguard the status-quo. To highlight the embodied Black body—to read all experience through the embodied Black body—is to maintain a sense of loss attached to new locations of possibility. It is to acknowledge the ongoing misery carved into these bodies over time—without losing sight of how these bodies still persist. If one thinks about the embodied body this way, one might also note a structural and programmatic possibility that Paris—like so many within the study of African American religion—is wont to express: The "African factor" points out a problem more than it solves a spiritual dilemma. That is to say, this theological-ethical connection between two traumatized geographies merging as a form of (meta)

---

42. This material on the ring shout is drawn from Pinn, "Sweaty Bodies in a Circle," 11–26.

physical encounter highlights (and also speaks against) the ongoing effort to destroy Black life.

If Saidiya Hartman is correct and the Black body has been constituted as a "weapon used against the enslaved," and I would add their descendants, perhaps dance becomes a way of reconstituting the embodied body and thereby forging new approaches to life, mocking anti-Black sociality?[43] Still, even if this is the case, this doesn't serve to end circumstances of demise, but instead entails an altered positioning in the world. Put differently, dance in the form of the ring shout doesn't end "possession" as a mode of ownership but rather it offers a different possession—one that is meant to highlight value by exposing new dimensions of existence not confined to the structures of disregard. What does dance say about the body? In light of what can be gleaned from Paris's book, one might argue for him it points to the aesthetic nature of the "African factor"—the manner in which religious sensibilities transverse the "middle passage" and are lodged in the development of Black spirituality. Namely, he might stress the ways in which the ring shout points to the continuation of African sensibilities—e.g., the presence of the gods within the community of devotion, the communal nature of religious engagement, and the embodied nature of the "African factor." For Paris these bodies do work, but what of these bodies *themselves*? What of this embodiment, and what of the ring shout when embodied bodies are highlighted over against the more abstract African-ness believed to be embedded in the dance and expressed through these bodies?

Clear and explicit reading of dance through the body promotes a different sense of aesthetics. Whereas for Paris, aesthetics has to do with the constitution of a moral community, through a turn to the body, aesthetics becomes more easily discussed in terms of beauty and wholeness grounded in physicality. This is to give keen attention to the material changes as bodies shift their occupation of time and space—speaking without words to life meanings. Blackness is presented through a different visibility, through a different intent—and by means of materiality. Such is an act that grounds vertical claims to horizontal expression, which is to say bodies matter in that they make knowable theological claims. The development of Paris's argument would suggest embodiment is of secondary concern to the theological-ethical structures of thought promoting abstract moral community. To be precise, thinking ideals trumps the material performance of those ideals—i.e., the nonmaterial over the material—although one might say the body is the limit of those ideals made visible, impactful, or "real." While this might be overstating the case, the "African factor" is dependent on the body

---

43. Hartman, *Scenes of Subjection*, 38.

but, at least implicitly, seeks a certain freedom from the existential "weight" of the embodied body.

Drawing from Robert Farris Thompson's "flash of the spirit" language, DeFrantz writes, "To enable the flash of the spirit, the dancer must be willing to become the thing that is being danced or being summoned."[44] While I hold to the importance of such an entanglement, in the context of this discussion of Paris's work, I shift the direction of impact. In relationship to the materiality of the "African factor" it is the nonmaterial that bends to the body because nonmaterial values are named and presented in relationship to the body. The nonmaterial is—in a sense—confined to embodiment as "flesh" sets the parameters of horizontal-vertical interaction. And because this is the case, religion within the context of the African diaspora, for example, presents this relationship in at least two ways: (1) denial of embodiment as important—i.e., the spiritualization of life; or (2) signifying of warped presentations of embodied African-ness and Blackness. By most accounts the latter is the religious orientation privileged by Paris and the scholars of African American religion he notes. But it is the latter restricted in part by a reluctance to fully engage the embodied body as material hermeneutic and cosmic map. In a word, the subjectivity sought within the liberationist agenda outlined by Paris requires a reframing of the embodied body as well as attention to metaphysical matters. The embodied body that was beaten, disregarded, pulled apart—both literally and figuratively—is turned to and revitalized, but it isn't celebrated. In this way, the body functions to only give (new) "life" to a signifying set of moral-ethical considerations.

We owe Paris a debt of gratitude in that he does a masterful job of highlighting this transformation; but it is done backward to the extent he highlights moral-ethical values and downplays their embodied expression, or materiality—the physicality of our "knowing" and "doing." Put another way, and to borrow language from Dana Mills, "in its ability to open up new worlds of meaning," she writes, "the body can open up new possibilities of being in the world, new spaces in which the subject can partake."[45] To dance is not to end resistance, to end confinement. Rather, dance—e.g., the ring shout—usurps the authoritative intent of anti-Black restriction *by moving*. How much more of what Paris intends to outline is available to us if we amplify and render central the work of the embodied (Black) body?

This is not to reduce the body to biology. No, it is recognition of the degree to which moral-ethical values (i.e., the "African factor") is discernible/knowable only by appreciating bodies *as embodied* bodies—in their

---

44. DeFrantz, "African American Dance," 98.

45. Mills, *Dance and Politics*, 25.

body-ness. This is to claim the "religious" significance of embodiment as mode of meaning making and conveyance. Both seen and ignored, the embodied body is a kind of physicality for a blackened *"mysterium tremendum"* and *"mysterium facinosum."*[46] Religious experience of concern to Paris can't be adequately named or compiled without attention to the embodied body's performance of theological-ethical adjustments and claims.[47] The body links vertical claims/desires and horizontal circumstances.

Dance is a medium across Black religious traditions—a medium that links worlds and gives material substance to psychic considerations. In this way, the embodied body is the entanglement of worlds—the physicality by means of which sociality has any significance. Both the stresses of life in an anti-Black social context and the ability to push against such dehumanization are born in and reflected through the embodied body. In fact, the embodied body was (and remains) the only means of knowing and communicating that is sure—that is consistently available. What does it mean to speak of gods in relationship to humanity without measuring that involvement through body language, through embodied signs? Possession, for instance, has no meaning outside the body—and possession of a sort is the fundamental aim of the ring shout. This aesthetic experience transforms theological discourse, rendering it a body language that highlights the intersection of two (horizontal and vertical) realms of meaning. In this context more is gathered concerning the theological claims of the community from the bend of the body, the sway of the arms, the frantic energy of leg movement, then from any written communication. From Africa to the Americas, the Black body communicated depths of meaning. Colonialism and white supremacy knew this and religious communities amplified this—rendering the embodied body both the source and content of deep yearnings across social worlds. Yet, what comes of all this? Freedom? Liberation? Freedom or liberation for all Black body-types?

BODY-TYPES: A CONCLUDING WORD

To the degree performance speaks of survival, I would have to agree with Mlondolozi Zondi in counter distinction to Paris's assumptions concerning liberation as "event." Reflecting on Black dance in another context in terms of continuity of presence, Zondi says, "Survival is the *afterlife of slavery*,

---

46. See Otto, *Idea of the Holy*.

47. I say this reflecting on and, to some extent, in conversation with Zondi, "Haunting Gathering."

and not its resolution or its transcendence."[48] Which is to say, there is no deep freedom found in the ability to withstand one's circumstances. Such an ability shouldn't be confused with liberation from those circumstances. Embodied bodies that withstand aren't to be confused with embodied bodies that overcome. Yet, in fairness, is liberation or freedom—often worded as "future"—possible for embodied beings within a world shaped by and orchestrated in accordance with anti-justice mechanisms? Can these bodies push hard enough to end up "outside" the limits of their existential setting and metaphysical "prisons"? One might say this is especially the case, and these questions are particularly compelling because embodied effort is the residue of ongoing disregard.

Display of and practices related to the embodied body can be said to constitute a mode of resistance *qua* the "African factor." However, this embodied resistance in relationship to certain forms of disregard can also serve to re-enforce other structures of injustice. How does the "African factor" present embodied bodies, when they aren't explicitly named? What, or better yet, who are they (Africans and their keen) prior to and outside of this particular theologized work? What is the grammar and vocabulary used to capture and describe the embodied body? And does this grammar/vocabulary assume certain modalities of masculinity or femininity as the proper representation of "right" bodies? One must think about this in complex ways, beyond cisgender normativity. Put another way, what are the capacities of these bodies assumed by Paris beyond their service as the storehouse of the "African factor"? This is a different arrangement of aesthetics in that it isn't about the wholeness of community (as Paris describes aesthetics) but rather the beauty, or "wholeness" (i.e., "symmetry") of the embodied body over against the social stigmas to which Black life in general and the "African factor" in particular are meant to respond. Stated yet another way, what is the "look" of the bodies—their capacities beyond the religious—reflected in Paris's work? How are they gendered? Sexed? Classed? Abled?

This raises a great deal for consideration, more than can be covered in this essay. But, even so, it is important to note before ending that the embodied body is also (and always) vulnerable within the religious context. All body work is not, of necessity, productive. Think about the ways in which gender can challenge access to participation and can shape in stereotypical ways the nature of the embodied body's reception both within ritual and after ritual. Think of the ways in which the expression of theological claims through the actions of the body can both challenge and embrace troubling social codes and standards. Isn't denial of the centrality of the embodied

---

48. Italics in original. Zondi, "Haunting Gathering," 263.

body, on one level, an adherence to the very "Western" structures of reality such religious practices were meant to disrupt? This can certainly be the case when Black religiosity is misunderstood as constituting a "fix," or a path to freedom from the structures of anti-Blackness that encouraged the very formation of Black religiosities as counter-narrative. Can Black religiosity somehow end the "othering" of Black people? No, one should be mindful of Mychal Denzel Smith's discouraging (for those assuming religion as ultimate corrective) but keen insight when saying, "There is no place where we have not been marked as other, where our otherness has not been used to justify our exploitation, and where our lives have not been defined by the limitations placed on them by whiteness."[49] Yet, all dance is not forced movement on slave ships, or the Jim Crow*ish* command to shuffle as a mode of belittling. Some dance is a statement of meaning signifying anti-Black dehumanization. There might be something religious—something of Black spirituality—in deciphering the difference. Such is one of the important lessons hidden in Paris's magisterial book.

BIBLIOGRAPHY

Andrews, Kehinde. *The New Age of Empire: How Racism and Colonialism Still Rule the World*. New York: Bold Type Books, 2021.

Bordo, Susan. "Bringing Body to Theory." In *Body and Flesh: A Philosophical Reader*, edited by Donn Welton, 84–99. Malden, MA: Blackwell, 1998.

———. *Unbearable Weight: Feminism, Western Culture, and the Body*. Berkeley: University of California Press, 1993.

Brown, Bill, ed. *Things*. A Critical Inquiry Book. Chicago: University of Chicago Press, 2004.

———. "Thing Theory." *Critical Inquiry* 28.1 (2001) 1–22.

Bruce, La Marr Jurelle. *How to Go Mad Without Losing Your Mind: Madness and Black Radical Creativity*. Black Outdoors. Durham: Duke University Press, 2021.

Covington-Ward, Yolanda, and Jeanette Selma Jouili, eds. "Introduction: Embodiment and Relationality in Religions of Africa and Its Diasporas." In *Embodying Black Religions in Africa and Its Diasporas*, 1–19. Religious Cultures of African and African Diaspora People. Durham: Duke University Press, 2021.

DeFrantz, Thomas F. "African American Dance—Philosophy, Aesthetics, and 'Beauty.'" *Topoi* 24.1 (2005) 93–102.

Fanon, Frantz. *Black Skin, White Masks*. Rev. ed. New York: Grove, 2008.

Gottschild, Brenda Dixon. *The Black Dancing Body: A Geography from Coon to Cool*. New York: Palgrave Macmillan, 2003.

———. Foreword to *Dancing in Blackness: A Memoir*, by Halifu Osumare, xi–xiv. Gainesville: University Press of Florida, 2018.

Harney, Stefano, and Fred Moten. *The Undercommons: Fugitive Planning and Black Study*. New York: Minor Compositions, 2013.

---

49. Smith, *Stakes Is High*, 7.

Hartman, Saidiya V. *Scenes of Subjection: Terror, Slavery, and Self-Making in Nineteenth-Century America*. Race and American Culture. New York: Oxford University Press, 1997.

Long, Charles H. "What Is Africa to Me? Reflection, Discernment, and Anticipation." In *The Collected Writings of Charles H. Long*, 247–59. New York: Bloomsbury Academic, 2018.

Malone, Jacqui. *Steppin' on the Blues: The Visible Rhythms of African American Dance*. Folklore and Society. Urbana: University of Illinois Press, 1996.

Mills, Dana. *Dance and Politics: Moving Beyond Boundaries*. Manchester: Manchester University Press, 2017.

Mott, Jason. *Hell of a Book: Or the Altogether Factual, Wholly Bona Fide Story of a Big Dreams, Hard Luck, American-Made Mad Kid*. New York: Dutton, 2021.

Olupona, Jacob K. Foreword to *Embodying Black Religions in Africa and Its Diasporas*, edited by Yolanda Covington-Ward and Jeanette Selma Jouili, vii–xiv. Religious Cultures of African and African Diaspora People. Durham: Duke University Press, 2021.

Otto, Rudolf. *The Idea of the Holy: An Inquiry into the Non-Rational Factor in the Idea of the Divine and Its Relation to the Rational*. New York: Oxford University Press, 1958.

Paris, Peter J. *The Spirituality of African Peoples: The Search for a Common Moral Discourse*. Minneapolis: Fortress, 1995.

Pinn, Anthony B. *African American Humanist Principles: Living and Thinking Like the Children of Nimrod*. Black Religion, Womanist Thought, Social Justice. New York: Palgrave Macmillan, 2004.

———. *Embodiment and the New Shape of Black Theological Thought*. Religion, Race, and Ethnicity. New York: New York University Press, 2010.

———. *The End of God-Talk: An African American Humanist Theology*. Oxford: Oxford University Press, 2012.

———. *Interplay of Things: Religion, Art, and Presence Together*. Religious Studies, African American Studies, Art. Durham London: Duke University Press, 2021.

———. "Sweaty Bodies in a Circle: Thoughts on the Subtle Dimensions of Black Religion as Protest." *Black Theology: An International Journal* 4.1 (2006) 11–26.

Smith, Mychal Denzel. *Stakes Is High: Life After the American Dream*. New York: Bold Type Books, 2020.

Spillers, Hortense J. "Mama's Baby, Papa's Maybe: An American Grammar Book." *Diacritics* 17.2 (1987) 64–81.

Zondi, Mlondolozi. "Haunting Gathering: Black Dance and Afro-Pessimism." *ASAP/Journal* 5.2 (2020) 256–66.

Chapter 3

Two Congolese Christians Epitomize Self-Initiation Principle in Their Quest for Justice and Fullness of Life

Nyambura J. Njoroge

INTRODUCTION: SOME MEMORIES[1]

IN THE EARLY 2000s, I was privileged to be part of the four-year collaborative project of sixteen Pan-African religious scholars spearheaded by Professor Peter Paris, which explored religion and poverty among the African people in five different countries: Ghana, Kenya, South Africa, Jamaica, and the United States. In the collection of essays published at the end of this project, *Religion and Poverty: Pan African Perspectives*, Paris contributed a thought-provoking essay, "Self-Initiation: A Necessary Principle in the African Struggle to Abolish Poverty."[2]

The four-year collaborative Pan-African religious scholars project was a rude awakening on how little I knew of the African story. The series of seminars, lectures, and visits to various locations of historical significance provoked a surge of anger in me. The first time I felt similar anger was during my first professional trip to apartheid South Africa in 1993. At the personal

---

1. These memories are based on the four-year collaborative Pan-African religious scholars project which took place for two weeks every August from 2001 to 2004. For further reference see Paris, *Religion and Poverty*.

2. See Paris, "Self-Initiation," 315–39.

level, it did not help that I was still grieving the death of my mother in April 1992 while in diaspora, away from family and close friends.

By design, Ghana was the kick-off country for the project. Despite having read about the slave trade and having interacted with many Africans in the diaspora, in particular, African Americans and Caribbeans, and reading some of their writings, visiting the site of the two world heritage monuments at Elmina and Cape Coast castles in Ghana blew my mind. Being in the presence of African American and Caribbean sisters and brothers as we toured the castles left us speechless, in tears, angry, memories that are etched in my whole being.

During the study project, I visited a bookstore at Johannesburg airport when I stumbled over Adam Hochschild's book on *King Leopold's Ghost*.[3] After spending Christmas break reading the book, my spiritual and professional life were never the same again. The content of the book is heart-wrenching. Together with some painful experiences during the study project, I found it very difficult and challenging to continue attending church worship for a while. Providentially, being a founding member of the Circle of Concerned African Women Theologians, which is committed to nurturing, mentoring, and motivating women to research, write, and publish, I poured my grief and anger into writing articles.[4] Equally important, as a theologian and a Christian social ethicist, I have grown to value the social-political memory of African countries, storytelling, and people's narratives—including those found in sacred scriptures and oral literature—in search of life-affirming practical theologies and ethics amid the insurmountable reality of political brutality, violence, despair, hopelessness, and violent death.[5]

Hence, the purpose of this chapter is to explore how two Congolese Christian leaders have applied the self-initiation principle as articulated by Peter Paris, in whose honor I make this contribution. In other words, the essay explores how some Congolese Christians have made a covenant with life in the deeply entrenched institutionalized violence and inhumanity of King Leopold's greed and terror in the post-independent Democratic Republic of Congo—commonly known as Congo-Kinshasa to distinguish it from its neighbor, Republic of Congo or Congo-Brazzaville.

---

3. See Hochschild, *King Leopold's Ghost*.

4. For instance, Njoroge, "Spirituality of Resistance and Transformation," 66–82; and Njoroge, "Bible and Christianity," 207–36.

5. For further reading on theology and Christian social ethics in Africa, see Katongole, *Sacrifice of Africa*.

COVENANT WITH LIFE

Monique Misenga Ngoie Mukuna and Denis Mukwege in their respective memoirs, *Cradling Abundance: One African Christian's Story to Empowering Women and Fighting Systemic Poverty* and *The Power of Women: A Doctor's Journey of Hope and Healing*, authoritatively introduce us to a people and in particular the women who have made a covenant with life in one of the most politically violent countries amid great wealth in Africa—Congo-Kinshasa.[6]

Both were born in the 1950s in Belgian colonial Congo during the rule of King Leopold II of Belgium. In their childhood they had encounters with Christian missionaries. Their parents embraced Christianity and Western education. Each followed their parents in nurturing the Christian faith and taking every opportunity to further their education amid politics of greed, plunder, brutality, violence, and death. Their God-given gifts and creativity were nurtured in patriarchal colonial churches and within African patriarchal cultural households. Remarkably, their parents embraced gender justice regarding household chores and educational opportunities. In other words, Maman Monique was given opportunities to go to school at an early age and to further her studies, contrary to the prevailing patriarchal cultural practices of marrying off teenage daughters.[7] On the other hand, uncharacteristically, at the time, Denis Mukwege's mother ensured that he undertook household chores, which he shared with his older sisters. Their upbringing laid a firm foundation and spirituality and ethics of resistance, transformation, and justice. They had the spirituality and ethics that empowered them to be socially engaged in crafting and making practical, nonviolent initiatives and life-transforming ethics.

From an early age, both demonstrated compassionate and courageous leadership qualities embedded in Christian faith and a prayerful life. Eventually, they became voices of hope, healing, joy, and life in the wilderness of brutality, violence, and death. Every step of the way, each must contend with insurmountable death-dealing realities. In "Breaking the Covenant of Violence Against Women," the South African theologians and scholars Tinyiko Sam Maluleke and Sarojini Nadar passionately depict what the Congolese must struggle with throughout their lives.

> The word "covenant" is usually reserved for the extraordinary love contract that God initiates with unworthy human

---

6. See Mukuna and McKee, *Cradling Abundance*; and Mukwege, *Power of Women*.

7. Elsie Tshimunyi McKee, the co-author of the *Cradling Abundance*, has taken time to explain how in Congo-Kinshasa names and titles are given before she settles with Maman Monique, which is used in this essay.

> beings—binding them to God and vice versa—in a resilient, powerful, and committed relationship. We propose to use this notion in a different sense in this essay—to describe an unspoken, unwritten but very real covenant between human societies and violence. It is a deadly covenant cultivated and reinforced in attitudes, teachings, practices and rituals that tear human societies apart even as they promise to preserve and sustain. Above all, this is a covenant of silence—silence about violence, especially violence against women . . .
>
> Given the great cloud and intricate network of witnesses and conspirators who subscribe to the covenant of death, standing up against this covenant of death and violence is costly. It often results in the isolation and rejection of those who dare to speak. Therefore, the voices of those who dare to stand up against covenant are often like voices in the wilderness.[8]

Both memoirs do not shy away from depicting a rich mosaic of how a deadly covenant in Congo-Kinshasa has been cultivated and sustained and how their respective self-initiatives were conceived, nurtured, and inspired to offer a counter covenant with life. In a wide variety of ways, each initiative has taken the gospel according to Matt 25 very seriously, by the way they welcome the "stranger and the naked" as they have focused on healing girls and women who are sexually violated and face insurmountable gender-based injustices and systemic poverty.

The dignity, power, and well-being of the African woman are at the heart of their initiatives. Storytelling by their grandmothers, mothers, fathers, and other key actors in their childhood fashioned their worldviews and their visions for a covenant with life. Providentially, both concretely applied the self-initiation principle in 1999 after the rebels and Rwandan forces invaded Congo in 1996 at the start of the First Congo War. However, the fact that both Maman Monique and Denis Mukwege have lived to eloquently narrate their stories and self-initiatives of hope and life to the international audience is nothing but a miracle.

MAMAN MONIQUE: A WOMAN CHIEF

"People are wealth" was a common mantra in my youth in rural Kenya, uttered in Gĩkũyũ language, "andũ nĩo indo." In my efforts to understand these words, I nurtured the love of reading feature stories, profiles, autobiographies, biographies, and memoirs. Eventually, I discovered that this

---

8. Maluleke and Nadar, "Breaking the Covenant of Violence Against Women," 7.

genre of literature tells much more than the individual in question. Without the friendship, enthusiasm, tireless commitment, and accompaniment of Elsie Tshimunyi McKee, the Archibald Alexander Professor of Reformation Studies and the History of Worship at Princeton Theological Seminary, who was born and raised in Congo-Kinshasa, Maman Monique's story may not have seen the light of day for many decades.

For ten years (2010–20), the two women spent countless hours piecing the stories together, including those of other key players, narrated in Tshiluba and Lingala, two Congolese languages with French translation. Painstakingly, the original conversations were taped—a few in video, mostly audio, which English readers now can "overhear," according to McKee. The tapes produced about 679 pages in French (169,696 words), so the reader is left to imagine the kind of cutting and editing that took place, let alone the translation to English. It is no wonder McKee asserts that "every story has a story." In the introduction "Why This Book Matters and Where It Fits In," McKee writes:

> The story I was hearing and seeing in Kinshasa in August 2010 began to take shape in my imagination. Who is this amazing woman? What else had she done? I wanted to know more. And the more I learned, the more I wanted to share the story of this remarkable Christian and her ministry. It is not just Maman Monique's work, though FEBA [*Femme, Berceau de l'Abondance, FEBA* acronym in French] would never have happened or survived without her. She and those she inspires are demonstrating that those on the margins, "second-class citizens" of their world, can be instruments of "cradling abundance" (John 10:10) for others. This story is a window on the shared faith, deep prayer life, and sheer grit and guts of so many African Christian women who confront all kinds of challenges: human and natural, political and economic, educational and spiritual, day in and day out. And they never give up, never stop caring, and never stop singing and hoping and working for life abundant in Jesus Christ, the Good Shepherd.[9]

Maman Monique is a powerhouse of courage, creativity, fruitfulness, joy and peace. At twenty years, her father was told, "What a child you have, what a daughter! No, she is not a daughter; she is a man! She saved us."[10] In a deeply entrenched patriarchal culture, what sounds like an insult was a great compliment in a context where a busload of passengers was confronted by

---

9. Mukuna and McKee, *Cradling Abundance*, 5.
10. Mukuna and McKee, *Cradling Abundance*, xii.

armed soldiers under the cruel rule of General Sese Seko Mobutu. The only person who dared challenge them was Maman Monique. Yet, women are not expected to demonstrate bravery, which is considered masculine.

Perusing through her childhood, which she brilliantly narrates, she learned the gifts of generosity, hospitality, and a prayerful life from her grandmothers, auntie, and father. But growing up in a family of ten sisters and three brothers, she learned early in life that, in her village, girls were not valued and were only good for marriage and childbearing. Literally, people believed her parents did not have children because the majority were girls. Consequently, her mother was a victim of violence from the people around her. Nevertheless, her parents would have none of it. All children were sent to school and Maman Monique (second-born and eldest daughter) and the last-born brother received university educations in pedagogy and economics, respectively.[11] Most significantly, she credits her father for the spirit of the self-initiation principle in her life.

> Our father also taught us vocational activities. I learned to sew at home, not at school. My father created a spirit of initiative in me. He said, "I do not want you to be unhappy or enslaved in life. I am teaching you vocational activities so that, even if you do not have a job from what you learn at school, you can work." That is what has always motivated me.[12]

Regrettably, when she was eight years old, at the dawn of independence from Belgium (1958–61), people started infighting and killing (mostly men) among Congolese people, and her father's life was threatened. Her relatives were displaced, and many were pushed into poverty. Her generous father took them in and provided shelter while educating others. Most importantly, Maman Monique acknowledges, "In our childhood, we lived in good conditions. I never knew a life of poverty, lack, because my father raised chickens, ducks, rabbits, goats, and cows and farmed all kinds of food crops. We drank fresh cow's milk; we never experienced famine."[13] These childhood experiences and education paved the way for her to become responsible and astute in navigating challenging circumstances as well as

---

11. I resonate with Maman Monique's story here. My parents had nine daughters, no son. Despite being church and community leaders, my parents were ridiculed, and my father was expected to take a second wife, to bear him son(s) who will inherit him. But none of this deterred them from educating us, beyond high school to the extent that two of us earned PhDs in theology and science.

12. Mukuna and McKee, *Cradling Abundance*, 30.

13. Mukuna and McKee, *Cradling Abundance*, 27.

making difficult choices about her profession as young educated Christian woman.

Her studies in pedagogy (teaching) and good command of the French language would have landed her lucrative government jobs after attending a world youth festival in East Berlin in 1973, which was government-sponsored. Nonetheless, the youth festival exposed her to new forms of sexual violence against women. Eventually, when she was offered to be part of a delegation traveling with President Mobutu's first trip to China, and she was warned that accepting the offer would lead her to death, she listened. In addition to her teaching career, she chose marriage. Within a year of her marriage, the couple was blessed with a son. Tragically, her husband died suddenly. As if that was not enough, her six-month-old son also died.

Heartbroken, depressed, and grieving, Maman Monique was nursed back to health through prayers and a supportive family. She later remarried and had nine children. She writes about these dark moments.

> My life has been richly blessed with Tatu Mukuna and our nine children, and I am deeply grateful to God. Yet what came before marked my soul and gave me a heart to reach out, to understand how to be with those who mourn. Infant and maternal mortality are high in Congo. Women often die from childbirth complications, and there are very few families which do not lose babies, at birth or before the age of five. Nothing prepares you for the sudden death of your first precious infant, as I know from experience, and when you are also newly widowed, the world seems to end.[14]

Their marriage was tested and tried by major illnesses of the children and the death of her father, which followed in 1981, but he did not die without teaching his beloved daughter a last lesson. Before he fell into a coma and died, he summoned her to the hospital. "I have considered all my children, and it is you who can be my heir. I want to leave you all the responsibility, all my possessions."[15] Maman Monique categorically said no and insisted that her brothers take that role, because she was afraid they would kill her. Finally, he said:

> Okay, if you do not want it, I will leave it to Kalala (the youngest son). But I will tell you something. You say that you are a girl. In the tradition of our village, a woman can be a chief of the village. . . . If she does not want to direct matters, she can give her power to her brother, but the brother is not the chief. He works

14. Mukuna and McKee, *Cradling Abundance*, 48–9.
15. Mukuna and McKee, *Cradling Abundance*, 59.

and comes and gives an accounting to his sister. They call this woman "*Ilunga Mbiya*"—a woman who is chief. So you cannot say that it is only boys who can direct; you can.[16]

WOMAN, CRADLE OF ABUNDANCE (*FEMME, BERCEAU DE L'ABONDANCE, FEBA*)

Maman Monique is a good listener, a quick learner, and a doer. For the last fifty years, she has diligently and fruitfully carried out multiple roles in the family, community, church, and ecumenical settings as a daughter, teacher, principal, wife, mother, village "chief," family manager, entrepreneur, churchwomen's mobilizer and organizer, activist, international ecumenical leader, peacemaker, advocate and founder and the mover of Woman, Cradle of Abundance (*FEBA*). She has been mentored by remarkable Christian women in her Presbyterian church and the Community of Protestant Churches nationally. Her church involvement as a church elder and leader of the women's department opened doors for her to be ecumenically engaged in the All Africa Conference of Churches, World Alliance of Reformed Churches (now World Communion of Reformed Churches), and World Council of Churches. Her business in marketing sewing products took her to other African countries, including Morocco and South Africa.

In all these church-related encounters she must contend with male dominated leadership and women who support the status quo, especially the wives of powerful church leaders. Moreover, she had to learn to work in contexts of violence.

> As a child I had grown up through the civil war on Congo. Then in 1965 General Mobutu took over in a military coup so our lives continued under a dictator. It was very dangerous to speak against him, but people helped each other to survive. In the 1990s in the context of my church responsibilities I became involved in responding to the turbulence and fighting, the struggles of displaced and destitute persons in neighboring countries. And then war came to Congo again in 1996, and rape and violence have spread everywhere.[17]

As a Christian, she also realized that the prevailing theology in the churches is disempowering to women who remain in systemic poverty, despair, and hopelessness due to a lack of knowledge and information. To bring

16. Mukuna and McKee, *Cradling Abundance*, 59–60.
17. Mukuna and McKee, *Cradling Abundance*, 96.

change to the women, Maman Monique applied the self-initiation principle to empower women through leadership seminars and income-generating projects by hosting intensive training workshops anchored in contextual Bible studies to address unyielding spiritual poverty. The encounter of weeping Mary Magdalene with Jesus at the garden (John 20:1–18) turned the tide.

Globally, the 1988 the World Council of Churches (WCC) declared the Ecumenical Decade of Churches in Solidarity with Women (1988–98). In Africa, women gathered in Lomé, Togo, in 1988 to launch the decade, and a delegation of thirty Congolese women attended, but Maman Monique did not attend. The theme was "Rise and Shine." In December 1998, at the end of the decade, there was a festival in Harare, Zimbabwe, to make an account of all that had been done.[18] During the ten years, women in different parts of the world wrestled with the challenges of injustices in the churches and in the society only to recognize that it was women in solidarity with women and not churches in solidarity with women.

Thirty Congolese women attended the festival led by Maman Monique. After the festival, she remained in Harare to participate in the general assembly of WCC as a delegate of her church. She was elected to the central committee of the WCC for eight years, an opportunity that gave her an international platform for learning, contributing, and flourishing. Most important, she witnessed the power of sisterhood—women's solidarity. She realized that women working within the church structures had manifold obstacles and that they had achieved very few Ecumenical Decade objectives. Rather, she observed that some of the most fruitful women's initiatives were nonprofits in their countries. As soon as they returned home, she initiated talks with a few women who attended the festival. The talks resulted in the founding of *Femme, Berceau de l'Abondance (FEBA)* on January 19, 1999. They chose Jesus' words in John 10:10, "I have come to give life, life abundant." They also identified the primary goal of raising consciousness and teaching women that they are human beings created in the image of God. Other specific goals were identified to fully address issues that were overlooked by Protestant denominational women's departments in the churches. *FEBA* is ecumenical, which includes Protestants, Catholics, African Instituted Churches, and Pentecostals.

Fundamentally, *FEBA* educates women that tolerating poverty is a sin and that they must do everything within their power and intellect to fight women's inferiority complex, illiteracy, domestic violence, unhygienic

---

18. I attended the festival. I was part of a small group that drafted a letter from the festival. See the report: World Council of Churches, "Your Story Is My Story," 90–99.

surroundings that enable communicable diseases, and material poverty. Maman Monique knows first-hand that education and lifetime learning from others is key to unlocking ignorance and poverty. Her approach is very practical. She works hard to tap the gifts and strengths of the women leaders in the churches and by inviting specialists. Bible stories and traditional Congolese proverbs are among the most effective tools of communication to overcome inexperience. Over the years, *FEBA* has offered training and education in economic literacy and microfinance, sexuality and HIV and AIDS, and agriculture, mostly focusing on unemployed young women. Because of the escalating war in eastern DRC, the 1994 genocide in Rwanda, and civil wars in other French-speaking countries, Maman Monique has been involved in peacemaking, ecumenical peace missions, and struggle for justice beyond her country, never giving up her hope and vision of life in its abundance. We now learn more about the escalating wars in eastern Democratic Republic of Congo (DRC) from the words of Denis Mukwege, who describes himself as "an accidental feminist and campaigner" of women's dignity and rights.

MEETING A COMPASSIONATE STRANGER

In 2018, Denis Mukwege, a renowned gynecological surgeon, was awarded the Nobel Peace Prize along with Nadia Murad, a Yazidi human rights activist and sexual violence survivor. It was so appropriate that he received the award alongside a sexual violence survivor as one recognized as the world's leading expert on treating rape injuries and his holistic approach to healing. Mukwege is a leading advocate for women's dignity, justice, peace, health, voices, and rights. His memories of childhood narratives, of how both his grandmothers died in childbirth of his parents and the near-death episode of his mother and himself in similar circumstances, are deeply embedded in his life and professional choices. His mother never forgot Majken Bergman, a Swedish Protestant missionary and a teacher who had chosen to live among the Congolese people in Bukavu, a rare European who chose to defy the apartheid arrangement of exclusive European-only, Asian-only, and African-only areas according to the rules of the Belgian colonial regime in the Congo. This pattern was extensively practiced in South Africa and Kenya with lasting negative impact.

As a child, Mukwege dreamed of becoming a pediatrician to save the lives of children like himself. Nevertheless, the more he witnessed the high rate of maternal mortality as he accompanied his father—the first Congolese Protestant pastor in Bukavu, eastern Congo—during his pastoral duties,

Mukwege discovered there was a deeper problem of devaluing women's lives. Sadly, the rivalry between Roman Catholic and European Protestant missionaries nearly cost Mukwege's life as he was denied treatment by a Catholic nun because he was a child of a Protestant pastor. However, the wise and quick actions of a compassionate stranger, Majken Bergman, saved his life. Later in life, Mukwege realized that her identity gave her power and responsibility. The manner in which Bergman lived her Christian life helped to shape his Christian morality and belief in the courage and power of extraordinary women who battled with multiple hardships and dehumanization.

Like Maman Monique, born in the 1950s, his childhood corresponded with the political decolonization process of many African countries. He faintly recollects accompanying his parents in 1960 to a political speech in Bukavu by Lumumba, who soon became the first prime minister and democratically elected leader of the independent Republic of the Congo. The tragic assassination of Lumumba on January 17, 1961, hardly six months into his office, drastically changed the young life of Mukwege and his family.

> In 1961, as boy of six, I sat in his church with my mother and sisters as heavily armed troops interrupted the service and dragged out a Swedish colleague of my father's on the orders of the local governor, who wanted to accelerate the departure of European settlers. I still recall the sound of military boots on the concrete floor, the frightened grimace of the Swedish pastor, and being too scared to turn around to look at the troops as they left. It was my first experience of violence. Papa was arrested a few days later and had a gun held to his head in the police station.[19]

He continues:

> These events would prepare me for other evacuations and periods of exile, for there have been many since then. I lost the illusion early that my parents, or our community, and still less the Congolese state, could shield me from danger. *If there is anything positive to say, it is only that it focused my mind on what was important: the health and safety of my loved ones.* Perhaps this explains why I've never been interested in accumulating possessions, knowing that they could be lost at any moment.[20]

Nonetheless, it was because of his father's pastoral ministry and its limitations to the sick and dying, whom he could only pray for but not

---

19. Mukwege, *Power of Women*, 18.
20. Mukwege, *Power of Women*, 18. My italics.

prescribe medication to, and his mother's persistent prayers that he became a doctor. Twenty years after this enriching encounter, Mukwege honored his parents by focusing on the well-being of his communities as a doctor after some detours into business in Kinshasa. With his mother's intervention, he ended up in a new medical school in Bujumbura, the capital of Burundi. After six years as a student doctor, Mukwege began his practice at a Swedish Pentecostal Mission hospital at Lemera, forty miles south of Bukavu. Instantly he came face to face with the maternal health-care crisis in rural Congo.

> In Lemera, I saw the consequences of neglect of women at the moment of childbirth, when they are at their most vulnerable and most powerful—when our Creator, through the design flaws of human anatomy, forces them to risk their own lives to deliver new ones.[21]

Mukwege set off on a journey of many discoveries, including the personal devastation caused by an obstetric fistula and that his actions could be the difference between life and death.[22] Like Maman Monique, his decisions and actions are exemplary of the self-initiation principle with a profound feminist conscience in their struggle against extreme poverty and violence meted out toward girls and women.[23] At the outset, in the introduction, Mukwege articulates his core convictions.

> I defend women because they are my equals—because women's rights are human rights, and I am outraged by the violence inflicted on my fellow humans. We must fight for women collectively. My role has always been to amplify the voices of others whose marginalization denies them opportunities to tell their stories. I stand at their side, never in front. . . . I am in many ways an accidental feminist and campaigner.[24]

PANZI HOSPITAL IN THE MIDST OF WAR

Growing up with a missionary-trained midwife mother operating a maternity clinic at home, I thought I had understood the vulnerability and power of rural women during pregnancy and childbirth, until I read *The Power of*

---

21. Mukwege, *Power of Women*, 26.
22. Mukwege, *Power of Women*, 27.
23. Mukwege, *Power of Women*, 35.
24. Mukwege, *Power of Women*, xiii.

Women, set in a military ruled country (Mobutu's thirty-two-year rule) and aftermaths of devastating wars with its neighbors. Painstakingly, Mukwege helps the reader to come to glimpse the beauty, riches, and resilience of women as well as the local and global primary actors who ignite and foment turmoil and violence that has become synonymous with the DRC. His memoirs put into perspective the Hutu-Tutsi political violence, massacres, and genocide in neighboring Burundi and Rwanda in the 1990s, including the involvement, greed, and failure of Western democracies and global actors such as the United Nations and how the Rwandan and Burundian political and economic violence spilled over into eastern DRC. In 1996, the hospital in Lemera was invaded, leaving many dead, and the hospital became a military camp. The massacre at the hospital was a prelude to a full-scale invasion of Congo by rebels from Rwandan, Ugandan, and Burundian forces, becoming the First Congo War.[25]

Eventually, in May 1997, Mobutu was ousted from power, with Laurent-Désiré Kabila becoming president with support from these neighboring countries with an overwhelming presence of Rwandan military and personnel in the new government. In August 1998, the Congolese people pressured Kabila to restore Congolese sovereignty with crucial military help from Angola and Zimbabwe and to a lesser extent from Namibia, Chad, and Libya. This became known as the Second Congo War.

In short, nine countries were involved in the conflict, which split Congo into three parts. The western third was under the control of Kabila, the north part run by Uganda-backed rebels, and the east, including Bukavu, was occupied by Rwanda.[26] Meanwhile, Mukwege and his family had taken refuge in Nairobi, Kenya. However, at the onslaught of this second war, they were back in Bukavu working on what was to become Panzi Hospital, a nonprofit hospital operated by the Community of Pentecostal Churches in Central Africa founded by Swedish Protestants. At the hospital, Mukwege has specialized in treating fistulas caused deliberately by men as well as performing cosmetic surgery to restore a sense of self to survivors of rape. The hospital has treated over sixty thousand survivors. To a large extent, his decisions and actions were and are shaped by events beyond his control, as he has sensitively and compassionately articulated in his journey of hope and healing in the midst of immeasurable suffering and needless deaths of millions of Congolese people in the last twenty-five years.

It is widely documented how rape or sexual violence of teenage girls and women is used as a weapon of war, and Mukwege has aided the reader

---

25. Mukwege, *Power of Women*, 50.
26. Mukwege, *Power of Women*, 58.

to put into perspective the plight of Congolese girls and women.[27] Through research and lifelong learning, he has established how rape in Congo is part of the process of ruthless exploitation and plundering of raw materials, among them coltan, cobalt, tantalum, and tin, for the electric products to sustain modern global economies and lifestyles. Rape is also part of the recruiting process of boys and young men for militias, which set up an elaborate system of sexual slavery. It also serves as a method of dispersing civilian populations around mining areas.

Reluctantly, Mukwege had an audience with some of the perpetrators of these hideous crimes, which opened his eyes to the unbroken chains of brutality and violence.

> The war on women's bodies in Congo has not been perpetrated by armies of psychopaths roaming the forests and acting out their sick sexual fantasies. . . . But the rapes should be understood as deliberate, conscious choices and a consequence of the disregard for the lives of women generally, which is the ultimate root cause. Only by understanding how and why this violence occurs can we try to mount a response at the individual and collective levels—and this holds true for Congo as much as it does for any peaceful country.[28]

Initially, attempts to bring perpetrators to account for their crimes through local military courts with army magistrates did not achieve much, but it was an opportunity to explain the daunting task undertaken by the Panzi team of professionals. This brief encounter with military judicial officials provoked the chief medical examiner at the military court in Kinshasa, the capital city of DRC, to visit Panzi Hospital in 2006. The women at the wing reserved for survivors of sexual violence were invited to ask questions or recount their own experiences. Several women volunteered to speak up, including a twelve-year-old girl. After retelling her heart-wrenching experience, the room fell completely silent. "How could anyone do this to a girl like that?" . . . "How is it possible?" muttered the shaken general. Immediately, the audience witnessed a near David-Goliath biblical episode.

> The general (six feet tall) could bear no more. He began to sob. Everyone's gaze turned from the girl to him. Then his knees buckled. He fainted, falling hard onto his back. It all happened so quickly that I was unable to react. There wasn't time to grab him under the arms. Shrieks rang out. The calm turned to commotion. I rushed forward and helped put him in the recovery

27. Mukwege, *Power of Women*, 108–12.
28. Mukwege, *Power of Women*, 101–2.

position. A colleague ran to get an oxygen mask. The women crowded around him, dozens of anxious faces, frozen with fear, looking down on his prone figure. Some of them began fanning him.[29]

The general regained consciousness. It was an unforgettable visit for Mukwege and his team, which yielded a positive impact. A few years later, Panzi Hospital created a new legal service as part of a "holistic care" program for survivors alongside medical care, psychological support, and socio-economic insertion programs. The legal area of the hospital is known as the "judicial clinic."[30] Nevertheless, despite this melodramatic event with the general, the military justice system took eight years to convict a few high-ranking political and military aggressors after forty-six girls between eighteen months and ten years old were raped with severe recto-vaginal injuries in Kavumu village between 2012 and 2015.[31]

It took the courage of Mukwege and his team to organize community gatherings in Kavumu village to fully understand why perpetrators had resolved to massacre children. In addition to the convictions of the few aggressors, the court condemned the Congolese state for failing in its duty to provide protection for citizens who had appealed for help. The government was ordered to pay damages to the victims. Regrettably, impunity, corruption, and complete breakdown of rule of law have resulted in millions of deaths and severe bodily injuries among thousands of girls and women.

POWER OF WORDS—POWER OF WOMEN

Denis Mukwege and his team at Panzi Hospital, like Maman Monique, made a "covenant with life." The natural progression of his self-initiation approach against incomprehensible violence and extreme poverty in the midst of a great wealth of minerals and fertile terrain compelled him to do more than being a gynecological surgeon who treated injuries and helped researchers from Human Rights Watch. He ensured whoever mattered in the community, including the United Nations (UN) agencies, knew about the situation on the ground and all the efforts made at the Panzi hospital to model holistic treatment. The encounter with the general and the twelve-year-old girl amplified the power of words and the power of women, which he captured brilliantly.

---

29. Mukwege, *Power of Women*, 130.
30. Mukwege, *Power of Women*, 160.
31. Mukwege, *Power of Women*, 159.

> Women have an ability to cut through the brittle exteriors of men, who pride themselves on projecting force and invulnerability. These macho masks are designed to be intimidating, but they can be pierced. They are no match for real inner strength.[32]

Without further ado, Mukwege resolved to be more than a doctor. He became an ambassador for the women to carry their stories as far as possible. One thing led to another. In September 2006, six months after the encounter with the general, he was addressing the UN General Assembly for the first time on a platform designated to address sexual violence. Despite gazing at the empty desk of the Congolese ambassador, his advisors, and the "dazzling void," the boycott of his presentation, and the patients at Panzi Hospital, he acknowledged it was an education on how women are often received whenever they find the courage to denounce their attackers.[33] Providentially, despite the outright opposition in the Congolese government to publicly discuss the rape crisis at the UN, Mukwege was invited for a public discussion on sexual violence at New York University. He was interviewed by Eve Ensler, the feminist playwright and creator of *The Vagina Monologues*, who has since changed her name to V.[34]

> She was the first person I met who felt no shame in talking about the vagina publicly or her personal history of sexual violence at the hands of her father. *We both shared the conviction that the reason vaginas were an object of so many taboos was so that men could continue to mistreat when behind closed doors.*[35]

In 2007, V visited Panzi Hospital, and as we say, the rest is his/her story! Her interaction with survivors of sexual violence at the hospital mutually opened their eyes and as Mukwege puts it, it was "a moment of communion and consciousness."[36] For V, it was worse than anything she had ever encountered in Bosnia, Afghanistan, or Haiti. For the Congolese women, they realized rape is not only in the villages and jungles of Congo but in the homes and on the streets of the richest cities of the world. The outcome of this encounter helped turn the vision of the survivors at the hospital into the City of Joy, a safe space for raped women that offers protection, education, and inspiration for its residents.[37] Its motto, written for all to read, is "Turn-

---

32. Mukwege, *Power of Women*, 132.
33. Mukwege, *Power of Women*, 137.
34. Mukwege, *Power of Women*, 86.
35. Emphasis added. Mukwege, *Power of Women*, 87.
36. Mukwege, *Power of Women*, 91.
37. For in-depth understanding and appreciation of City of Joy, watch a 2018

ing pain into power."³⁸ As much as they involved professional engineers and contractors, the women survivors were part of the construction team, which spoke volumes.

> It demonstrated what would become one of our central messages to each future resident: that women are so much more powerful and capable than the positions and roles they are assigned in society. Female builders were unheard of in the Congo, as they are on most construction projects worldwide. The main contractor agreed to take them on with an attitude of utter bafflement, convinced that sooner or later he would have the satisfaction of telling us that women were indeed ill-suited to building walls or doing carpentry. . . . At the end, some of their male colleagues confessed that the women had inspired them and pushed them to improve and work harder. "This is the story of men and women in the workplace through history," V joked afterward.³⁹

With increased awareness and donations, women survivors are helped to start their own businesses, and others go back to school and become agents of change with the power to make a difference. All donations are channeled through the Panzi Foundation, and the women are encouraged to participate in and lead mutual solidarity organizations (MUSOs) and microfinance initiatives for shared savings schemes. MUSOs are open to everyone but administered by survivors.⁴⁰

In the midst of fruitful and positive initiatives like City of Joy, more disheartening massive atrocities and several attempted assassinations have not deterred Mukwege from drawing from the inner strength and the power of the girls and women not just in Congo but globally. He has intensively educated himself on the many movements, initiatives, and campaigns against sexual violence in different countries and internationally, lest we assume the plight of the Congolese people is an isolated case. In light of this, Mukwege has continuously urged the international criminal justice systems and the United Nations to up their efforts against sexual violence. It is no wonder that Mukwege has also earned himself several awards besides the Nobel

---

Netflix original documentary in association with Impact Partners and Artemis Rising Foundation, *City of Joy*, which captures how Denis Mukwege, V, Christine Deschryver, and the women survivors build the City of Joy from scratch, its launch in 2011, and how the women protected Mukwege when his life was in danger.

38. Mukwege, *Power of Women*, 92.
39. Mukwege, *Power of Women*, 93.
40. Mukwege, *Power of Women*, 97.

Peace Prize in 2018. But his enviable global aura has not deterred him from remaining grounded in Bukavu, eastern DRC.

Back at the hospital, he faced deeper challenges, which triggered additional approaches in offering holistic treatment. This time around, he noticed about 15 percent of all children delivered in one year (about three thousand) were out of rape, with some being rejected by their mothers. In addition to the City of Joy, he created a specialized center, Maison Dorcas, to offer accommodation, care, and psychological support for these mothers and their children. As a result, with extraordinary efforts, the majority of the women giving birth to children out of rape at Panzi Hospital succeed in accepting them, but there are many who do not. Tragically, children born out of rape face the fate of their mothers, the problem becoming multigenerational.[41] Amazingly, part of the reason Mukwege and his team never give up is that their compassionate advocacy and healing ministry are in high demand. Like Maman Monique and her team, the Panzi team lives out the gospel of John 10 and Matt 25.

Throughout his professional life, Mukwege has learned not to run away from difficult circumstances. He is a critical thinker and works diligently with others in the community to look for practical solutions. As he did in Kavumu village, whose children suffered severe bodily injuries, he identified another village, Shabunda (similar in size to Belgium), to evaluate the performance of the justice system and to learn from the survivors what they needed urgently from the government. Once again, he drew many lessons from this encounter. Still, the most unexpected and inspiring discovery is when he was led to the middle of the town to a statue that had been erected in tribute to the survivors of the area.[42]

> It was unsettling to behold, but immensely powerful in what it captured and symbolized. Our guides explained that the statue had been placed facing eastward toward Congo's neighbors, Rwanda in particular, which the community viewed as the source of their misfortune and fear.[43]

Yet, the most profound effect of Shabunda on survivors occurred during their final encounter.

> Our final interview was with the oldest woman we met, a sixty-one-year-old widow who had been abducted for six days and gang-raped in the jungle. . . . She began by telling us about her

---

41. Mukwege, *Power of Women*, 150.
42. Mukwege, *Power of Women*, 190.
43. Mukwege, *Power of Women*, 190.

experience, and once she had finished, I asked what she needed. "I don't need anything," she replied. Her eyes flashed with indignation. "But I want one thing. We women deserve respect. We give birth, we bring up children, we work. But we are being humiliated. I was humiliated by children. The same age as my grandchildren. Nothing can remove this shame, nothing. But what I want is for the president to come here and apologize in public. I want him to come and recognize our suffering and the crimes against us. That would help me heal, that would make me feel respected again by people here," she said.[44]

Fast forward, ten years later, Mukwege received the Nobel Peace Prize in the company of Nadia Murad, a sexual violence survivor. Finally, Mukwege used this new platform to fulfill one of his deferred dreams after encountering survivors at Shabunda. In the supportive environment after the Nobel award, Angela Merkel, Germany's chancellor, sponsored a proposal for a global fund for survivors of sexual violence at the UN Security Council, which was approved in April 2019 as part of Resolution 2467. Nadia Murad and Mukwege publicly launched it six months later.[45] On his part, with the US$500,000 check he received for the Nobel award, he bought property in Kinshasa, the Congolese capital, and opened a new facility for survivors, drawing from lessons learned in Bukavu. Mukwege has continuously reflected on his journey of becoming a feminist in a predominantly patriarchal society and how men can be creatively engaged to play their part. After his father died, he officially became the head of the family, according to tradition. He fully understands the significance of customs and ceremonies of life but, most insightfully, he knows it is important to question them.

> We must open our eyes to their impact. Whenever we reinforce the message that boys are more capable, more deserving, or more valuable, we perpetuate injustice—and ultimately violence—against women. Why do I say violence? What is the link between the division of domestic chores, inheritance traditions, or funeral ceremonies and rape? It is that the more boys and men are made to believe they are superior, that their lives matter more, that more likely they are to conclude that they have a right to dominate and mistreat other people's daughters and sisters physically. *It is not just* fathers who entrench gender biases in children. Mothers, too, are responsible.[46]

---

44. Mukwege, *Power of Women*, 191–92.
45. Mukwege, *Power of Women*, 209.
46. Emphasis added. Mukwege, *Power of Women*, 216.

In light of his convictions and Christian moral responsibility, in 2010, he began working with tribal chiefs to initiate voluntary seminars for husbands and unmarried men in several villages. His main objective is to introduce positive masculinities in families and in communities. He has also invested in a critical understanding of leadership at different levels and in institutions, communities, and society at large. He believes change must come from the top to energize and influence those who are led and at the bottom of the ladder. As a Christian, son of a pastor, and a pastor in his own right in a small church in Bukavu, he insists we must acknowledge the role of religion in enforcing male dominance and female submissiveness.[47] Moreover he believes feminism and faith are compatible concepts. It is no exaggeration; Denis Mukwege leads by example and passionately believes in women's power and leadership, women who, on many occasions, literally protected him.

CONCLUSION: *UBUNTU* PAR EXCELLENCE

I have met both Monique Misenga Ngoie Mukuna and Denis Mukwege in very different contexts but never in their homeland of the Democratic Republic of Congo. In various ways, I learned about their deep Christian witness and moral responsibilities. Still, nothing prepared me for what I was to discover through their writings and the confessions of people they have impacted. From the beginning, I was struck by the way they both made a covenant with life in the midst of immeasurable suffering and violent deaths. Throughout their writings, we come face to face with the power of women and their incredible resolve to stay alive against all odds. No matter what happens, Mukwege and Maman Monique never stop caring, doing, hoping, and healing.

As an African, Christian, and feminist woman theologian and ethicist reflecting on how they each practice a "self-initiation approach" in their struggle against insurmountable injustices against girls and women in one of the richest countries with huge deposits of essential minerals and other natural resources, the concept of *Ubuntu* par excellence stayed with me and inspired me. Their ways of thinking, questioning, reasoning, and practicing their faith embody not only Christian morality but also the hallmarks of Ubuntu, humanness, justice, communitarianism, solidarity, interdependence, generosity, and compassion. Both have worked tirelessly and with lots of risks for their dear lives to transform pain into power and life in its fullness. They both espouse humility, ingenuity, respect, and dignity, which

---

47. Mukwege, *Power of Women*, 242.

offer hope and healing to thousands of Congolese girls and women who walk the valley of death-dealing injuries.

Clearly, Monique Misenga Ngoie Mukuna and Denis Mukwege demonstrate that we must take the initiative to dismantle African patriarchy and its deadly consequences in order to become empowered, resourceful, and life-giving. We have what it takes: the power of women, men, and our allies working together, drawing from our faith and the African Indigenous ideology of *Ubuntu*.

BIBLIOGRAPHY

Hochschild, Adam. *King Leopold's Ghost: A Story of Greed, Terror, and Heroism in Colonial Africa*. Boston: Houghton Mifflin, 1998.

Katongole, Emmanuel. *The Sacrifice of Africa: A Political Theology for Africa*. The Eerdmans Ekklesia Series. Grand Rapids: Eerdmans, 2011.

Maluleke, Tinyiko Sam, and Sarojini Nadar. "Breaking the Covenant of Violence Against Women." *Journal of Theology for Southern Africa* 114 (2002) 5–17.

Mukuna, Monique Misenga Ngoie, and Elsie Tshimunyi McKee. *Cradling Abundance: One African Christian's Story of Empowering Women and Fighting Systemic Poverty*. Downers Grove: IVP Academic, 2021.

Mukwege, Denis. *The Power of Women: A Doctor's Journey of Hope and Healing*. New York: Flatiron Books, 2021.

Njoroge, Nyambura J. "The Bible and African Christianity: A Curse or a Blessing?" In *Other Ways of Reading: African Women and the Bible*, edited by Musa W. Dube, 207–36. Atlanta: Society of Biblical Literature, 2001.

———. "A Spirituality of Resistance and Transformation." In *Talitha Cum! Theologies of African Women*, edited by Nyambura J. Njoroge and Musa W. Dube, 66–82. Pietermaritzburg: Cluster, 2001.

Paris, Peter J., ed. *Religion and Poverty: Pan-African Perspectives*. Durham: Duke University Press, 2009.

———, ed. "Self-Initiation: A Necessary Principle in the African Struggle to Abolish Poverty." In *Religion and Poverty: Pan-African Perspectives*, 315–39. Durham: Duke University Press, 2009.

World Council of Churches. "'Your Story Is My Story, Your Story Is Our Story': The Decade Festival, Harare, November 1998." In *Ecumenical Decade: Churches in Solidarity with Women, World Council of Churches*, 90–99. Geneva: Justice, Peace and Creation Team, WCC Publications, 1999.

Chapter 4

Environmental Racism, Global Warming, and Human Flourishing

Rubén Rosario Rodríguez

In his 2012 presidential address to the American Theological Society, Peter J. Paris traced the historical arc of Black theologies in the United States from the religion of the enslaved Africans who constructed an alternative to the religion of white slave-holding Christians to the rise of the independent Black churches that nurtured and empowered the public theology of the civil rights movement, to the articulation of Black and womanist theologies within the theological academy, to argue that the unifying thread throughout this history—even as Black theologies adapted to ever-changing sociopolitical realities—was the desire to always "remain faithful to the liberating faith they had inherited from their ancestors."[1] Thus, in articulating a theological ethics that confronts the widespread problem of environmental racism, it is vital to engage these emancipatory theologies and allow the Black church tradition to frame an adequate response.

As Nimi Wariboko contends, the focal point of all Peter Paris's scholarly works is the problem of racism, providing both analysis and critique by means of a methodology grounded in the African American experience of racism "and the responses to it in black religious practices in ways that evade and challenge the American theological enterprise."[2] Wariboko expounds

---

1. Paris, "Theologies of Black Folk in North America," 385.
2. Wariboko, "Evasion of Ethics," 215.

eloquently about Paris's approach, "Like the old spirituals, Paris's ethical analyses are conversations with America about blacks' experience of pain and suffering, struggle and striving, and the unity of protest and hope in their religious thought—all carried out in plaintive tones and sad rhythms."[3] Formed within this Black church tradition, Paris sees the ultimate goal of theological reasoning as the advancement of human flourishing:

> In my perspective, ethics always takes as its point of departure some concrete actions, deeds, practices performed by persons or groups of persons. In this sense, ethics is always empirical and its aim is to discern the nature of the good or the right or the appropriate inherent in some actual occasion and to describe its limits and possibilities; i.e., what values are sacrificed or not allowed to see the light of day and the difference it would make were things to be otherwise.[4]

Accordingly, a Christian theological response to environmental racism in the twenty-first century must work to overcome the obstacles, policies, and institutions that impede African American flourishing or risk betraying the public-facing and politically engaged Black church tradition.

For generations, scientists and ecologically minded theologians have been warning about the impending environmental collapse. As astrophysicist and planetary scientist Carl Sagan noted in an open letter to people of faith over thirty years ago, "Some of the short-term mitigations of these dangers such as greater energy efficiency, rapid banning of chlorofluorocarbons or modest reductions in nuclear arsenals are comparatively easy and at some level are already underway."[5] Quite early in the environmental movement, the connection was made between racial and economic disparities and levels of exposure to pollutants, giving rise to a growing body of academic work, especially in the social sciences, documenting the correlation between environmental degradation, race, and poverty.[6] There is a general consensus that climate change disproportionately affects those who suffer from socioeconomic inequalities, reflecting generations of colonialism, racism, and political marginalization of oppressed peoples. As a result of economic globalization, environmental racism—a form of systemic racism whereby communities of color are unduly burdened with exposure to health hazards as a result of policies and practices that force them to live in proximity to sources of toxic waste such as sewage works, mines, landfills,

---

3. Wariboko, "Evasion of Ethics," 215.
4. Wariboko, "Evasion of Ethics," 216.
5. Sagan et al., "Preserving and Cherishing the Earth."
6. See Bullard, *Dumping In Dixie*; and *Unequal Protection*.

power stations, major roads and emitters of airborne particulate matter—has become a worldwide problem.[7] The COVID-19 global pandemic further exposed existing racial and economic disparities heightening the need for a theological response that seeks to move beyond *political* emancipation, which often merely perpetuates existing power structures, in favor of *human* emancipation that seeks to preserve the basic dignity of every human life. In the words of Brazilian liberationist Rubem Alves, what is needed is a theological vision guided by the question, "What does it take to make and keep life human in the world?"[8]

James H. Cone (1938–2018), arguably the most influential Black liberation theologian of the past fifty years in the theological academy, explicitly connects the history of white supremacy in the United States to the ecological devastation facing communities of color: "For over five hundred years, through the wedding of science and technology and in the name of God and democracy, White people have been killing people of color and exploiting their homelands in every nook and cranny of the planet."[9] This culture of domination, facilitated by the "mechanistic and instrumental logic" of capitalism, is the same "logic that led to slavery and segregation in the Americas, and colonization and apartheid in Africa," which is now responsible for widespread environmental devastation.[10] Not surprisingly, considering the role of white supremacy in perpetuating this culture of domination, the Black poor "are the first to get hit and the worst affected" when it comes to environmental destruction.[11] In the North American context, the environmentalist movement has resisted analyzing climate change and environmental degradation through the lens of racism, thereby allowing the underlying culture of domination to remain unchecked. Or, as Cone encapsulates the problem in his inimitable style, "The leading environmentalists, mostly middle- and upper-class Whites, are unprepared culturally and intellectually to dialogue with angry Blacks about the hard facts of racism."[12] One of those hard facts is the unquestioned link between racism and the victims of environmental catastrophe. Therefore, Cone challenges both the Black church tradition and the mainstream environmental movement to work together against their common enemy—the culture of

---

7. See Bhattacharyya et al., *Race and Power*; and Westra and Lawson, *Faces of Environmental Racism*.

8. Alves, *Theology of Human Hope*, 53.

9. Cone, "One Earth, One Struggle," 20.

10. Cone, "One Earth, One Struggle," 20.

11. Cone, "One Earth, One Struggle," 20.

12. Cone, "One Earth, One Struggle," 20.

domination: "If Blacks and other hard-hit communities do not raise these ethical and political questions, they will continue to die a slow death on the planet while White environmentalists will simply continue to protect their own at the cost of poor people of color."[13]

Like Cone, Peter Paris presents African and African American ethics as an alternative to the dominant white Christian ethics that prioritizes humanity above the rest of the creation and white European humanity above the rest of humankind. Appealing to the spirituality of African peoples in the diaspora, though adapted to the North American context and influenced by both African and American cultural forces, the ensuing ethical worldview values the "preservation and promotion of community" above all else, while understanding community through an African cosmological lens that entails "a sacramental view of life in general. And of human life in particular. Yet African anthropocentrism does not imply either the superiority of humans over other forms of life or a denial of the supremacy of the deity over all existence. Nor does it constitute a rationale justifying wanton exploitation of humans over natural resources."[14] A crucial distinction between Western Christianity and the spiritual vision of African peoples— even under the brutal yoke of slavery where African religious practices "were rigorously controlled and stringently forbidden"[15]—is the lack of an Augustinian doctrine of original sin that condemns the whole of humanity. This denial of predestination suggests that even a seemingly inevitable future, such as the looming environmental collapse, "does not imply human passivity. Instead it informs persons about the possibilities that they are either capable or incapable of realizing."[16] In other words, African spirituality is both utopian and pragmatic, thriving on hope because it embraces the human capacity to dream of a better future then takes the necessary steps to make those dreams reality. Consequently, "African thought, including that of theology and ethics, arises out of problems of daily experience, and it is pursued for the purpose of discovering practical solutions for everyday problems. In short, African theology and ethics are practical sciences in the service of the community's well-being."[17]

Paris argues for a distinctive form of social ethic "deeply rooted in and reflective of" the spirituality of African and African American peoples embodying "the four constitutive spheres of African experience, namely:

13. Cone, "One Earth, One Struggle," 22–23.
14. Paris, *Spirituality of African Peoples*, 130–31.
15. Paris, *Spirituality of African Peoples*, 130.
16. Paris, *Spirituality of African Peoples*, 132.
17. Paris, *Spirituality of African Peoples*, 132.

God, community, family, person."[18] Furthermore, these four spheres are fully interdependent such that no single one "can flourish apart from all the others."[19] As a practical discipline, ethics requires concrete solutions for real-world problems, and its goal is the common good through the uplifting of all. Yet, for this common moral discourse to develop, it is vital for members of different social groups to embrace shared values and goals. Given the history of racism and environmental degradation resulting from the culture of white supremacy—as James Cone has argued—an ethic that provides practical solutions to the problem of environmental racism must begin by directly confronting anti-Black racism. Accordingly, an African and African American ethics is explicitly political. At the same time, because the goal is the building of the common good and the creation of mutually beneficial social relations, the virtue of forgiveness, even in the face of "slavery, segregation, colonialism, and apartheid," is key.[20]

Drawing upon the example of African and African American moral exemplars—specifically Nelson Mandela and Martin Luther King Jr.—Paris elevates the virtue of forgiveness on the principle that even "evildoers are capable of moral transformation."[21] Mandela, who suffered unjust imprisonment and torture at the hands of the white South African government, and Dr. King, whose family home was bombed by white supremacists, each embodied the virtue of forgiveness without compromising the need for repentance and moral accountability by their oppressors. Furthermore, such virtue emanates from a deep spirituality that is open to the work of transcendence in the practical, everyday world: "Africans view religious devotion and good moral habits as necessary conditions for the prevention and the solution of most practical problems in daily life," while at the same time it is "inconceivable for Africans to think of human existence apart from its dependent relationship on God, the divinities, and the ancestral spirits."[22] King, for example, admonished "his followers not to fight hate with hate but with love and forgiveness. The way of love and forgiveness is not, as is often thought, the way of weakness but of strength because it is not, as often thought, the way of weakness but of strength because it is not a natural response but rather a response that manifests a second [divine] nature."[23] Consequently, the virtues and practices needed to reverse environmental racism

18. Paris, *Spirituality of African Peoples*, 130.
19. Paris, *Spirituality of African Peoples*, 130.
20. Paris, *Spirituality of African Peoples*, 148.
21. Paris, *Spirituality of African Peoples*, 151.
22. Paris, *Spirituality of African Peoples*, 131.
23. Paris, *Spirituality of African Peoples*, 151.

in the United States must be encouraged and nurtured in the public sphere across all social groupings in order to bring about concrete change. The biggest challenge to Paris's practical approach to social ethics is overcoming the hatred and resentment of the bigoted and racist other who refuses dialogue let alone cooperation: "The converse of the virtue of forgiveness is the vice of hatred, which repudiates any possibility of reconciliation with one's enemies and which views one's enemies as demonic. The leadership style that emanates from such a vice is isolationist, chauvinist, and belligerent, easily disposed to acts of retaliation."[24] It is at this most basic level—to bring about the desired conversion of the hate-filled other—that human effort engages and depends on divine assistance.

As a political theology, the spirituality of African and African American peoples presents itself as pragmatic, recognizing that the Black churches live in a polis that extends beyond the local community affirming the shared humanity of others—even those labeled enemies—while undertaking projects that uplift the common good. At the same time, there is a profound realization that the common good cannot be built on a foundation of injustice, and so the emphasis on the liberation of the oppressed and marginalized by means of transformative social projects—like dismantling segregation and working toward equity in public education for example—can be seen as the *necessary* precondition for a common moral discourse. Thus, Peter Paris can claim that for Africans and African Americans justice "is the supreme virtue because it is the sum of all the virtues."[25] Since the ultimate goal of an African social ethic is the preservation and promotion of community, anything that dehumanizes another human being is by definition destructive of community and must be resisted, for genuine community cannot exist without "inclusive equality, wherein the well-being of all the community's members is assured."[26] In practical terms, when discussing the problem of environmental racism, social structures and cultural practices that perpetuate domination of the other, whether manifest as racism or the exploitation of nature, demand repentance and conversion.

Ecowomanism, a theological movement arising from the experiences and perspectives of African American women, is an approach to environmental justice that "centers on the perspectives of women of African descent and reflects upon these women's activist methods, religious practices, and theories on how to engage earth justice."[27] Drawing upon the unifying

---

24. Paris, *Spirituality of African Peoples*, 151.
25. Paris, *Spirituality of African Peoples*, 152.
26. Paris, *Spirituality of African Peoples*, 153.
27. Harris, "Ecowomanism," 5.

themes of African spirituality Peter Paris has documented in his many works, ecowomanism argues that environmental justice has always been a priority for Black women due to the "deep value of the earth as sacred, and the interconnection of black women's bodies to the body of the earth, a religious worldview that translates across the African diaspora."[28] This emergent movement thus serves as a case study for analyzing how the Black church tradition confronts the problem of environmental racism and articulates a solution faithful to the emancipatory tone of its African spiritual heritage.

Central to ecowomanism is the need for Black women's voices to assert themselves in the conversation about environmental justice, serving as a prophetic voice "speaking truth to power and cutting through normative practices of white supremacy."[29] A key aspect of the ecowomanist narrative is its analysis of the culture that has allowed the exploitation of the natural world alongside the exploitation of Black bodies—especially Black women's bodies—to conclude that the "crisis of climate change facing us all" stems from the "logic of domination that has functioned to privilege white men and white communities over communities of color."[30] Ecowomanists have many allies within the ecotheology movement, especially when it comes to deconstructing and rejecting the patriarchal narrative of white supremacy, including feminist theologians like Rosemary Radford Ruether and Elisabeth Schüssler Fiorenza, Latin American liberationists like Ivone Gebara and Leonardo Boff, and the process theology of Catherine Keller, who describes the current ecological crisis as humanity's "moment of self-contradiction."[31] The ecofeminist perspective of Brazilian liberation theologian Ivone Gebara is highly critical of the complicity of Christian patriarchal theologies "in the persistent domination of women and the unchecked exploitation of natural resources," arguing that not enough has been done to address the role of Christian colonialism in "the destruction of indigenous divinities" by denying "other religious rapprochements" their due as "equally truthful," and ignoring the important role Indigenous and African religious narratives can play in fostering an "egalitarian and solidary dialogue."[32] Clearly the work of Gebara has much in common with ecowomanism as both seek to dismantle the white, Eurocentric, and colonial narrative that has predominated

28. Harris, "Ecowomanism," 6.
29. Harris, "Ecowomanism," 7.
30. Harris, "Ecowomanism," 7.
31. Keller, *Political Theology of the Earth*, 2.
32. All translations from the Spanish my own. Gebara, *Intuiciones ecofeministas*, 28.

Western Christianity by giving voice to previously silenced narratives relating to humanity's place in the natural order that affirms humankind's interdependence with the planet. Like African spirituality, Gebara's liberationist theology embraces a sacramental interrelationality between humanity and planet Earth enabled by the love of a compassionate and caring God: "Transcendence is that feeling of always belonging to something greater—much greater—whose full breadth we barely know and are unable to express. . . . the human experience of transcendence is also the experience of beauty, the majesty of nature, and all its relationships and interdependencies."[33]

Given the long suffering and tragic history of African descended peoples in the Western hemisphere—dragged from their native land to a life of brutal bondage and exploitation—ecowomanism critically interrogates the Christian tradition and its role in the racialization of Black peoples by asking fundamental questions with broad implications for the ecological crisis:

> More specifically, ecowomanism asks the questions, what liberating theological precepts are upheld to empower black peoples to know their innate worth as earthlings, and as parts of creation designed by God who deserve to be honored and celebrated even in the face of white supremacy and racism? What earth honoring faith practices embedded within African religious life are helpful to undergird African and African American peoples' identity and connection to and with the earth?[34]

In an era when Black activism and speaking truth to power has helped the nation confront its racist crimes and begin to affirm that Black Lives Matter, ecowomanism raises awareness of the double oppression of racialization and ecological degradation that wreaks violence against Black bodies and Black communities then "tries to get at the root, dismantling the logic of domination that might keep these oppressive systems in place . . . Linking social justice to earth justice becomes central when crafting climate solutions and raising consciousness."[35]

The study by the Michigan Civil Rights Commission (MCRC) of the Flint water crisis exposes the deep connections between racial and environmental exploitation by concretizing the realities of environmental racism that have impacted communities of color, especially women, since the rise of modern industrialization. In January 2016, multiple states of emergency for the city of Flint, Michigan, were declared by the mayor, the governor of Michigan, and the president of the United States. These declarations turned

---

33. Gebara, *Intuiciones ecofeministas*, 136.
34. Harris, "Ecowomanism," 8.
35. Harris, "Ecowomanism," 9.

the nation's attention to the Flint water crisis after extremely high levels of lead were found in the city's drinking water. Ultimately, the MCRC concluded that to understand the Flint water crisis it is necessary to look at Flint's history: "We believe the underlying issue is historical and systemic, dates back nearly a century, and has at its foundation race and segregation of the Flint community. These historical policies, practices, laws and norms fostered and perpetuated separation of race, wealth and opportunity."[36] The voices of those directly affected—especially the voices of African American mothers in Flint like Nakiya Wakes—drew nationwide attention to the problem of environmental racism and generated civic outrage and an outpouring of support. Wakes describes the trauma of miscarrying twins, then coming home from the hospital to find a letter from "the City of Flint stating that pregnant women and people fifty-five and older should not be drinking the Flint tap water. For me, that warning came too late. My family and I moved to Flint in 2013 and had been drinking the water ever since. We were still drinking the water."[37] She had her other children tested and their lead levels were at 5.0: "Anything 5 and higher is considered to be high lead levels. My daughter's hair was falling out. . . . My son developed behavioral problems in school."[38] Yet, despite her personal suffering and loss, Nakiya Wakes drew empowerment from the crisis in Flint and responded in the way so many African American women before her have done, by becoming a prophetic voice for change: "All of this made me realize that my voice and the voice of my community should be heard. I believed then and I believe now that everyone who knew about this contamination of the water and failed to do anything about it should be held accountable for their actions."[39]

In solidarity with the Black and brown citizens of Flint, Michigan, Latina theologian Ahida Calderón Pilarski examines the Flint water crisis through an Old Testament prophetic lens, focusing her analysis on three passages from the prophet Jeremiah that refer to "poisoned" water (Jer 8:14; 9:15; and 23:15). YHWH is angered because of the people's infidelity: "For my people have committed two evils: they have forsaken me, the fountain of living water, and dug out cisterns for themselves, cracked cisterns that can hold no water" (Jer 2:13 NRSV). First, by rejecting God who is the living water, then by trying to provide water for themselves by digging cisterns, the people of Israel continue to place their trust in earthly things—even when those material things prove unreliable. Later, the people lament their sins:

---

36. See Michigan Civil Rights Commission, "Flint Water Crisis."
37. Wakes, "Testimonies," 143.
38. Wakes, "Testimonies," 143.
39. Wakes, "Testimonies," 143.

"for the Lord our God has doomed us to perish, and has given us poisoned water to drink, because we have sinned against the Lord" (Jer 8:14 NRSV). The prophet repeats the condemnation a second time: "Behold, I will feed this people with bitter food, and give them poisonous water to drink" (Jer 9:15 NRSV). According to Jeremiah, the rebellion among God's chosen people was spread by God's own corrupted prophets: "I am going to make them eat wormwood, and give them poisoned water to drink; for from the prophets of Jerusalem ungodliness has spread throughout the land" (Jer 23:15 NRSV). Pilarski links this last prophetic statement, in which the leadership of Israel is held responsible for polluting the land and spreading their ungodliness and apostasy like contagion, to the crisis in Flint by comparing the systemic corruption that led to the environmental destruction primarily affecting minority communities to the disobedience of God's prophets, who were tasked with preaching truth to power but instead spoke self-serving lies that brought destruction down on all the people. While in Jeremiah it is God who poisons the water to punish the ungodly, in both instances—ancient Israel and modern day Flint—it is a failure of leadership that ultimately poisoned the water, revealing "a multi-generational chain of unjust actions, and these realities necessitate, as a counter-response, an integral commitment to intergenerational justice in the household—or God's creation, if one is to address it from a theological and biblical perspective."[40]

It is incredibly ironic—not to mention exceedingly unjust—that in such crises the burden of speaking truth to power and challenging the status quo all too often falls on the victims themselves. As Robert Bullard, author of *Dumping In Dixie: Race, Class, and Environmental Quality*, has noted, it was African American churches—specifically a group of Black church women—who first drew national attention to the realities of environmental racism through direct action and civil disobedience in the little town of Afton, North Carolina, back in 1982, by laying their bodies on the road to prevent dump trucks carrying highly toxic chemicals (PCB) from depositing them in local landfills, marking "the first time anyone in the United States had been jailed trying to halt a toxic-waste landfill."[41] The courage of these activists, born of necessity, contrasts sharply with the enduring apathy of elected officials and the systems in place that supposedly exist to protect citizens. In the words of Flint mother turned activist, Nakiya Wakes, "I feel like Governor Rick Snyder and everyone involved should be held accountable and responsible. They chose saving money over saving the lives of their people. We have been lied to for too long. We do not trust our government

---

40. Calderón Pilarski, "What Do Prophets Have to Say About Poisoned Water?," 63.
41. Bullard, *Dumping In Dixie*, 31.

anymore. It is time for Flint to get justice. Three years later and we are still on bottled water. It is a disgrace. We live in the United States of America and cannot drink clean water."[42]

After the Second World War and under the shadow of the racist ideology of Nazism, formerly colonized nations in the new international community embraced the work of the United Nations and its agencies. From its onset, the United Nations Educational, Scientific and Cultural Organization (UNESCO) focused its energies on the problem of racism, addressing the structures of power that perpetuate racism, and producing the 1950 "Statement on Race" and the 1967 "Statement on Race and Racial Prejudice." The first statement affirmed a scientific consensus rejecting the notion of biologically distinct races by declaring that "mankind is one: that all men belong to the same species, *Homo sapiens*."[43] The second UNESCO statement goes further, acknowledging the social construction and arbitrary usage of race as a descriptive term: "Many anthropologists stress the importance of human variation, but believe that 'racial' divisions have limited scientific interest and may even carry the risk of inviting abusive generalization."[44] The 1967 statement concludes that the primary means of combating racism involves "changing those social situations which give rise to prejudice, prevent the prejudiced from acting in accordance with their beliefs, and combating the false beliefs themselves."[45] It is within this cultural moment that we must locate the civil rights movement in the United States, not as a local or regionalized crisis, but as part of a larger globalized struggle for decolonization and political empowerment.

The Argentinian exile Enrique Dussel, best known for his pioneering work *Philosophy of Liberation*, describes European colonization as an ideological totality that facilitated the conquest and colonization of America, Africa, and Asia by disguising "oppression" behind the promise of "progress." In Dussel's critique of global capitalism, the racialized tone of this imperialist project becomes most obvious whenever white Europeans encounter Black and brown "others" impeding their path to political and economic domination: "We were told, 'being is, not-being is not' (Parmenides). 'How innocent!' or 'How abstract!' they said. No! Such a colonizer! The not-beings are the barbarians because they are-not. And because the not-being is not, only the being is—What happens next? The Other is placed (as an object) in the world, and the only world 'that is' is the one that has

---

42. Wakes, "Testimonies," 144.
43. Kuper, *Race, Science and Society*, 343.
44. Kuper, *Race, Science and Society*, 360.
45. Kuper, *Race, Science and Society*, 362.

dominion over all."⁴⁶ Dussel's rejection of Enlightenment rationalism, neoliberal economics, and Euro-American colonialism draws inspiration from Latin American liberation movements (including liberation theology), and offers a humanist re-reading of Karl Marx against the social structures that continue to subjugate Indigenous, African-descendent, and other marginalized peoples in Latin America.

Much like the African and African American social ethics championed by Peter Paris, Dussel's politics of liberation offer a counternarrative that exposes the underside of capitalism in which racism, patriarchy, universal surveillance, and ever-widening social and economic disparities are the human cost of doing business. Dussel argues that capitalism as a social system is inherently flawed because the free market works for the top 10–20 percent of the population but not for the starving majority, and offers instead a politics of liberation that builds a new consensus that will transform existing institutions and build new ones that above all aspire "toward the advancement of the life of the community, of the people, of humanity!"⁴⁷ Yet, by embracing the phenomenological description of otherness in the work of Emmanuel Levinas, and inspired by real-world liberation efforts of Indigenous and Afro-descendent peoples, Dussel embraces racial identity as an integral part of encountering the Other *as other* without having to subsume the Other under one's own totalizing metanarratives while committing himself to social projects that uplift the community as a whole.

African American Christianity has developed in critical opposition to the religion of the white slaveholders in much the same way that the continent of Africa has embraced Christianity despite the hurtful legacy of the cultural imperialism of European colonialism, so that today, "most Africans on the continent now claim Christianity as their own."⁴⁸ Furthermore, throughout the history of the Black church tradition, the struggle for African independence has "been a source of inspiration for the African American Independent Church Movement," and the African American civil rights movement has impacted Black consciousness movements in Africa and vice versa.⁴⁹ As African and African American social ethics continue to confront the climate crisis, especially the disproportionate harm environmental degradation causes Black peoples and Black communities around the world, it becomes necessary to transcend local contexts and recognize

---

46. All translations from the Spanish my own. Dussel, *Introducción a la Filosofía*, 43.
47. Dussel, *Twenty Theses on Politics*, 61.
48. Paris, *Spirituality of African Peoples*, 158.
49. Paris, *Spirituality of African Peoples*, 158.

the global extent of the damage done by climate change and other forms of ecological devastation. Consequently, as affected communities work for practical solutions that build up the common good, it is crucial to encourage solidarity and emphasize practical wisdom.

Peter Paris defines practical wisdom as "excellence of thought that guides good action."[50] Within African cultures practical wisdom is passed from one generation to the next by example and practice: "Children imitate the activities and styles of their primary mentors—parents, older siblings, adult family members, teachers," valuing the importance of a large extended family and other "intergenerational adults in the upbringing of their children."[51] Sadly, the most harmful consequence of racism and white supremacy in the United States is the breakdown of this extended family within African American communities, first by the brutal realities of slavery, later due to the socio-economic consequences of multiple generations living in extreme poverty. Nevertheless, as Black voices assert themselves in the ecological debate, it is vital to draw upon the inherited wisdom of these ancestors, and recognize that no single leader can embody said wisdom. Therefore, what is needed are leaders who, before passing judgment, are willing to "listen well to all who have relevant information pertaining to the issue at hand. Such a person must be open-minded. He or she must shun premature closure . . . the person of practical wisdom seeks a solution that reconstitutes the unity of the community without any undue sacrifice."[52]

We have seen such practical wisdom—grounded in the community's well-being—during the Flint water crisis, as well as in the organizing work of the Black Lives Matter movement. In response to the acquittal of George Zimmerman, who shot teenager Trayvon Martin to death in a gated Sanford, Florida, community, Black Lives Matter (BLM) was founded by three Black activists, Alicia Garza, Patrisse Cullors, and Opal Tometi, as "an ideological and political intervention in a world where Black lives are systematically and intentionally targeted for demise."[53] BLM first came to national prominence in the aftermath of the murder of African American youth Michael Brown by a white police officer in Ferguson, Missouri, on August 9, 2014. Not an explicitly theological movement, and not linked to any single confessional tradition, BLM has often invoked Martin Luther King Jr. to differentiate, situate, and defend itself from external criticism. Responding

---

50. Paris, *Spirituality of African Peoples*, 144.

51. Paris, *Spirituality of African Peoples*, 144.

52. Paris, *Spirituality of African Peoples*, 145.

53. For an introduction to and defense of the movement, see their website: Black Lives Matter, "About."

to criticism that their involvement in the Ferguson protests that turned into rioting betrayed the nonviolent legacy of Dr. King, the movement's founders contend that they are reclaiming King's "Letter from a Birmingham City Jail" and his infamous address at Riverside Church in New York City, "A Time to Break Silence," in order to drive home the urgency of the situation in which Black bodies continue to be brutalized and murdered by agents of the state with impunity. BLM thus stands on the same principled call to "direct action" that brought Dr. King to Birmingham in 1963, because there "comes a time when the cup of endurance runs over, and men are no longer willing to be plunged into an abyss of injustice where they experience the blackness of corroding despair"; BLM organizers have learned from "painful experience that freedom is never voluntarily given by the oppressor; it must be demanded by the oppressed."[54] As Peter Paris has argued, such leadership exemplifies the Black religious tradition and is notable for lifting up the voices of the silenced and marginalized, most notably because they refuse to be defined solely as powerless victims. Rather, the hallmark of African and African American social ethics is the recognition that Blacks are moral agents who respond to injustice by doing something to improve the situation for all members of the community nurtured by a rich heritage: "Suffice it to say that the religious spirit that slaves nurtured and promoted in various secret assemblies was undoubtedly subversive if, for no other reason, than the fact that the slaves were engaged in constructing a means of helping themselves by coopting the religion of the slaveowners."[55]

If for no other reason than their communities are always the hardest hit, Black churches need to come to terms with the fact that racism and poverty are also ecological issues. As James Cone has argued, "No longer can environmentalism afford to be an elitist or White middle-class issue centered around the comfort and security of White suburbia. A clean, safe environment is a human and civil right that today is in jeopardy for poor people of color."[56] And as Peter Paris contends, the truest form of the African and African American moral tradition is distinguished by its commitment to liberating the oppressed. Accordingly, a Black ecological ethics is not in competition with a Black theology of liberation. Rather, it is a manifestation of Black liberation given the intersection of racist oppression and environmental exploitation under the stranglehold of white supremacy. In solidarity with their Black and brown brothers and sisters around the world, Black voices—like those in Flint, Michigan—need to prophesy against the

54. King, "Letter from a Birmingham City Jail," 292–93.
55. Paris, *Spirituality of African Peoples*, 39.
56. Cone, "One Earth, One Struggle," 23.

corruption and ungodliness of modern capitalism and cultural imperialism, or risk "further subjugating peoples of color who often contribute the least to climate change, but pay the highest cost."[57]

BIBLIOGRAPHY

Alves, Rubem. *A Theology of Human Hope*. St. Meinrad, IN: Abbey Press, 1969.
Black Lives Matter. "About Black Lives Matter." N.d. https://blacklivesmatter.com/about/.
Bhattacharyya, Gargi, et al. *Race and Power: Global Racism in the Twenty-First Century*. London: Routledge, 2002.
Bullard, Robert D. *Dumping in Dixie: Race, Class, and Environmental Quality*. 3rd ed. London: Routledge, 2018.
———. *Unequal Protection: Environmental Justice and Communities of Color*. Reprint. San Francisco: Sierra Club Books, 1994.
Calderón Pilarski, Ahida. "What Do Prophets Have to Say About Poisoned Water? A Latina Reflection on Racial Ecojustice in the Flint Water Crisis." *Journal of Hispanic/Latino Theology* 24.1 (May 15, 2022) 37–63.
Cone, James H. "One Earth, One Struggle." *The Other Side*, Feb. 2004, 20–23.
Dussel, Enrique. *Introducción a La Filosofía de La Liberación Latinoamericana*. México: Editorial Extemporaneos, 1975.
———. *Twenty Theses on Politics*. Translated by Geo Maher. Latin America in Translation/En Traducción/Em Tradução. Durham: Duke University Press, 2008.
Gebara, Ivone. *Intuiciones ecofeministas: Ensayos para repensar el conocimiento y la religión*. Translated by Graciela Pujol. Madrid: Editorial Trotta, 2000.
Harris, Melanie L. "Ecowomanism: An Introduction." *Worldviews* 20.1 (2016) 5–14.
Keller, Catherine. *Political Theology of the Earth: Our Planetary Emergency and the Struggle for a New Public*. New York: Columbia University Press, 2018.
King, Martin Luther, Jr. "Letter from a Birmingham Jail." In *A Testament of Hope: The Essential Writings and Speeches of Martin Luther King Jr.*, edited by James Melvin Washington, 289–302. San Francisco: HarperSanFrancisco, 1991.
Kuper, Leo, ed. *Race, Science and Society*. New York: Columbia University Press, 1975.
Michigan Civil Rights Commission. "The Flint Water Crisis: Systemic Racism Through the Lens of Flint." Feb. 17, 2017. https://www.michigan.gov/documents/mdcr/VFlintCrisisRep-F-Edited3-13-17_554317_7.pdf.
Paris, Peter J. *The Spirituality of African Peoples: The Search for a Common Moral Discourse*. Minneapolis: Fortress, 1995.
———. "The Theologies of Black Folk in North America: Presidential Address to the American Theological Society, March, 2012." *Theology Today* 69.4 (2013) 385–402.
Sagan, Carl, et al. "Preserving and Cherishing the Earth: An Appeal for Joint Commitment in Science and Religion." Global Forum of Spiritual and Parliamentary Leaders Conference in Moscow, Russia, January 1990. https://fore.yale.edu/sites/default/files/files/Preserving%20and%20Cherishing%20the%20Earth.pdf.
Wakes, Nakiya. "Testimonies: The Flint Water Crisis." *Anglican Theological Review* 100.1 (2018) 143–49.

57. Harris, "Ecowomanism," 13.

Wariboko, Nimi. "The Evasion of Ethics: Peter Paris Feels the Spirituals." *Toronto Journal of Theology* 27.2 (Sept. 2011) 215–34.

Westra, Laura, and Bill Lawson, eds. *Faces of Environmental Racism: Confronting Issues of Global Justice*. New York: Rowman & Littlefield, 2001.

Chapter 5

The Impact of Afro-Brazilian Spirituality on Brazilian Culture and Christianity[1]

Raimundo C. Barreto

PETER PARIS HAS ARGUED that, in spite of their diversity around the world, all African peoples both in the continent and in the diaspora are connected by a common African worldview and spirituality.[2] At the heart of his argument is the claim that the violence and horror of slavery, colonization, and even Christianization were not able to obliterate the African cultural as well as the African moral and religious values from those transplanted to the Americas and their descendants. In other words, in the history of religion in the Americas, Africans brought to the Americas and their descendants must not be treated as *tabula rasa*. In the same way, as the Europeans who invaded the Indigenous lands now known as the Americas brought their religion and spirituality to these shores, so did Africans, regardless of the fact that they came to these lands against their will. In fact, their faith and moral values were key elements in their capacity to cope with the inhuman oppression of slavery and, in the depths of their souls, resist it. However, as Paris's work has shown, the preservation of an African worldview and spirituality in the diaspora was never pure. As it commonly happens to culture and

---

1. This chapter reworks some ideas initially shared at the 2015 Conference of the Yale-Edinburgh Group on the History of the Missionary Movement and World Christianity, New Haven, CT, June 25–27, 2015, which also appeared as Barreto, "Brazil's Black Christianity."

2. See Paris, *Spirituality of African Peoples*; and Paris, *Virtues and Values.*

religion anywhere, as a result of the interaction with a new environment, the African consciousness that sustained those who survived the so-called Middle Passage had to adapt to the new demands, giving birth to an African American consciousness.³

This chapter does not discuss Paris's groundbreaking work on the common traits of an African identity. Nevertheless, in line with it, and with a particular focus on the reality of Brazil, it shows the lasting cultural and religious impact of the African presence in Brazil. My claim here is that Brazilian Christianity, just like Brazilian culture at large, has been largely influenced by African spirituality. Brazilian scholar Reginaldo Prandi has compellingly argued that despite its numerical decline, Afro-Brazilian religions occupy a central place in the permanent construction of Brazilian culture.⁴ As I will show in this paper, that contribution has also occurred in the religious field, extending far beyond the number of faithful practitioners of Afro-Brazilian religions such as Candomblé and Umbanda, influencing different streams of Brazilian Christianity.

Studies in world Christianity over the past two decades have shed light on how different Christian expressions have emerged, evolved, and changed in formerly colonized countries. The impressive growth of African Christianity and its diaspora in the twentieth century is on the forefront of this still incipient field of studies.⁵ Yet, Latin American Christianity has not received sufficient attention in the studies of world Christianity.⁶

Very early in the colonial era, Latin America was claimed as a Christian continent, meaning a Catholic one. In post-colonial Latin America, despite internal disputes, that Catholic dominance remained, and Latin American culture continued to be referred to as Catholic.⁷ In 1910, 95 per-

---

3. Paris, *Virtues and Values*, ix.

4. Prandi argues that in spite of continuous numerical decline (only 0.3 percent of the Brazilian population identified themselves as affiliated with an Afro-Brazilian religion in the 2010 census), the cultural contribution they have made to Brazilian identity (in music, dance, culinary, theater, cinema, literature, poetry, aesthetics, and mythical imagination, to mention a few areas) is unparalleled. In comparison to that, he argues, the cultural impact made by evangelicals in Brazil so far is insignificant. See Prandi, "Sobre Religiões Afro-Brasileiras,"11.

5. Amos Yong speaks of the "out of Africa" thesis as a possible "'new reformation' of a global reality," referring to Allan Anderson's suggestion that the renewal of African Christianity will have a worldwide impact similar to that of the Reformation. See Yong, "Out of Africa?," 315; and Anderson, *African Reformation*.

6. Todd Hartch's description of Latin American Christianity as being "neither newly Christian nor truly 'non-western'" is telling in relation to the insufficient attention Latin America has received so far in the studies of world Christianity. Hartch, *Rebirth of Latin American Christianity*, 2.

7. Prandi, "Religions and Cultures," 265.

cent of all Latin Americans professed to be Catholic.[8] In the second half of the twentieth century, though, the Latin American religious scene experienced significant changes. Still, Christianity remains the dominant religion, and Catholicism continues to hold a place of privilege as a majority religious group.

Beginning in the 1960s, Catholicism has experienced an unprecedented decline, and Protestantism, particularly in the form of Pentecostalism, has become a major player in the region, currently accounting for almost 20 percent of all Latin American Christians.[9] Contrary to stereotypes, Pentecostalism has shown over the years that it is not an otherworldly religion. As a sign of its this-worldliness, it has become a significant political actor in the Latin American public square.[10]

Because of its increasing social visibility, Pentecostalism has attracted more scholarly attention than other Latin American religious movements. However, Latin America has experienced religious change and revitalization in a variety of ways in the past few decades. Todd Hartch argues that Protestant growth in Latin America has contributed to sparking Catholic renewal.[11] To cope with the growth of Pentecostalism, Catholicism is experiencing new vigor in multiple ways, especially in regard to its rediscovery of the Bible and the engagement of its laity. Additionally, the contributions coming from Indigenous churches to Latin American Christianity are not insignificant. In contrast to the first round of evangelization, when most Indigenous people in Latin America were coerced into conversion, now, at a time when Indigenous traditional spirituality and identity experience a revitalization, Latin American Indigenous peoples who profess Christianity are seeking to make sense of their Christian faith in light of their own historical and communal struggles, and without necessarily breaking with their Indigenous values and traditions.

The religious scene in Latin America, thus, is becoming increasingly diverse, and the resurgence of traditional Afro-Latin American and Indigenous religions in the region enormously contribute to the religious plurality one sees in the region today. However, scholarship about the developments within Latin American Christianity is still very limited among world Christianity scholars; literature addressing how the revitalization of Indigenous

---

8. Pew Research Center, "Religion in Latin America."

9. Pew Research Center, "Religion in Latin America."

10. See Dodson, "Pentecostals, Politics, and Public Space in Latin America," 25–40. For the increasing, although ambiguous, political presence of Evangelicals and Pentecostals in Latin America, see Freston, *Evangelical Christianity and Democracy in Latin America*.

11. Hartch, *Rebirth of Latin American Christianity*, 4.

and African worldviews and spiritualities has impacted and transformed different streams of Latin American Christianity is nearly nonexistent, particularly in the Anglophonic world.[12]

This chapter seeks to work on that gap by focusing particularly on the effervescence of Afro-Brazilian spirituality in the context of the ongoing interaction between Afro-Brazilian religions and different expressions of Brazilian Christianity. In it, I examine those relations with particular attention to the interface between religion, identity, and race in Brazil. At a time when the Brazilian religious landscape is increasingly plural, understanding the Afro-Brazilian contributions for the formation of the Brazilian cultural and religious mosaic is crucial. More than highlighting religious change, this chapter also sheds light on the agency of Afro-Brazilian peoples and communities as social and cultural actors who have not only resisted colonial and neocolonial tendencies to whiten Brazilian culture but have also uniquely contributed to the formation of Brazilian identities in the midst a dynamic and continuous relationship with their African heritage. In spite of centuries of discrimination, persecution, and suppression, Afro-Brazilian spirituality has become a significant force in the Brazilian cultural and religious landscape.[13]

RACE AND RACISM IN BRAZIL

Brazil is known for having the largest presence of African peoples outside of the African continent. According to Vanessa Barbara, "Afro-Brazilians—people who self-identify as black or brown—make up 53 percent of our population, a total of about 106 million individuals. It is the world's largest black population outside Africa and the second largest after Nigeria."[14] Such a significant African presence in Brazil results from an intense and long slave trade. In the course of more than three centuries, almost 4.9 million enslaved Africans were trafficked to Brazil, "over ten times as many as went

---

12. Among the limited resources on the resurgence of Indigenous spirituality, one may see Cook, *Crosscurrents in Indigenous Spirituality*. Also see Cleary and Steigenga, *Resurgent Voices in Latin America*. Most essays, though, particularly in the second book, are written by non-native authors.

13. As Paris has shown in his work identifying common values and virtues of the African and African American experience, one can also identify a particular kind of moral agency among the African diaspora. Although moral agency is certainly present throughout the following pages, a specific focus on this aspect of the Afro-Brazilian experience is beyond the scope of this chapter.

14. Barbara, "In Denial over Racism in Brazil."

to mainland North America and almost as many as the total number who went to the entire Caribbean and North America combined."[15]

Despite this remarkable African presence in Brazil, the study of Brazilian Christianity has not devoted enough attention to the significant contributions made by Afro-Brazilians to Brazil's religious, cultural, and sociopolitical milieu.[16] Even Latin American liberation theology, which emerged as a refreshing prophetic voice in the continent in the late 1960s, has not given due importance to the racialization of oppression in the region.[17] To this date, there are not many books on the history of Latin American Christianity from the perspective of the Afro-Brazilian and Indigenous peoples.[18]

The rise of Latin American liberation theology in the late 1960s reflected what Gustavo Gutiérrez called "the irruption of the poor" in history. By that, he meant the resurgence of subjects who had previously received little attention from those controlling academic and theological discourses.[19] "The poor," "the oppressed," and "the marginalized" are categories chosen by liberation theologians to describe the presence of these new

---

15. Kananoja, *Central African Identities and Religiosity in Colonial Minas Gerais*, 4. More data on the transatlantic slave trade can be found at Slave Voyages, "Trans-Atlantic Slave Trade."

16. This is particularly true for Anglophonic scholars, but not exclusively. Few scholars of Christianity writing in Portuguese have paid attention to race and racial relations. One of the few historians who have done so is Eduardo Hoornaert. See Hoornaert, *Cristianismo Moreno do Brasil*.

Another important initiative that stimulated the conversation about Black identity and religion in Latin America was the Consultation on Black Culture and Theology in Latin America, organized by the Ecumenical Association of Third World Theologians (EATWOT) in São Paulo, Brazil, in 1985. CEDI published the procedures of that consultation. See Associacao Ecumenica de Teologos do Terceiro Mundo (ASETT), *Identidade Negra e Religiao*.

17. In his introduction to the fifteenth anniversary revised edition of *A Theology of Liberation*, Gustavo Gutiérrez acknowledged the limitations of the almost exclusively socio-economic categories used by the first liberation theologians to address oppression and injustice in the early 1970s, and welcomed the contributions made by Black, Hispanic, Amerindian, and feminist theologies to expand the views of liberation theologians. He still maintained, though, the centrality of the socio-economic dimension of "the poor," this time using it as an expanded category, which also included racial, cultural, and gender concerns. "The world of the poor is a universe in which the socio-economic aspect is basic but not all-inclusive." Gutiérrez, *Theology of Liberation*, xxi.

18. There are few reinterpretations of the Latin American history, and even fewer of the Brazilian religious history, from the perspective of Native Americans, Afro-Latin Americans, women, and the poor, as counterpoints to dominant top-down approaches; see Horna, *People's History of Latin America*; Hoornaert, *Historia da Igreja no Brasil*; and Fagundes Hauck, *Historia da Igreja no Brasil*.

19. Gutiérrez, *Theology of Liberation*, xx.

"active agents of their own destiny" as the new protagonists in Latin American history.[20] According to Paulo Freire, their ingress in the historical process as responsible subjects "who know and act," as opposed to being objects, "which are known and acted upon," required *conscientização*, i.e., an attitude of awareness through which the oppressed learn "to perceive social, political, and economic contradictions, and to take action against the oppressive elements of reality."[21]

Whereas Freire's pedagogy was an important contribution to raise awareness among the oppressed peoples in Latin America concerning the nature of their plight, and their agency in the process of their own liberation, it seems to assume that the oppressed has no agency before their *conscientização*. In contrast to that, I submit that subaltern people do not lack agency, even when they do not articulate it in sophisticated rational ways, particularly through writing. When it is not articulated in ways sanctioned by the Western intelligence, oppressed people's agency as subjects is often overlooked, ignored, or silenced in academic and religious Eurocentric discourses. Speaking of the failure of academic discourses to understand the agency of enslaved Afro-Latin American subjects, Andres Perez y Mena says, "For the Eurocentric, the enslaved are presumed brawn, without consciousness."[22]

James Scott has shown that those who are subjugated or oppressed continue to have self-determination. Scott speaks of the "daily tactics of resistance,"[23] concealed techniques of resistance that have been used by different subjugated peoples throughout history, including African Americans and Native Americans. Likewise, Afro-Brazilians have always been social, cultural, and religious agents whose agency is often neglected by those controlling academic discourse.

In the 1980s, Latin America, including many of its liberation theologians, experienced a cultural turn. The dominant socioeconomic reductionism of liberation theology's early days began to be questioned, and an emphasis on new cultural agents using a variety of hermeneutical lenses to interpret and act upon their own history began to emerge.[24]

In the late 1990s, decolonial theories provided further language and categories to explain how a colonial/modern epistemological displacement "removed 'the other' from the production of an effective history of

---

20. Gutiérrez, *Theology of Liberation*, xxi.
21. Freire, *Pedagogy of the Oppressed*, 513–14, 511–12.
22. Perez y Mena, "Cuban Santería, Haitian Vodun, Puerto Rican Spiritualism," 20.
23. Scott, *Weapons of the Weak*, xvi.
24. See, for instance, Sommer, *Cultural Agency in the Americas.*

modernity," and how history itself had become a "product of the West in its actions upon others."[25] Previously unheard narratives began to create a demand for fresh theological reflection. But, more than that, decolonial theories linked the colonial history of Latin America to the formation of a new global power: "colonial/modern Eurocentered capitalism."[26] This new global matrix of power that emerged concomitantly with the conquest of Latin America racialized oppression. Decolonial theory, thus, aggregates an essential connection missed by liberation theology: it connects colonial and neocolonial domination to the origin of the idea of race. As Aníbal Quijano states, the new model of global power, which had Latin America as its first space/time, codified

> the differences between conquerors and conquered in the idea of "race," a supposedly different biological structure that placed some unnatural situation of inferiority to the others. The conquistadors assumed this idea as the constitutive, founding element of the relations of domination that the conquest imposed.[27]

Quijano shows that this modern meaning of race was not known before the colonization of America. America (South and North) was its first laboratory. As the European conquistadores assumed this idea of race as foundational, people in America were racially classified, taking European superiority as the norm. The whole of life in the continent, and later in the world, was ordered accordingly, including the structures of labor and slavery.[28]

J. Kameron Carter makes an important contribution to the analysis of modern racial discourse and practice by placing "their genesis inside Christian theological discourse and missiological practice, which themselves were tied to the practice of empire in the advance of Western civilization."[29] As Carter argues, "modernity's racial imagination is religious in nature."[30] His impressive work painstakingly demonstrates "how the discourse of theology aided and abetted the processes by which 'man' [sic] came to be viewed as a modern racial being."[31]

The history of religion in Brazil is part of that larger picture. A narrative that recovers the relation between religion, race, and coloniality/

---

25. Bhambra, "Postcolonial and Decolonial Dialogues," 116.
26. Quijano, "Coloniality of Power, Eurocentrism, and Latin America," 533.
27. Quijano, "Coloniality of Power, Eurocentrism, and Latin America," 533.
28. Quijano, "Coloniality of Power, Eurocentrism, and Latin America," 534.
29. Carter, *Race*, 3.
30. Carter, *Race*, 5.
31. Carter, *Race*, 3.

modernity is of particular importance in the Brazilian scenario, because Brazilian elites have done more than most other dominant groups in the Americas to hide racism. Discussions about race and racism remain limited in Brazil. Brazilian elites have made a great effort to glorify the myth of racial democracy, which portrays racial relations in Brazil as uniquely cordial. In Brazil, racism is often denied, and racists are rarely identified. One of the most common strategies used to deny racism in Brazil is to compare Brazil's racial relations and legislation to segregationist regimes. Such discourse, however, only masks a deeply rooted and persistent racism that continues to impact racial relations in the country.[32]

The idea of racial democracy in Brazil has historically been connected to the ideological project of whitening the Brazilian population. The significant presence of Black and brown people in the makeup of Brazil was treated as a problem that needed to be solved, particularly after the abolition of slavery in 1888 and the establishment of the Republic in 1889. In contrast to the US, though, the Brazilian republican government believed in a genetic solution for the "negro problem," namely miscegenation.[33]

Maria Jose Barbosa explains that through a consistent process of racial miscegenation, "the Brazilian elite hoped that already by the third generation the children of interracial marriages would have lost most of the physical characteristics that would classify them as direct descendants of Africans."[34] Referring to an article written by Theodore Roosevelt after his trip to Brazil in 1914, she mentions Roosevelt's visit to the National Museum of Rio de Janeiro "where he was shown a famous picture that represented the ideal of 'whitening': in the background of the painting an old black lady and a lighter-skinned man, and at the center stands out a mother phenotypically mixed with a white boy on her lap."[35]

Instead of adopting a policy of racial segregation, which would keep African descendants separated, Brazilian political and economic elites adopted a policy of miscegenation, which intended to absorb the darker skinned segment of its population into the lighter skinned one. In contrast to the US, where the one-drop rule implied that miscegenation meant degradation, corruption, and impurity, in Brazil miscegenation was a sort of redemption, which would solve "the problem" of race in the country. The

---

32. See Walker Huntley, Prefacio, 12.

33. Somerlate Barbosa, "'Aves Que Aqui Gorjeiam Não Gorjeiam Como Lá?,'" 235.

34. Translation is mine. Somerlate Barbosa, "'Aves Que Aqui Gorjeiam Não Gorjeiam Como Lá?,'" 235.

35. Somerlate Barbosa, "'Aves Que Aqui Gorjeiam Não Gorjeiam Como Lá?,'" 235. The article Roosevelt wrote was titled "Brazil and the Negro" (1914). It appeared in the *Outlook*, the *Chicago Defender*, and the *Philadelphia Tribune*.

Brazilian whitening program included several actions, such as waves of European immigration, and the encouragement of the spreading of more "enlightened" European religious practices, in contrast to African ones.

That assimilationist "solution," though, did not work. A racial divide continues to be pervasive in Brazil.

> The pervasiveness of slavery, the lateness of its abolition, and the fact that nothing was done to turn former slaves into citizens all combined to have a profound impact on Brazilian society. They are reasons for the extreme socioeconomic inequality that still scars the country today.[36]

The accumulative impact of slavery and racial discrimination has turned race into a "significant dimension of inequality in Brazil."[37] Even without "a clear 'color line,' Brazilian society is founded on an explicit belief in white superiority, although not white supremacy."[38] As Thomas Skidmore points out, the Brazilian elite's response to the issue of race was ingenious. They "accepted the doctrine of innate white superiority, but then turned the white supremacist argument on its own head by affirming that in Brazil the white was prevailing through miscegenation."[39]

Furthermore, again in contrast with the US, Brazilian racism is based not on blood, but on the phenotype, on the color of one's skin. Thus, in Brazil, in the same nuclear family, a darker-skinned child can suffer racial prejudice from his/her parents or lighter-skinned siblings and have a harder time navigating structural racism in ways that his/her lighter-skinned siblings will not experience.

The thesis of miscegenation has altered the demographic makeup of the Brazilian population and might have prevented more conflictive relations. Nevertheless, it has worked against Black Brazilians, the majority of whom remain on the lower economic strata of the population. Besides masking systemic racial prejudice and preventing most Blacks from ascending to the

---

36. The Economist, "Race in Brazil."

37. Cleary, "Race, Nationalism and Social Theory in Brazil."

38. See Skidmore, "Fact and Myth." Skidmore writes, "Brazil never had the option, at least after the mid-colonial era, to enforce racial endogamy, or its implicit biracial assumptions, because too many persons of color (primarily mixed bloods) had entered free society.... Relatively few had penetrated to the top of the society... yet the moral and social legitimacy for drawing a sharp color line was already lost. Enforced racial endogamy and segregation were practical impossibilities." "Fact and Myth," 5.

39. Also, "This assimilationist ideology, commonly called 'whitening' by the elite after 1890 had taken hold by the early twentieth century" and continued to be Brazil's predominant racial ideology throughout the twentieth century. Skidmore, "Fact and Myth," 5.

upper classes, it has encouraged them to accept their share as "the norm" and stay quiet.[40]

It took some time for Brazilian scholars to question the myth of racial democracy. In the 1960s, Florestan Fernandes began to address the flaws of this doctrine, accusing it of being a "dissimulated defense of the attitudes, behavior, and 'aristocratic' ideals of the 'dominant race.'"[41] The formation of the Brazilian Black movement in the course of the twentieth century uniquely contributed to exposing the extent to which racism has persisted as one of the most vicious problems impacting the lives of a large number of Brazilian citizens.[42]

The Unified Black Movement, formed in 1978, has succeeded in impacting public policy. Some concrete successes can be seen in the following examples: (1) the passing of November 20, the birthday of *Quilombo* leader Zumbi, as the National Day of Black Consciousness in 1988; (2) the inclusion of anti-racist laws in the 1988 Brazilian constitution; (3) the adoption of affirmative action; (4) the creation of police stations specialized in racial crimes; (5) the sanctioning of a federal law in 2003, which made the teaching of Afro-Brazilian history and culture in schools nationwide obligatory; (6) and the creation of SEPROMI, Secretaria de Promoção da Igualdade

40. Somerlate Barbosa, "'Aves Que Aqui Gorjeiam Não Gorjeiam Como Lá?,'" 244.

In the 1930s, sociologist Gilberto Freyre developed a comprehensive theory of miscegenation as the foundation of Brazilian identity. For him, Brazilian society results from a singular historical experiment that brought together three different peoples and cultures, intermingling their traditions, beliefs, and idiosyncrasies. Having received his training in the US, Freyre wrote that he had background ethnological and anthropological theories that affirmed European supremacy. As a result, he held a positive view of the Brazilian cultural and racial mixture. Furthermore, he also had a religious contrast to offer. For him, Brazilian miscegenation was only possible because of the plasticity and flexibility of a Catholic culture that had more capacity of assimilation than a Protestant culture would ever have. Despite his genius, Freyre's theory was seriously flawed, as anthropologist Darcy Ribeiro shows. Writing the preface for the Spanish edition of one of Freyre's most important books, Ribeiro criticizes Freyre for speaking from the perspective of the oppressor since his analysis prioritizes the patriarchal and polygamous pattern of the Portuguese family in Brazil rather than the view of women, slaves, and natives in that process. Ribeiro, "Prólogo y Cronologia," ix–xlii.

41. Somerlate Barbosa, "'Aves Que Aqui Gorjeiam Não Gorjeiam Como Lá?,'" 240. See also Fernandes, *Integração do Negro na Sociedade de Classes*, 205.

42. The Black movement in Brazil is the successor of Black anti-slavery resistance, which can be traced back to the colonial times. As a movement, though, it begins to establish itself in the turn of the twentieth century. The rise of the *imprensa negra* (Black press), in the 1920s, and of *Frente Negra Brasileira* (Brazilian Black Front), in 1931, were some of the first expressions of the *Movimento Negro Brasileiro* (Brazilian Black Movement), which evolved in the following decades, being unified in 1978. For a brief history of this movement, see do Nascimiento and Larkin Nascimento, "Reflexoes Sobre o Movimento Negro no Brasil, 1938–1997," 203–36.

Racial do Estado, to deal with public policies for Black men and women in 2006.[43]

There is still a long way ahead to change the impact of five centuries of racial discrimination and more than three centuries of slavery. A recent report shows that in spite of the absolute gains in reducing the gap in poverty rates between 2004 and 2012, Afro-Brazilians remain the most marginalized people among the overall Brazilian population.

> In absolute terms, the likelihood of being in poverty declined between 2004 and 2012, but the relative gap with the white population remained almost unchanged.[44]

Between 1999 and 2001, a study was conducted to identify the impact of race or ethnic origin on mortality patterns in the state of São Paulo. This study, published with the title "The Color of Death," showed that Black and brown women comprised the majority among the deaths from pregnancy, childbirth, and postpartum complications.[45] Similarly, a criminological study published in October 2004 brought attention to the fact that the homicide mortality rate among Afro-Brazilians was 87 percent higher than that of white Brazilians in the years 1999 and 2000.[46]

> [Afro-Brazilians] are also more likely to be victims of police killings; a study by the University of São Carlos showed that 58 percent of all people killed in the state of São Paulo by the military police were black. They make up 62 percent of all people incarcerated nationwide.[47]

This data shows the terrible impact of racism on the daily life (and death) of Black Brazilians. Black women are especially affected by discrimination of gender and race. Refusing to be silent about it, Brazilian Black women have organized to tell their stories and to participate in political decision making.[48]

---

43. Somerlate Barbosa, "'Aves Que Aqui Gorjeiam Não Gorjeiam Como Lá?,'" 241–42.

44. Rodriguez Takeuchi and Mariotti, *Who Is Being Left Behind in Latin America?*, 12.

45. Batista et al., "Cor da Morte." See also Wood et al., "Color of Child Mortality in Brazil, 1950–2000."

46. Soares and Borges, "Cor da Morte," 27–31.

47. Somerlate Barbosa, "'Aves Que Aqui Gorjeiam Não Gorjeiam Como Lá?,'" 241–42.

48. See Crenshaw, *Intersecionalidade na Discriminação de Raça e Gênero*.

RELIGION AND RACE IN BRAZIL

Religion has played ambiguous roles in the plight of Afro-Brazilians. Enslaved Africans were baptized either before boarding the ships to cross the Atlantic or upon their arrival as part of a larger process meant to detach them from their African roots and heritage. Aline Hernandez describes a ritual, which occurred before boarding:

> Before boarding a ship, prisoners sold as slaves to slave traders were forced to walk around a baobab tree, known as the oblivion tree, to lose memory of their family ties, language, customs, and their belonging to a given place and culture.[49]

Silencing the memories of Africa was part of the systemic domination imposed on enslaved Africans by the colonizer.[50] However, the attempt to erase African memories from the Africans trafficked to Brazil failed terribly. The *colonizadores* failed to understand the depth of African identity and social agency.

As Peter Paris has stated so well, "Africans brought their worldviews with them into the diaspora, and as a result of their interaction with their new environments, their African worldviews were gradually altered into a new-African consciousness."[51] Integral to that worldview was African spirituality.[52] Such spirituality took different forms in the new surrounding environment.

The development of the African spiritual legacy in Brazil happened in a hostile environment. However, in contrast to the colonizer's expectation, the conversion of Afro-Brazilians to Christianity, forced or not, also entailed the aggregation of new elements from their worldview to an incipient Brazilian Christianity, contributing to its subsequent transformation. The agency and participation of Afro-Brazilians in the formation of the Brazilian religious landscape demands more attention from scholars studying Brazilian Christianity.

In the world in which the conquest of the Americas took place, for all agents involved, religion permeated all aspects of their lives. For the conquistadores, it was not different. They did not distinguish between their

---

49. The translation is mine. Hernandez, "Historias por Escrever," 84.
50. Hernandez, "Historias por Escrever," 84.
51. Paris, *Spirituality of African Peoples*, 24.
52. I borrow Paris's definition of spirituality as "the animating and integrative power that constitutes the principal frame of meaning for individual and collective experience." For him, spirituality "is synonymous with the soul of a people: the interpreting center of their power and meaning." Paris, *Spirituality of African Peoples*, 22.

religion and their politics or economic interests.⁵³ Under the influence of the myth of the Reconquista, both the Portuguese and the Spanish conquistadores believed that they had a mandate from God to protect the Catholic faith against all unbelievers. Their enterprise in the Americas was perceived as "a sacred trust so that they could bring their religion to the benighted people in these lands."⁵⁴

González and González illustrate the pervasiveness of religion in the mindset of the conquistadores.

> And they brought their religion and its institutions. The latter were patterned after what had developed in the Old World as new territories were conquered. The invaders brought their religion in much the same way as they had earlier brought it to southern Spain during the Reconquista and to the Canary Islands—by force of arms. The conquistadores were not only men in armor riding horses and carrying firearms. They were also men in clerical garb riding mules and carrying crosses. And it was not only the men in armor who became rich; there were also clerics who invested in various enterprises of conquest and thus became wealthy.⁵⁵

From the perspective of the Amerindian peoples, the arrival of the conquistadores in Latin America also represented the arrival of their God and their religion. However, their encounter with European Christianity became an encounter with prolonged distress. The lands known as *Abia Yala*⁵⁶ were reasonably well developed and larger than those of their conquerors, who knew nothing about the people who inhabited them.⁵⁷ For the native peoples in the Americas, the "discovery" of Latin America became "an invasion,

---

53. González and González, *Christianity in Latin America*, 3.

54. González and González, *Christianity in Latin America*, 3.

55. González and González, *Christianity in Latin America*, 3.

56. This is a name given by the Amerindians, in Kuna, a native dialect, to Latin America. It means "ripe land, big motherland." After the conquest, the Spaniards imposed the Italian name America to the "new land." Wagua, "Present Consequences of the European Invasion of America," 56.

57. Before the European invasion, there were three well-developed empires in Latin America: Mayas, Aztecs, and Incas. When the Europeans arrived in 1492, the Indigenous population was about one hundred million people, whereas Portugal had around one million inhabitants and Spain and England about three million each. The capital of the Aztec Empire, Tenochtitlan, had three hundred thousand inhabitants. In Europe, only Paris was bigger than the capital of the Aztecs. Also, "the Roman empire at its greatest extent was not greater than the Inca Empire." Richard, "1492," 59.

an enormous act of violence against million . . . one of the greatest genocides in the history of humanity."[58]

> [It represented] the beginning of the tribute, the beginning of the alms, what made the hidden discord appear, the beginning of the fighting with firearms, the beginning of the outrages, the beginning of being stripped of everything, the beginning of slavery for debts, the beginning of the debts bound to the shoulders, the beginning of the constant quarreling, the beginning of the suffering.[59]

For the survivors of the genocide that decimated the Indigenous population within a few decades, the memory of their painful encounter with Christianity would not go away.[60] To this day, their human and cultural rights continue to be violated. Whatever remained of their lands in Brazil continues to be invaded. Indigenous and peasant community leaders who dare to confront their oppressors are killed.[61] In other words, the structural violence perpetrated against the native peoples during the European invasion of Latin America is still a daily reality for most Indigenous peoples in the entire region.

Along with the material/physical conquest, there was also a spiritual/cultural one, aimed at destroying "the basic foundations of the indigenous cosmology."[62] As David Tavarez and John F. Chuchiak have stated, "The conversion of the indigenous peoples of Latin America to Catholicism and the eradication of their ancient beliefs and religious rituals were as important to most Spaniards as the military conquest."[63] Over the centuries, Amerin-

---

58. Richard, "1492," 59.

59. Richard, "1492," 60.

60. Wagua, "Present Consequences of the European Invasion of America," 47–56.

61. Only in 2014, Global Witness documented 116 killings of environment and land defenders in 17 countries around the world. Brazil was the worst affected country, with 29 deaths. Indigenous communities continue to take the hardest hit in land-related conflicts, which tend to isolate peasants and Indigenous communities by branding them as anti-development groups standing over against the pro-development powerful corporations. See Global Witness, "How Many More?"

According to David E. Toohey, just in the opening decade of the twenty-first century, 1,150 activists were murdered in the Amazon region. According to him, ranchers tend to be responsible for the murder of Indigenous peoples. See Toohey, "Indigenous Peoples, Environmental Groups," 73, 88.

62. Dussel, *History of the Church in Latin America*, 42.

63. Tavarez and Chuchiak, "Conversion and the Spiritual Conquest," 66.

dians have been imposed the Iberian worldview and turned into "marginal elements of the new society."[64]

The Africans taken to Brazil experienced similar pain. On top of being uprooted from their homes and lands, physically enslaved, turned into a commodity, tortured, raped, and killed in the trade process, they were supposed to leave their culture, their ways of life, and their religion behind.

> The entrance of the enslaved Africans in the . . . Portuguese territories was made, then, through evangelization and the reception of baptism. They received a new name, the water of baptism and salt as a sign of liberation from original sin, while the baptismal minutes recorded their condition as captives and the name of their owner . . . . The process of making the new slave included the individual's desocialization . . . . In this long process of enslavement of Africans, baptism was a central criterion in the making of a new slave.[65]

In spite of isolated voices denouncing the inhumanity of slavery, most Christians did not oppose the enslavement of Africans. On the contrary, even Catholic priests "practiced slavery and kept slave women as their mistresses."[66] Slavery was rooted in a value system. In racialized Latin America, being non-white became synonymous with being less than white. Non-European ways of living, thinking, and knowing were perceived as lacking and inferior.

Although Protestants only became part of that scene in the eighteenth century, they did not challenge that view of race. In his important study of slavery and Protestant missions in imperial Brazil, José Carlos Barbosa says:

> Just like the Catholic Christians who colluded with the conquistadors and were protected by their weapons and favors, pretending that they were presenting the radical Jesus of Nazareth to the inhabitants of the Land of the Holy Cross but turned a deaf ear to the pitiful appeals of blacks, so too, the Protestants failed to hear the insistent supplications coming from blacks scattered across all the fields of Brazil.[67]

---

64. Dussel, *History of the Church in Latin America*, 42. Amerindians were deemed as "an inferior social class." Dussel, *History of the Church in Latin America*, 43.

65. Castro Maia, "Nova Interpretação da Chegada de Escravos Africanos à América Portuguesa." Such a description of "making a slave" rigorously follows the instructions of the *Ordenações Filipinas* promulgated in 1603. See Hunold Lara, *Ordenações Filipinas*, 308.

66. Carvalho, *Struggle for Democracy in Brazil*, 7–8.

67. Barbosa, *Slavery and Protestant Missions in Imperial Brazil*, xix.

Like their Catholic counterparts, Protestant missionaries and converts believed that ignorance of "true religion" was the cause of the social problems of the nation. Therefore, evangelization and conversion, meaning rupture with one's superstitious past, were the solution.[68] Most Protestants shared the Eurocentric understanding of white superiority and accepted slavery as a necessary evil.[69] However, there was also a direct support of slavery, particularly among US southerners who immigrated to Brazil after the Civil War. As Barbosa states, "The southerners were encouraged by the prevailing system of large-scale slave ownership in Brazil."[70] As for their motivations to go to Brazil, he affirms, "An argument that was quite convincing was the possibility of reproducing and perpetuating the southern society demolished by the Civil War."[71] González and González mention that some of those southern white North Americans who refused to accept the emancipation of slaves in the US even "brought their slaves with them and tried to build in Brazil plantations similar to those they had owned in the lands of the Confederacy."[72] Among them, there were Baptists, Methodists, and Presbyterians who would later receive spiritual and material support, including missionaries, for the purpose of evangelizing Brazilians.[73]

FROM RELIGIOUS MONOPOLY TO RELIGIOUS HYBRIDITY AND PLURALITY

Lísias Nogueira Negrão describes the Brazilian religious landscape as being monolithically Catholic during the empire and religiously pluralistic in the republic.[74] That description is accurate only if one thinks about the dominance of Catholicism as the official religion imposed by the Portuguese Crown on the inhabitants of the colony.[75] The royal patronage which governed the relationship between the Portuguese Crown and the Vatican

---

68. Barbosa, *Slavery and Protestant Missions in Imperial Brazil*, 135. For Protestants conversion included also breaking with Catholicism, which they perceived as a corrupted form of Christianity.

69. Barbosa, *Slavery and Protestant Missions in Imperial Brazil*, 45.

70. Barbosa, *Slavery and Protestant Missions in Imperial Brazil*, 58.

71. Barbosa, *Slavery and Protestant Missions in Imperial Brazil*, 58.

72. González and González, *Christianity in Latin America*, 200.

73. González and González, *Christianity in Latin America*, 200.

74. Nogueira Negrão, "Trajetórias Do Sagrado," 115–32.

75. Nogueira Negrão, "Pluralismo e Multiplicidades Religiosas no Brasil Contemporaneo," 262.

legitimized the temporal interests of the Portuguese empire.[76] Such alliance gave the Portuguese Crown the control over the Brazilian church, as it appointed its clergy and kept them dependent on the royal power.[77] The sector of the church that remained faithful to the interests of the Vatican was the monastic order of the Jesuits, which ended up being expelled from the country in 1759.[78] The irregularity of the clergy's presence in many parts of the country made room for the rise of popular Catholicism, which retained many elements of Indigenous and African-derived spirituality.[79] Yet, Catholicism was still the imposed official religion.[80] However, with those gaps in the catechesis, Catholic indoctrination was weakened. At one point, in Brazil, as Negrão states, "the appearance of being Catholic mattered more than being really a Catholic."[81]

> It was vital to go to Mass and pray publicly, observe the holy days, baptize their business with Catholic saints names. To escape enslavement or having to journey deep into the hinterlands where they were hunted by the pioneers, Amerindians were predisposed to accept the settlements where they were christened and indoctrinated. Blacks continued to honor their ancestors and deities by identifying them with Catholic saints and performing their rituals before altars; Jews, attended Mass and prayed correctly.[82]

Without the close presence of clergy, the Indigenous dwellers of rural villages and districts and Afro-Brazilians, both slave and free, were able to preserve their own religious beliefs and practices. There were spaces within

---

76. Nogueira Negrão, "Pluralismo e Multiplicidades Religiosas no Brasil Contemporaneo," 262.

77. Nogueira Negrão, "Pluralismo e Multiplicidades Religiosas no Brasil Contemporaneo," 262.

78. Nogueira Negrão, "Pluralismo e Multiplicidades Religiosas no Brasil Contemporaneo," 262.

79. Nogueira Negrão, "Pluralismo e Multiplicidades Religiosas no Brasil Contemporaneo," 263.

80. Nogueira Negrão, "Pluralismo e Multiplicidades Religiosas no Brasil Contemporaneo," 263.

81. Nogueira Negrão, "Pluralismo e Multiplicidades Religiosas no Brasil Contemporaneo," 263.

82. Nogueira Negrão, "Pluralismo e Multiplicidades Religiosas no Brasil Contemporaneo," 263.

and outside the Catholic church which allowed for the practice of a hybrid faith.[83] Popular Catholicism became increasingly dark-skinned and autonomous.[84]

The beginning of the nineteenth century brought the opening of the ports to trade with the British, allowing Protestant services to be held on Brazilian soil. However, proselytizing was not allowed. Only later, Emperor D. Pedro II allowed freedom of worship for native Brazilians and the free activity of North American missionaries. The Republican Constitution of 1889 secured the separation of church and state and created favorable conditions for the formation of a pluralistic and secular society by the turn of the twentieth century.[85]

However, the legacy of colonial and imperial Catholicism was preserved. Most Brazilians continued to declare themselves Catholic, although on their own terms. Many descendants of Africans and Indigenous people created hybrid religious expressions in which Catholicism coexisted with non-Christian beliefs and practices like Candomblé and Umbanda.[86]

In different ways, Candomblé, Umbanda, and some expressions of popular Catholicism and of Pentecostalism retained elements of the African worldview brought to Brazil by the almost five million enslaved Africans. As Mikelle Smith Omari-Tunkara has pointed out:

> The cumulative cultural cognizance and worldviews of enslaved Africans transported to the New World during the trans-Atlantic slave trade (1538–1888) remain operative within the sacred spaces of Candomblés, although new cultural forms were and continue to be invented.[87]

Candomblé temples, houses of Umbanda, Catholic Black brotherhoods, and Black Pentecostal temples became symbolic spaces of resistance, reinterpreting and recreating the African worldview in new ways, thus renewing its significance to Afro-Brazilian peoples. Speaking of the role played by Candomblé, Omari-Tunkara says:

---

83. Nogueira Negrão, "Pluralismo e Multiplicidades Religiosas no Brasil Contemporaneo," 264. One of those internal spaces emerged with the formation of Catholic brotherhoods, sisterhoods, and orders, which gathered mainly Black Brazilians.

84. Nogueira Negrão, "Pluralismo e Multiplicidades Religiosas no Brasil Contemporaneo," 265.

85. Nogueira Negrão, "Pluralismo e Multiplicidades Religiosas no Brasil Contemporaneo," 265.

86. Nogueira Negrão, "Pluralismo e Multiplicidades Religiosas no Brasil Contemporaneo," 265.

87. Smith Omari-Tunkara, "Candomblé."

Thus, Candomblés are not only creative, but dynamic "political entities" as they directly or indirectly operate as "centers of cultural resistance and power." Such resistance is based on African precepts and epistemological frames remaining active despite persistent, often elusive efforts by the wider Luso (Portuguese)-Brazilian society.[88]

Can Pentecostalism also claim its cultural agency as a Black religion? Just as popular Catholicism has allowed Black and brown Brazilians to embrace Catholicism in their own terms, Pentecostalism has played a similar role in the context of Brazilian Protestantism. By the turn of the twentieth century, historical Protestant groups such as Baptists, Presbyterians, Congregationalists, Episcopalians, Lutherans, Mennonites, and Methodists had failed to reach out to the Brazilian masses. Protestantism only found a broader space in the hearts of the Brazilian masses with the rise of Pentecostalism, especially in metropolitan areas at the end of the first decade of the twentieth century.[89] Pentecostalism's impact on the Brazilian religious landscape would be more clearly felt toward the end of the twentieth century.

Up to the mid-1940s, though, Catholics still accounted for a total of 95 percent of the population over against only 2.6 percent of Protestants and 1.9 percent of other religions. A decline in Catholic numbers began to become apparent toward the end of the past century and the beginning of the twenty-first century.

A 2013 report published by the Pew Research Center illustrates the demographic changes in the major religious groups in Brazil between 1970 and 2010.[90] The report shows that up to 1970, 92 percent of all Brazilians identified themselves as Catholics. Only 5 percent of the 95 million Brazilians then claimed to be Protestants, and only 2 percent were affiliated with other religions.[91] By 2010, the situation had drastically changed. Roman Catholics remained the absolute majority. However, in 2010 only 65 percent of the Brazilian population claimed to be Catholic. Those identifying themselves as Protestants (*Evangelicos*) were now 22 percent. The Brazilians affiliated with other religions, including Afro-Brazilian religions, represented now 5 percent of the more than 200 million Brazilians, and the number of people who are not affiliated to any particular religion raised from 1 percent

---

88. Smith Omari-Tunkara, "Candomblé."

89. Nogueira Negrão, "Pluralismo e Multiplicidades Religiosas no Brasil Contemporaneo," 266.

90. Pew Research Center, "Brazil's Changing Religious Landscape."

91. Pew Research Center, "Brazil's Changing Religious Landscape."

to 8 percent of the Brazilian population.[92] Between 1991 and 2010, historical Protestants, grew from 3 to 4 percent. Unclassified Protestants increased in the same period from 1 to 5 percent. Unsurprisingly, Pentecostals experienced a significant growth during that time. In 1991 they represented 6 percent of the Brazilian population. By the 2010 census they had increased to 13 percent of the population, or something around 25 million people.[93]

Although Pentecostalism is a religious phenomenon impacting different social classes in Brazil, it particularly attracted the poorer urban populations. Taking into consideration Brazil's racial inequalities and the larger Pentecostal presence among the poor, some Black Brazilians have claimed Pentecostalism as a Black religion. Marco Davi de Oliveira, a Black Baptist pastor and theologian, has argued that Pentecostalism is the largest Black religion in Brazil today, given the fact that there are more Blacks in Pentecostal temples each Sunday than in Catholic churches or *terreiros* of Candomblé.[94] He goes on to say that whereas historical Protestantism ignored Black Brazilians, Pentecostalism made an option for them, based on its liturgy, singing, proximity of the poor, language, and an ecclesiastical posture that he sees lacking in both historical Protestant churches and the Catholic hierarchy.[95] Although de Oliveira briefly mentions the African American origins of the US Pentecostalism, in Azusa Street, his argument is mainly based on the history and reality of Black people in Brazil and the lack of spaces to discuss their pain, their struggle, and their freedom within historical Protestant churches, which, in his view, have made an option for the elites. José Honório das Flores Filho equally refers to a Black Pentecostal vocation in the periphery of Brazilian urban centers (shantytowns or favelas).[96]

Another voice claiming the Blackness of Brazilian Pentecostals is Hernani da Silva, the founder of the Brazilian Evangelical Black Movement (*MNE, Movimento Negro Evangelico*) and a long-standing member of the Pentecostal Brasil Para Cristo Church.[97] Although the *MNE* is not exclu-

---

92. Pew Research Center, "Brazil's Changing Religious Landscape." The Protestant/Pentecostal boom particularly between 1991 and 2010 was impressive. However, two other pieces of information on this report are also worth noting. The number of people openly identifying themselves with non-Christian religions also grew significantly as did the number of Brazilians with no religious affiliation.

93. Pew Research Center, "Brazil's Changing Religious Landscape."

94. Oliveira, *Religião Mais Negra do Brasil*.

95. Oliveira, *Religião Mais Negra do Brasil*, 20.

96. Flores Filho, "Vocação Da Periferia," 111.

97. For an introduction to this movement, see Burdick, "Why Is the Black Evangelical Movement Growing in Brazil?," 311–32.

sively Pentecostal, it has a number of Black Pentecostal participants, including da Silva, its main leader. MNE is only one face of multifaceted similar initiatives. In the six years I served as a Baptist pastor in Salvador, Bahia, between 2004 and 2010, I was involved in the Black Evangelical movement of the state of Bahia (*MONEBA, Movimento Negro Evangelico da Bahia*), led by a Black lawyer from the Assemblies of God and a Black Baptist charismatic pastor. There are many other local and regional expressions of this movement, many times working independently of other similar movements. Common among these initiatives is the reclaiming of Blackness (negritude) by Black Pentecostals and Evangelicals.

An immediate impact that this movement has made on its participants is the reconsideration of the relationship between Black Pentecostals/Evangelicals and the Unified Black Movement, mostly led by participants of Afro-Brazilian religions. Evangelicals and Pentecostals in general tend to see participants of Afro-Brazilian religions through negative lenses. Many Pentecostals equate, for instance, Candomblé *orishas* with demonic spirits. When approaching a person who is related to Afro-Brazilian religions, they want to evangelize them, which might include "delivering" or exorcising them from demonic influences.[98] Black Pentecostals participating in the Black Evangelical Movement, on the other hand, have developed a more open view, which allows them to look for common ground at least on the level of political alliances in the struggle for civil and human rights, in spite of religious differences.

Black Pentecostals/Evangelicals such as Hernani da Silva and Marco Davi de Oliveira are developing a "theology of African roots" that can help them "articulate an anti-racist message in clear, theologically sophisticated biblical terms."[99] Along with that, they are also retelling the story of Brazilian Protestantism from an Afro-Brazilian perspective. They fully represent the irrupting of new subjects whose voices were previously silenced and who are now re-situating their own history by telling it from a different place of enunciation.

Whereas most books on the history of Brazilian Christianity take the work of Scottish Presbyterian missionary Robert Reid Kalley as the starting point of the first Portuguese-speaking Protestant congregation in Brazil (1855), Hernani da Silva gives that credit to Black preacher Agostinho Jose Pereira, who founded a Portuguese-speaking Protestant church in Recife, in 1841. By doing that, da Silva turns a Brazilian Black evangelist and a Black Protestant church into the cornerstone of Brazilian Protestant

---

98. See Almeida, "Guerra das Possessões," 323.
99. Burdick, "Why Is the Black Evangelical Movement Growing in Brazil?," 325.

history.[100] Through the lenses of the Evangelical Black Movement, the history of Protestantism in Brazil gains a new accent and new emphases; it recovers the memories of previously unheard Black Protestants, including some women.[101] Also, as he retells the history of Brazilian Christianity from an Afro-Brazilian perspective, he denounces white colonial Christianity and its support of slavery and racism, whereas recovering often overlooked Christian anti-racist and Black movements in Brazil and elsewhere.[102] Evangelical and Pentecostal mobilization for racial justice is timely, particularly when hate crimes against practitioners of Afro-Brazilian religions are on the rise.[103]

However, in contrast with exclusivist discourses proffered from Pentecostal pulpits, in the day-to-day life in Latin America, one finds, as Andrea Althoff suggests, great "fluidity of religious traditions at the grassroots level" in Pentecostal communities, which makes room for the coexistence of apparently contradictory religious identities. Referring to her study of Pentecostal practices among the Maya, she states:

> When I asked a Mayan indigenous Pentecostal about Mayan spirituality, he categorically rejected these practices. However, when I asked him if it is possible to protect a child against the evil eye with a necklace of pepper—a method that is common in that area—he agreed that it is possible and added that this is a type of medicine.[104]

Her findings point to a "very practice-oriented view of faith" among those Mayan Pentecostals, which in many ways are similar to what Lísias Nogueira Negrão encountered among economically dispossessed Catholics in Brazil as indicated earlier.[105]

BELONGING, CHANGE, AND AGENCY IN BRAZILIAN CHRISTIANITY

With all of this in mind, how are we to understand the complex and plural Brazilian religious landscape? It is not enough to speak about a change from Catholic monopoly to religious plurality. The apparent monolithic

---

100. Silva, *Movimento Negro Evangelico*, 9.
101. Silva, *Movimento Negro Evangelico*, 10.
102. Silva, *Movimento Negro Evangelico*, 18.
103. Sullivan and Barros, "Followers of Afro-Brazilian Religions Feel Under Attack."
104. Althoff, *Divided by Faith and Ethnicity*, 260.
105. Althoff, *Divided by Faith and Ethnicity*, 261.

Catholicism of colonial and imperial times was never so hermetic and unified as some might think. Throughout the history of Brazil since the Portuguese conquest, the process of Christian evangelization has resulted in religious encounters and exchanges, involving several parties. Decimated Indigenous subjects and the enslaved Afro-Brazilians have been active participants in those encounters and exchanges. In the case of the enslaved Africans, they reinterpreted their worldview and spirituality in light of the new reality and of the new challenges. Such encounter, however, was never among equally standing parties. It was a violent encounter; a military invasion. Christianity played a key role in legitimizing the violence of the conquistadores and in colonizing the minds and souls of Black and brown Brazilians. It contributed to the racialization of oppression and to the attempt to eradicate the religious traditions of the conquered dark-skinned peoples.

Against all odds, however, the spirituality of the African peoples in Brazil not only survived but also became an important element of resistance and creativity for Afro-Brazilians. Whenever they converted to Christianity, Afro-Brazilians have also brought their symbols, languages, deities, and bodily expressions to a Christianity they have embraced in their own terms. Lacking sufficient priests to enforce strict vigilance of the religious practices of the subaltern peoples, the Catholic Church ended up providing spaces for Afro-Brazilians to practice their Christian faith, which were turned into spaces of creativity and resistance. Enslaved Africans and their descendants have used Catholic symbols, saints, and festivities to fulfill their obligations to the *orishas* and practice their own religion.[106] That has particularly impacted popular forms of Christianity in Brazil, which are now reclaiming their African roots.

There is significant mobility, fluidity, and hybridity in the Brazilian religious landscape.[107] In his research on popular religiosity in the city of São Paulo, Lísias Negrão identified duplication or even the multiplicity of beliefs and belongings, as well as varied dynamics of individuals' religious paths and trajectories.[108] Negrão concludes that in the contemporary Brazilian religious landscape, the phenomenon of dual belonging or confession has not only persisted but, in fact, increased and diversified.[109]

---

106. Perez y Mena, "Cuban Santería, Haitian Vodun, Puerto Rican Spiritualism," 17.

107. Nogueira Negrão, "Pluralismo e Multiplicidades Religiosas no Brasil Contemporaneo," 261–79.

108. Nogueira Negrão, "Pluralismo e Multiplicidades Religiosas no Brasil Contemporaneo," 269.

109. Nogueira Negrão, "Pluralismo e Multiplicidades Religiosas no Brasil Contemporaneo," 270.

A large number of those people converting to Pentecostalism come either from popular Catholicism or from Afro-Brazilian religions. Conversion does not necessarily imply a clear-cut break with the past. The motives to follow or change religion might be extremely pragmatic. And the failure to see a particular need satisfied might lead to new changes of loyalty.[110] Such a pragmatic attitude was also noticed in the early study of Brazilian Pentecostalism done by Waldo Cesar and Richard Shaull. Among the Pentecostals they examined in a favela in Rio de Janeiro, many were searching for responses to their practical and immediate needs. Studies of Brazilian Christianity need to take seriously these variations in the non-religious motivation for religious belonging, and religious change in Brazil, particularly considering the religious fluidity among those at the margins of the Brazilian society. There is a life of its own in sectors of society that have been often neglected and marginalized. Edwin David Aponte has asserted that the margins are "border areas with other concurrent cultural areas of alternate discourse and activity," and "places where individuals and communities craft and live out multiple identities and experiences that challenge dominant categories of perceiving, knowing, living, and storytelling."[111] Brazilian Christianity is predominantly a dark-skinned Christianity, emerging in one of those marginalized spaces full of creativity. Its complex nature combines elements of African, Indigenous, and Euro-American spiritualities into a unique intercultural milieu whose wealth is just beginning to be explored.

In significant parts of Brazil, the poor are for the most part the descendants of the millions of enslaved Africans brought to Brazil and the descendants of the hundreds of Indigenous peoples who lived in the land prior to the arrival of the Portuguese caravels in 1500. The spirituality of the African peoples who arrived in the lands now known as Brazil continues to inform the tens of millions of Brazilians who identify as Afro-descendant. That spirituality took a variety of forms, reinventing itself as a continuous source of resilience and resistance in light of centuries of physical, psychological, and cultural oppression.

On the ground, encounters between Afro-Brazilians and equally suppressed Indigenous peoples led to the formation of merging Black and brown identities, which combined into multiple popular religious traditions, later infused with popular Christianity, as this chapter shows. The conversion to Christianity, although meant to erase the practice of traditional religions, ended up infusing Brazilian popular Christianity—both Catholic and

---

110. Nogueira Negrão, "Pluralismo e Multiplicidades Religiosas no Brasil Contemporaneo," 276.

111. Aponte, "View from the Margins," 86.

Protestant—with values, beliefs, and practices inherited from African and Indigenous traditional religious practices. Despite the paradox of exclusivist discourses, which continue to be produced in many Catholic and Protestant circles in Brazil, more than five centuries later, it is undeniable that Brazilian culture, spirituality, and religious practices—especially among the poor—are deeply and irretrievably infused with African-derived practices. As Afe Adogame has repeatedly said in reference to the relationship between the African continent and the African diasporas—of which Brazil is the largest contingent—"One cannot fully understand Africa without its diaspora, neither can we understand the African diaspora in isolation. This is more so as the African Union (AU) now characterizes the Africa diaspora as the sixth region of Africa."[112] By contrast, one can say that it is impossible to fully understand Brazilian religion, including Christianity, without its African legacy. While many in Brazil continue to associate Christianity with the West and its empires, the claim Black Brazilians are increasingly making on Christianity as a Black religion is not only pertinent but crucial to the understanding of Christian practices and beliefs among the more than half of the Brazilian population which identify as Black or brown.

BIBLIOGRAPHY

Adogame, Afe. "Mapping African Christianities Within Religious Maps of the Universe." *Princeton Seminary Bulletin* 33 (2016) 39–65.

Almeida, Ronaldo de. "A Guerra das Possessões." In *Igreja Universal do Reino de Deus: os novos conquistadores da fé*, edited by Ari Pedro Oro et al., 321–43. São Paulo: Paulinas, 2003.

Althoff, Andrea. *Divided by Faith and Ethnicity: Religious Pluralism and the Problem of Race in Guatemala*. Boston: De Gruyter, 2014.

Anderson, Allan H. *African Reformation: African Initiated Christianity in the 20th Century*. Trenton, NJ: Africa World Press, 2001.

Aponte, Edwin David. "View from the Margins: Constructing a History of Latina/o Protestantism." In *Hispanic Christian Thought at the Dawn of the 21st Century: Apuntes in Honor of Justo L. González*, edited by Alvin Padilla et al., 85–97. Nashville: Abingdon, 2005.

Associacao Ecumenica de Teologos do Terceiro Mundo (ASETT). *Identidade Negra e Religiao*. Rio de Janeiro: CEDI, 1986.

Barbara, Vanessa. "Opinion: In Denial over Racism in Brazil." *New York Times*, Mar. 23, 2015. https://www.nytimes.com/2015/03/24/opinion/vanessa-barbara-in-denial-over-racism-in-brazil.html.

---

112. Adogame, "Mapping African Christianities Within Religious Maps of the Universe."

Barbosa, José Carlos. *Slavery and Protestant Missions in Imperial Brazil: "The Black Does Not Enter the Church, He Peeks In from Outside."* Translated by Fraser G. MacHaffie and Richard K. Danford. New York: University Press of America, 2008.

Barreto, Raimundo C. "Brazil's Black Christianity and the Counter-Hegemonic Production of Knowledge in World Christianity." *Studies in World Christianity* 25.1 (Apr. 1, 2019) 71–94.

Batista, Luís Eduardo, et al. "A Cor Da Morte: Causas de Óbito Segundo Características de Raça No Estado de São Paulo, 1999 a 2001." *Revista de Saúde Pública* 38.5 (Oct. 2004) 630–36.

Bhambra, Gurminder K. "Postcolonial and Decolonial Dialogues." *Postcolonial Studies* 17.2 (2014) 115–21.

Burdick, John. "Why Is the Black Evangelical Movement Growing in Brazil?" *Journal of Latin American Studies* 37.2 (2005) 311–32.

Carter, J. Kameron. *Race: A Theological Account*. Oxford: Oxford University Press, 2008.

Carvalho, José Murilo de. *The Struggle for Democracy in Brazil: Possible Lessons for Nigeria*. Port Harcourt: Port Harcourt University and SEPHIS, 2002.

Castro Maia, Moacir Rodrigo de. "Uma Nova Interpretação Da Chegada de Escravos Africanos à América Portuguesa (Minas Gerais, Século XVIII)." Presented at the Anais do XXVI Simpósio Nacional de História, São Paulo, 2011. http://www.snh2011.anpuh.org/resources/anais/14/1308192610_ARQUIVO_TextocompletoANPUHjunho2011.pdf.

Cleary, David. "Race, Nationalism and Social Theory in Brazil: Rethinking Gilberto Freyre." *David Rockefeller Center for Latin American Studies*, n.d., Working Paper 99–09 edition.

Cleary, Edward L., and Timothy J. Steigenga, eds. *Resurgent Voices in Latin America: Indigenous Peoples, Political Mobilization, and Religious Change*. New Brunswick: Rutgers University Press, 2004.

Cook, Guillermo, ed. *Crosscurrents in Indigenous Spirituality: Interface of Maya, Catholic, and Protestant Worldviews*. Studies in Christian Mission. Leiden: Brill, 1997.

Crenshaw, Kimberele. *A Intersecionalidade Na Discriminação de Raça e Gênero*. Brasilia: UNIFEM/Programa Igualdade, Gênero e Raça, 2002.

Dodson, Michael. "Pentecostals, Politics, and Public Space in Latin America." In *Power, Politics, and Pentecostals in Latin America*, edited by Edward L. Cleary and Hannah W. Stewart-Gambino, 25–40. Boulder: Westview, 1997.

Dussel, Enrique. *A History of the Church in Latin America: Colonialism to Liberation 1492–1979*. Grand Rapids: Eerdmans, 1981.

The Economist. "Race in Brazil: Affirming a Divide." Jan. 28, 2012. https://www.economist.com/the-americas/2012/01/28/affirming-a-divide.

Fagundes Hauck, João. *Historia Da Igreja No Brasil: Ensaio de Interpretacao a Partir Do Povo*. Petropolis: Vozes, 1980.

Fernandes, Florestan. *A Integração do Negro na Sociedade de Classes*. São Paulo: Editora Nacional, 1964.

Flores Filho, José Honório das. "A Vocação Da Periferia Pelo Pentecostalismo e o Negro Pentecostal Na Área Do Mutirão Em Bayeux Em Meio à Segregação e Pobreza." *PLURA—Revista de Estudos de Religião* 7.1 (2016) 111–35.

Freire, Paulo. *Pedagogy of the Oppressed*. Translated by Myra Bergman Ramos. 30th anniversary ed. Kindle. New York: Bloomsbury, 2000.

Freston, Paul, ed. *Evangelical Christianity and Democracy in Latin America*. Evangelical Christianity and Democracy in the Global South. Oxford: Oxford University Press, 2008.

Global Witness. "How Many More?" April 20, 2015. https://www.globalwitness.org/en/campaigns/environmental-activists/how-many-more/.

González, Ondina E., and Justo L. González. *Christianity in Latin America: A History*. Kindle. Cambridge: Cambridge University Press, 2008.

Gutiérrez, Gustavo. *A Theology of Liberation: History, Politics, and Salvation*. 15th anniversary ed. Maryknoll, NY: Orbis, 1988.

Hartch, Todd. *The Rebirth of Latin American Christianity*. Oxford: Oxford University Press, 2014.

Hernandez, Aline. "Historias Por Escrever: Um Museu Virtual Sobre a Influencia Negra Na Vida Sociopolitica Nos Campos de Cima Da Serra." *Dialogo* 22 (2013) 81–92.

Hoornaert, Eduardo. *Historia Da Igreja No Brasil: Ensaio de Interpretacao a Partir Do Povo*. Petropolis: Vozes, 1976.

———. *O Cristianismo Moreno Do Brasil*. Petropolis: Vozes, 1991.

Horna, Hernán. *A People's History of Latin America*. Princeton: Markus Wiener, 2013.

Hunold Lara, Silvia. *Ordenações Filipinas, Livro V*. São Paulo: Companhia das Letras, 1999.

Kananoja, Kalle. "Central African Identities and Religiosity in Colonial Minas Gerais." PhD diss., Åbo Akademi University, 2012.

Nascimiento, Abdias do, and Elisa Larkin Nascimiento. "Reflexoes Sobre o Movemento Negro No Brasil, 1938–1997." In *Tirando a Mascara: Ensaios Sobre o Racismo No Brasil*, edited by Antonio Sergio Alfredo Guimaraes and Lynn Walker Huntley, 203–36. São Paulo: Editora Paz e Terra, 2000.

Nogueira Negrão, Lísias. "Pluralismo e Multiplicidades Religiosas No Brasil Contemporaneo." *Sociedade e Estado* 23.2 (2008) 261–79.

———. "Trajetórias Do Sagrado." *Tempo Social* 20.2 (Nov. 2008) 115–32.

Oliveira, Marco Davi de. *A religião mais negra do Brasil: por que mais de oito milhões de negros são pentecostais*. São Paulo: Editora Mundo Christão, 2004.

Paris, Peter J. *The Spirituality of African Peoples: The Search for a Common Moral Discourse*. Minneapolis: Fortress, 1995.

———. *Virtues and Values: The African and African American Experience*. Facets. Minneapolis: Fortress, 2004.

Perez y Mena, Andres I. "Cuban Santería, Haitian Vodun, Puerto Rican Spiritualism: A Multiculturalist Inquiry into Syncretism." *Journal for the Scientific Study of Religion* 37.1 (1998) 15–27.

Pew Research Center. "Brazil's Changing Religious Landscape: Roman Catholics in Decline, Protestants on the Rise." July 18, 2013. https://www.pewresearch.org/wp-content/uploads/sites/20/2013/07/Brazil-religious-landscape-full.pdf.

———. "Religion in Latin America: Widespread Change in a Historically Catholic Region." Nov. 13, 2014. https://www.pewresearch.org/wp-content/uploads/sites/20/2014/11/Religion-in-Latin-America-11-12-PM-full-PDF.pdf.

Prandi, Reginaldo. "Religions and Cultures: Religious Dynamics in Latin America." *Social Compass* 5.33 (2008) 264–74.

———. "Sobre Religiões Afro-Brasileiras." *Horizonte* 11.29 (2013) 10–12.

Quijano, Aníbal. "Coloniality of Power, Eurocentrism, and Latin America." Translated by Michael Ennis. *Nepantla: Views from South* 1.3 (2000) 533–80.

Ribeiro, Darcy. "Prólogo y Cronologia." In *Casa-Grande y Senzala: Introducción a La Historia de La Sociedad Patriarcal En El Brasil*, by Gilberto Freyre, ix–xlii. Caracas: Biblioteca Ayacucho, 1977.

Richard, Pablo. "1492: The Violence of God and the Future of Christianity." In *1492–1992: The Voice of the Victims*, edited by Leonardo Boff and Virgilio P. Elizondo, 59–67. London: SCM, 1991.

Rodriguez Takeuchi, Laura, and Chiara Mariotti. *Who Is Being Left Behind in Latin America?* ODI report. London: Overseas Development Institute, 2016. http://cdn-odi-production.s3-website-eu-west-1.amazonaws.com/media/documents/10282.pdf.

Scott, James C. *Weapons of the Weak: Everyday Forms of Peasant Resistance*. New Haven, CT: Yale University Press, 2000.

Slave Voyages. "Trans-Atlantic Slave Trade—Estimates." n.d. https://www.slavevoyages.org/assessment/estimates.

Silva, Hernani da. *O Movimento Negro Evangelico: Um Mover Do Espirito Santo*. São Paulo: Selo Editorial Negritude Crista, 2010.

Skidmore, Thomas E. "Fact and Myth: Discovering a Racial Problem in Brazil." Kellogg Institute working paper 173, April 1992. https://kellogg.nd.edu/sites/default/files/old_files/documents/173_0.pdf.

Smith Omari-Tunkara, Mikelle. "Candomblé." In *African American Studies Center*, edited by F. Abiola Irele and Biodun Jeyifo. Oxford University Press, 2010. https://oxfordaasc.com/view/10.1093/acref/9780195301731.001.0001/acref-9780195301731-e-47792.

Soares, Glaucio Ary D., and Doriam Borges. "A Cor Da Morte." *Ciencia Hoje* 35 (2004) 27–31.

Somerlate Barbosa, Maria Jose. "'As Aves Que Aqui Gorjeiam Não Gorjeiam Como Lá?' As Abordagens Raciais No Brasil e Nos Estados Unidos." *Afro-Hispanic Review* 29.2 (2010) 235–48.

Sommer, Doris, ed. *Cultural Agency in the Americas*. Durham: Duke University Press, 2006.

Sullivan, Zoe, and Lydia Barros. "Followers of Afro-Brazilian Religions Feel Under Attack." *Al Jazeera America*, Sept. 14, 2014. http://america.aljazeera.com/articles/2014/9/13/prejudice-againstcandombleworshippersincreasesinbrazil.html.

Tavarez, David, and John F. Chuchiak. "Conversion and the Spiritual Conquest." In *Religion and Society in Latin America: Interpretive Essays from Conquest to Present*, edited by Lee M. Penyak and Walter J. Petry, 66–82. Maryknoll: Orbis, 2009.

Toohey, David E. "Indigenous Peoples, Environmental Groups, Networks and the Political Economy of Rainforest Destruction in Brazil." *International Journal of Peace Studies* 17.1 (2012) 73–97.

Wagua, Aiban. "Present Consequences of the European Invasion of America." In *1492–1992: The Voice of the Victims*, edited by Leonardo Boff and Virgilio P. Elizondo, 47–56. London: SCM, 1991.

Walker Huntley, Lynn. Prefacio to *Tirando a Mascara: Ensaios Sobre o Racismo No Brasil*, edited by Antonio Sergio Alfredo Guimaraes and Lynn Walker Huntley, 11–17. São Paulo: Editora Paz e Terra, 2000.

Wood, Charles H., et al. "The Color of Child Mortality in Brazil, 1950–2000: Social Progress and Persistent Racial Inequality." *Latin American Research Review* 45.2 (2010) 114–39.

Yong, Amos. "Out of Africa? Pentecostalism in Africa, the African Diaspora, and to the Ends of the Earth." *Pneuma* 35.3 (2013) 315–17.

Chapter 6

Strengthening the Ties That Bind
Examining Peter J. Paris's Search for a Common Moral Discourse Among African Peoples and Its Implications for World Christianity

Moses O. Biney

INTRODUCTION

Scholarship on African and African American theology and ethics diverges significantly in their foci and goals. Though rooted in the same African ancestry, distinct historical, socio-cultural, and political experiences have shaped the theological and ethical perspectives of continental and diaspora Africans in different ways. While African theology emerges primarily from and is shaped by Indigenous African experiences, African American theology is deeply influenced by the African diaspora, especially the context of enslavement, segregation, and the civil rights movement in the United States. These mainly epistemological differences are linked to deep-seated philosophical differences regarding the role of the African past with the American present. In other words, the differences in foci reflect the perennial debate over African retentions in African American religion and culture, that is, the extent to which elements of African culture have been preserved, transformed, or integrated into African American religious practices, rituals, and broader cultural life after the transatlantic slave trade.

With many Africans from the continent migrating to the United States and North America and many Africans from the diaspora, especially African Americans, seeking to reconnect with their African heritage, scholarship that creates opportunities for a common theological and moral discourse among African peoples is more than needed. By understanding and appreciating these divergencies and disagreements, we can foster a richer, more inclusive theological discourse that can address the challenges faced by both communities. One scholar who attempts to do this is Peter J. Paris.

This chapter seeks to do three interconnected things. First it examines Peter J. Paris's contributions to the fields of theology and ethics and, second, explores and interrogates his vision of unity and ethical discourse among African peoples. Third, it outlines some broader implications for the study of world Christianity, particularly among African peoples in a diverse and interconnected world driven by migration and transnationalism.

To fully appreciate the work of Paris and other scholars who have written about African and African American theology and ethics, it is critical to have a general overview of the context within which he and others wrote. This is what I will present in the next section.

COMMON GROUND: CONFRONTING COLONIAL AND RACIST SCHOLARSHIP

A common agenda for many African and the African diaspora scholars in the twentieth and twenty-first centuries was to confront and call out the Eurocentric and imperial bent of Western theology and ethics. For several centuries these disciplines have privileged European culture—its perspectives, philosophies, and experiences—over that of other cultures. Scholarship in theology, ethics, and even world Christianity has largely been shaped by Eurocentric and patriarchal notions of creation and human existence. Factors such as the political and economic dominance of European powers, and its attendant colonialism and racism, and the exclusive use of Western languages and texts in global theological education have contributed immensely to this situation. Colonial powers, it must be noted, often imposed their own religious and moral values on colonized peoples, thus shaping the way that non-Western cultures are perceived.

Western Christian scholarship, for example, has traditionally focused on the study of the Bible and other Christian texts mostly written in European languages and from a European perspective. This has led to the neglect of the religious and cultural traditions of Africa, Asia, the Middle East, and Latin America and the preponderance of Western categories and research methods in these disciplines. In some ways, Western Christian scholarship has been used to justify Western imperialism and racism and has led to the marginalization of non-Western cultures in the study of theology and ethics.[1] In fact, theologies and moral principles from non-Western cultures are often treated as inferior to European ones. African and Black theology, for instance, have generally not gained comparable traction and respect as European ones in the academia.

Since the last century, however, there has been a growing number of African and African American theologians and scholars who have challenged Western theology and ethics. These scholars have called attention to the Eurocentric bias of these disciplines and the need to give voice to African perspectives, and methods of study. They have, among other things, argued that traditional Christian theology must shed its colonial and patriarchal perspectives and methods of study.

Working in a variety of academic fields, such as biblical studies, systematic theology, ethics, and liberation theology, these scholars have developed new theological frameworks that are rooted in their own cultures and experiences and helpful for creating a more inclusive and equitable understanding of Christianity. As Peter J. Paris points out rightly:

> In retrospect, it is clear that the second half of the twentieth century constituted a veritable watershed in academic scholarship. Often, for the first time the voices racial and ethnic minorities, so-called third world peoples, and white women were clearly heard challenging Western scholarship in humanities, the so-called social sciences and the professions. Their forceful criticisms centered on epistemological questions. Most importantly, they critically analyzed the presuppositions underlying traditional Western scholarship, which hitherto had privileged white-male bias to the detriment of all other groups.[2]

Prominent among these scholars are John Mbiti, a pioneer in African theology, who argued that African theology should be rooted in African culture and experience and not in the Eurocentric assumptions of traditional Christian theology; Desmond Tutu, the first Black Anglican archbishop of Cape Town, South Africa, an anti-apartheid activist who points

---

1. Here are some examples of how the theology and ethics of African cultures have been marginalized. (a) The work of African theologians, such as John Mbiti, Desmond Tutu, Kwame Bediako, and Mercy Oduyoye, has often been overlooked by Western scholars. (b) The ethical teachings of Indigenous cultures have often been dismissed as "primitive" or "uncivilized." And (c) the perspectives of women and other marginalized groups have often been excluded from theological and ethical discourse.

2. Paris, *Spirituality of African Peoples*, 2.

out that Christians have a responsibility to fight against all forms of injustice, including racism and colonialism; James Cone, the founder of Black liberation theology who maintains that Black Christians need to develop a theology that is rooted in their own experience of oppression; Emilie M. Townes, a Black American womanist theologian who argues for womanist theology, that is, a way of doing theology that is rooted in the experience of Black women. Others are Mercy Oduyoye, Kwame Bediako, and Peter Paris, whose contributions to development of post-colonial African and African American theology and ethics are notable. For the purposes of this chapter, I shall now shift focus to the Peter J. Paris, his scholarship, and his contributions to the fields of theology and ethics.

PETER J. PARIS: SCHOLARSHIP

Paris's scholarship focuses on Christian social ethics, African and African American religion and ethics, and some intersections with other fields of study.[3] His writings offer a profound understanding of the history, sociopolitics, theology, and ethics of Black people. Through his study of Black religious institutions, Black religious and political leaders, and Black spirituality, he offers a practical understanding of ethics. Indeed, Paris's teaching and research in social ethics explores "ethics that matter," as captured in the title of a recent collection of essays in his honor.[4] Through his books and scholarly articles, he provides insights that challenge many Western-centric views of ethics and morality.

Paris's philosophical perspectives and goals are often clearly revealed in the introductions to his books and essays. In *Black Religious Leaders:*

---

3. I first met Peter J. Paris in Accra, Ghana, in fall of 1997 when visiting a friend, one for whom I served as teaching assistant at the University of Ghana. Dr. Paris had at the time taken a sabbatical from Princeton Theological Seminary and was teaching ethics for a semester at Trinity Theological Seminary. What felt like a chance meeting at the time led to decades of being his student, mentee, and friend. During our first and subsequent meetings in Ghana, he showed great interest in my studies, particularly a dissertation I was writing for the award of a MPhil in religion at the University of Ghana. He spent about three hours in steaming hot weather discussing with me helpful ideas for my dissertation, which explored the traditional Akan methods and processes for conflict resolution. He also encouraged me to apply to Princeton Theological Seminary (PTS) for a master's program. Later in the fall of 1998, we met again in PTS when I was admitted into their ThM program and later into the PhD program. Throughout my studies he served as my academic advisor and mentor. This full disclosure is aimed at showing my personal relationship with Paris, which offers me a better understanding of his ideas beyond his writings and also to indicate his connections with Africa and its people.

4. Riggs and Logan, *Ethics That Matters*.

Unity in Diversity, Paris states the ethical presupposition underlying his scholarship this way:

> A presupposition operating throughout this study is that an inquiry in social ethics should begin with some actual, concrete problems arising among human beings in their public actions. That is to say, such investigation should begin with conflicting views about the good humans can and should do. The conflicting views are problematic for human action in that they can limit and threaten the possibility for creativity. The result of such an investigation should be some resolution of the problem or a restatement of the problem in order to liberate the agents and their activities and to establish thereby the conditions for more creative enterprise. In short, the subject matter of our inquiry is human action, and the goal of that inquiry is the enhancement of human action.[5]

Also, in his introduction to *The Spirituality of African Peoples: A Search for a Common Moral Discourse*, he states among other things that:

> Historical experience shapes the nature of theology and ethics. Since religion and morality are respectively the subject matter of theology and ethics, a plurality of one (that is either religion or morality) implies a plurality of the other (that is, either theology or ethics). As with all living phenomena, both religion and morality continually change while preserving their basic identities.[6]

Writing specifically about African theology and ethics, Paris points out that:

> Much of African thought including theology and ethics, arises out of problems of daily experience and it is pursued for the purpose of discovering practical solutions for everyday problems. In short, African theology and ethics are practical sciences in the service of the community's well-being. Hence both are intrinsically political.[7]

One social problem Paris seeks "practical solutions" to is poverty. In his introduction to his edited volume book, *Religion and Poverty: Pan-African Perspectives*, based on interdisciplinary research conducted by a Pan-African group of scholars, Paris writes:

---

5. Paris, *Black Religious Leaders*, 31–32.
6. Paris, *Spirituality of African Peoples*, 21.
7. Paris, *Virtues and Values*, 9.

> Thus, since African peoples shared the common historic experience of oppression in one form or the other, much common ground exist for moral discourse about these and related matters.... The general purpose of this study was to develop a common moral discourse by studying religion and poverty through the multiple lenses of our academic disciplines. Further, the group embraced a Pan-African consciousness similar to the one devised more than a century ago by various scholars and leaders of Africa, the West Indies and United States. As those early Pan-Africanists eagerly nurtured and promoted African unity in their common quest for political independence from European colonialism, so we also share in the common desire to eradicate poverty among African peoples everywhere.[8]

Based on these quotations and many of his writings, we can surmise that for Paris, ethics is contextual, practical, and aimed at communal problem-solving. In other words, the true nature, goals, and effectiveness of ethical principles and systems can best be understood when they are studied in cultural and social contexts where they are used to solve real and practical challenges.

In some ways, his understanding of ethics reflects some of Aristotle's ideas. Both scholars, for instance, emphasize the importance of virtues in life. For Aristotle, virtue is the "mean" between extremes. Courage, for example, is a virtue that lies between recklessness and cowardice. This is the doctrine of the mean, where virtue is about finding the right balance between deficiencies and excesses. Like Aristotle's doctrine of the mean, Paris discusses the African notion of harmony and balance. Yet, while Aristotle focuses on the balance within an individual, Paris's balance emphasizes the interconnectedness of individuals within the community. While Aristotle emphasizes individual flourishing, Paris puts a strong emphasis on communal ethics, underlining the importance of the community in determining ethical values and behaviors. For Paris, the well-being of the community often supersedes individual desires.

Paris, in his writings and presentations, elucidates the complex, diverse, yet interconnected ethical and spiritual systems of African and African American communities. By drawing from the rich tapestry of African traditions, rituals, and stories, Paris creates a narrative that celebrates the communal, reciprocal, and sacred nature of African ethical systems. He strongly asserts that despite their cultural diversity, African societies share a common moral discourse that is deeply influenced by their collective histories, social structures, and spiritual beliefs. In the next section, I outline and

8. Paris, *Religion and Poverty*, 4.

discuss some of the moral principles Paris considers common to African and African American peoples.

PARIS'S CONCEPTS OF AFRICAN MORAL AND SPIRITUAL DISCOURSE

Central to Paris's work, as hinted earlier, is the exploration of African ethical thought as a rich reservoir for global ethical reflection. He has consistently sought to understand and highlight the moral and spiritual richness of African and African diaspora communities. Again, he underscores the communalism inherent in many African societies, positioning it as a counter-narrative to Western individualism. For Paris, a common moral discourse must attend to these communal values, considering ethics as rooted in the well-being of the community. Paris also brings to the fore the intersections of religion and ethics, emphasizing how faith traditions, particularly within African and African American contexts, shape moral considerations.

His work has emphasized the importance of ethical and spiritual discourse as a unifying and empowering tool for African peoples globally. Among the key ethical concepts found in Paris's work are the following:

1. Communal Ethic: Paris has consistently emphasized the significance of the community in African ethical systems. Unlike the Western emphasis on individual rights and freedoms, African morality, according to Paris, is fundamentally communal. This is articulated in his book *The Spirituality of African Peoples*, in which he delineates how the well-being of the community, as well as its stability and harmony, is prioritized over individual ambitions.[9]

2. Virtue Ethics: In his writings, virtues such as wisdom, courage, and compassion are not just personal attributes but are realized and actualized within the communal context.[10]

3. Ethics of Care and Responsibility: Stemming from the communal nature of African moral thought, there's an emphasis on care and responsibility toward others. The responsibilities of care are tied to one's identity and place within the community.

4. Sacredness of Life: Paris frequently underscores the sacredness of life, which is a defining feature of African spiritual discourse. This

---

9. Paris, *Spirituality of African Peoples*, 101–5.
10. Paris, *Spirituality of African Peoples*, 18, 136.

reverential view of life is deeply intertwined with ethics, shaping moral obligations toward fellow human beings, animals, and the environment. This perspective is seen in his discussion about African rituals and traditions, which often celebrate and affirm the sanctity of life.[11]

5. Reciprocity: In Paris's view, African ethics is built on the principle of reciprocity. This principle emphasizes mutual obligations and reinforces the idea of collective well-being. He touches upon this in *Black Religious Leaders: Conflict in Unity*, which highlights the idea that the success and well-being of one individual are tied to the well-being of others.[12]

6. Role of Ancestors: Paris points out that respect for ancestors and the guidance they provide plays a pivotal role in individual and community decision-making. His examination of the ancestral veneration practices sheds light on how morality is often derived from the wisdom of those who came before.[13]

7. Integration of Christianity and Traditional Beliefs: Paris also believes that African Christian ethics is a unique synthesis of biblical teachings and traditional African moral and spiritual values. His work *The Social Teaching of the Black Churches* is a testament to this, where he probes into the theological and ethical dimensions of Black churches and how they echo this synthesis.[14]

CONVERGENCIES: PARIS'S VIEWS ON INTERCONNECTIVITY AMONG AFRICAN PEOPLES

Paris in *The Spirituality of African Peoples: The Search for a Common Moral Discourse*, writes:

> Africans and African Americans share a common worldview, which comprises a cosmological whole that unites all of life in and among the realms of the spirit, history, and nature. Hence it follows that all knowledge in their daily lives should presuppose this fundamental holism.[15]

---

11. Paris, *Spirituality of African Peoples*, 101–17.
12. Paris, *Black Religious Leaders*, 31,
13. Paris, *Spirituality of African Peoples*, 51.
14. Paris, *Social Teaching of the Black Churches*, 99–102.
15. Paris, *Spirituality of African Peoples*, 129.

This is a bold and controversial assertion considering the disagreements that exist among scholars regarding the African survivals and continuities of African culture and religion among African Americans. Nonetheless, he argues convincingly, based on his review and analysis of the works of many African and African American scholars, that such continuities exist. Regarding African and African social ethics, Paris identifies six moral virtues—beneficence, forbearance, practical wisdom, improvisation, forgiveness, and justice—as building blocks and convergent values. Drawing upon a combination of historical analysis, cultural observations, ethical theories, and his own personal experiences, he highlights the interconnectedness of these virtues and how they have been shaped by, and in turn, shape the lived experiences of African and African American communities.

Beneficence, which he sees as the most highly praised virtue among these African peoples, refers to acts of kindness or charity, where individuals go beyond their duty to help others. Paris suggests that this virtue is prevalent in African societies, where there's a strong emphasis on mutual assistance, generosity, and caring for the welfare of others. African American communities, with their long-standing traditions of mutual aid societies, church support, and community upliftment, also exemplify this virtue.

Second is the virtue of forbearance, which involves patience, restraint, and tolerance in the face of adversity or provocation. Paris argues that given the historical adversities faced by both African and African American communities—such as colonization, slavery, and racial discrimination—forbearance has been essential for survival. This quality is often seen in the way these communities respond with resilience and unity instead of being consumed by anger.

A third virtue is practical wisdom. Paris emphasizes the importance of this virtue, which involves a sense of discretion, discernment, and the ability to make prudent decisions based on experience. Traditional African societies, with their respect for the wisdom of elders and their oral traditions, place great importance on this virtue. Similarly, in African American communities, practical wisdom has been essential in navigating complex socio-political landscapes.

Next is improvisation. This virtue pertains to the ability to adapt, innovate, and make do with available resources. Paris observes that, historically, African societies have shown a remarkable ability to adapt to changing circumstances, be it environmental, political, or social. African American culture, particularly in areas like music (e.g., jazz) and art, exemplifies the spirit of improvisation, turning constraints into creative expressions.

Paris underscores the importance of forgiveness in both African and African American traditions. The capacity to forgive, even in the face of grave injustices, is seen as a powerful virtue that fosters reconciliation and community healing. Whether it is post-apartheid South Africa's Truth and Reconciliation Commission or the broader African American quest for civil rights and social justice, forgiveness plays a crucial role in paving the way forward.

Lastly, justice is central to Paris's understanding of African and African American ethics. For both communities, the quest for justice—be it in the face of colonization, slavery, segregation, or ongoing systemic racism—is a driving force. Paris emphasizes that justice in these contexts is not just about retribution but also about restoration and ensuring the dignity and rights of all community members.

STRENGTHENING TIES IN AFRICAN SOCIETIES

In his writings, Paris calls for dialogue and mutual understanding among African peoples and the integration of traditional African ethical values into modern African societies. This implies building upon Indigenous concepts of justice, governance, and social welfare to formulate policies that are not only efficient but also culturally resonant. He not only talks the talk, but also walks the walk. Through his research, teaching, preaching, traveling, and networking, he always looks for ways of connecting African peoples in Africa and North America.

I recall, for instance, that in 2001 he brought together African, Caribbean, and African American students at Princeton Theological Seminary at the time for a discussion. The central purpose for this discussion was to explore the challenges and opportunities for establishing a more cordial relationship between these peoples. One main finding during the meeting was that there was lack of knowledge of each other's history and culture and that any assumption that all Blacks share the same culture and worldview was inaccurate. However, it was also established that we had several commonalities in the areas of history, spirituality, music, food etc. Also relevant are his several travels to and teaching in Africa, the Pan-African project on Religion and Poverty, mentioned earlier.

In a presentation for the Kwaku Boakye Memorial Lecture at First Presbyterian Church, Irvington, New Jersey, on February 17, 2008, titled "Values and Experiences That All African Peoples Share," Paris outlined twenty-three values and experiences, both positive and negative, he saw as common among African peoples.[16] Responding to a question, about how

---

16. Paris, "Values and Experiences That All Africans Share." Among these values and experiences are the following: (a) African peoples share the common experience

African peoples might think about imagining, building, and enhancing organized structures for social, political, economic, religious, and cultural interactions, Paris reflects on his own experience and work in Africa. He writes:

> One year after Ghana gained its independence from colonial rule, in 1958, Dr. James Robinson, Pastor of the Morningside Presbyterian Church in New York City founded a multi-cultural program called "Operation Cross-roads Africa." Its purpose was to provide opportunities for students in the United States to live, work and study with students in various countries of Africa. The first years' experience witnessed 60 American students going to Nigeria, Ghana, Liberia, Sierra Leone, and Senegal. I was privileged to go to Nigeria. In each place we met with an equal number of African students and together worked on a community project, visited various homes and public sites. Through discussions with our peers and lectures from invited guests we received a general introduction to the culture. We, in turn, told the African students about the United States. Many life-long friendships developed. It was on that occasion that I met Modupe Oduyoye who would eventually become Mercy Oduyoye's husband. We became life-long friends. He later studied theology at Yale University, and I later returned to Nigeria for a three-year period to work with the Student Christian Movement there. My daughter was born there. Everyone involved in that program has been influenced by the experience in countless

---

of embracing a religious worldview that views the cosmos as sacred, and consequently, they reject a purely secularist or humanist orientation; (b) African peoples share the common experience of viewing religious and moral practices as more important than religious doctrines and beliefs; (c) African peoples share a common experience of bestowing greater value on habits of spending money in order to celebrate and enjoy family and communal life than in saving and investing their monies. The former is thought to express the moral virtue of a generous spirit, while the latter connotes the vice of selfishness. These reasons may be mere rationalizations for the habit of conspicuous consumption. (d) African peoples share a common vulnerability toward tribalism and classism, both of which contain the seeds of genocide; (e) African peoples share a common disdain for those in their own group who become criminals. These include drug addicts, the homeless, the imprisoned, prostitutes, drug dealers, corrupt police, and other public authorities; (f) African peoples everywhere share the experience of being viewed as a whole as among the poorest people on the planet; (g) African peoples share a common attitude of patriarchal privilege which perceives men and their work on a higher plane than women and their work. This implies a routinized division of labor between them, which begins in the family and expands to the community at large. Though matrilineal family structures among the Akan peoples constitute a corrective to such customary practices, they are not widespread either in Africa or abroad. Clearly, patriarchalism is a negative value that is widely shared among African peoples.

ways. At that time very little was known in the United States about the African continent.[17]

I have quoted Paris at length here for two important reasons. First to show his personal engagement with the peoples and cultures of continental Africa and, second, to underscore the fact that his understanding of their spirituality and desire for moral dialogue derives from his personal bonds with Africa.

MIGRATION, TRANSNATIONALISM, AND SPIRITUALITY OF AFRICAN PEOPLES

Religion, or the belief in transcendent divine power, in Paris's view, is the most important connector between Africans on the continent and those in the diaspora.[18] This assertion has not gone unchallenged. Anthony Pinn, for instance, raises concerns about this "religious imperialism." For Pinn, there is no basis to support Paris's claim that traditional Africans had no atheists among them. While he does not necessarily refute the significance of religion in the life of continental and diaspora Africans, he finds the use of "African Spirituality" as a framework for discussing the connections between Africa and its diaspora is too narrow.[19] This, he believes creates a dissonance in *The Spirituality of African Religions*. He writes:

> Paris seeks a broad and flexible theory of life meaning(s) but limits the possibility through a grammar of religiosity that is rather fixed, and one that takes as paradigmatic a god(s) centered framework.[20]

I consider Pinn's critique important, not necessarily because of the reasons he gives. He may be right about Paris's overstatement of the fact, but there are no reliable statistics available, for instance, to determine the percentage of non-religious people among traditional Africans. So, rather than the past, my concern is about the present and the future. The important questions we must wrestle with, among others, are "Is spirituality still the most important connector between African peoples?" "How evident is this

---

17. Paris, "Values and Experiences That All Africans Share."
18. A similar view is held by Albert J. Raboteau in his book, *Slave Religion: The "Invisible Institution" in the Antebellum South*. Raboteau writes, "One of the most durable and adaptable constituents of slave culture linking African past with American present, was religion." See Raboteau, *Slave Religion*, 4.
19. Pinn, "Maps of Meaning," 14.
20. Pinn, "Maps of Meaning," 14.

among continental Africans and the 'New' African diaspora?" and "What are the possible non-spiritual avenues for strengthening ties between African peoples?" These questions obviously cannot be fully answered in this short essay. However, I want to highlight here some changing dynamics in African diaspora spirituality, particularly in the United States, due to migration and transnationalism.

In the last fifty plus years, what generally was called the African diaspora by many scholars has changed. Due to the influx of immigrants from Africa and the Caribbean especially since the 1970s, the African diaspora no longer refers to the descendants of African slaves but also includes African immigrants of all generations. A large percentage of these immigrants, many of whom are Christians and Muslims, have brought with them their own brands of religions that they practice and propagate. They have founded churches, mosques, and temples that cater to their spiritual, social, and cultural needs and that of their children and grandchildren in many cities and towns. They generally, therefore, resist pressures to completely assimilate into American social-cultural and religious life and are therefore simultaneously embedded in both their home countries and the United States. On the other side of the coin, African and Caribbean Americans are connecting more with Africans on the continent through travel, education, mission work, and business. In fact, several African countries are now making it easier for them to visit and become residents of the countries.

Nonetheless, it is not clear that African peoples are connecting more than they did in the past mainly based on their religious affiliation, practices, and congregational formations. What is true, though, is that there are similarities between much of the worldview and practice of religion of these continental Africans and those in the diaspora (both old and new). Spirituality offers both groups a connection to a shared African heritage and identity, serving as a reminder of common roots and histories. While the specifics of religious practice may vary, the underlying spiritual principles and values often resonate with notions of community, resilience, and reverence for ancestors that are significant in many African cultures. Also true is the fact that continental Africans and diaspora Africans are connected in other cultural areas such as through music, dance, art, and cuisine.

Though Peter Paris's *Spirituality of African Peoples* deals primarily with the relationship between Africans and African Americans, it provides useful ideas for the study of the spirituality of new African immigrants. It calls for an understanding of spirituality that does not dichotomize the sacred and the secular but sees them as interrelated. Such is the general worldview of many Africans, as John S. Mbiti and other African scholars have pointed out. Additionally, he shows the possibility of studying the spiritual and moral connections that exist between the old and new African diasporas and a methodological example for doing so. This has wider implications for disciplines such as world Christianity.

SOME IMPLICATIONS FOR WORLD CHRISTIANITY

The study of world Christianity has until recently focused on the history of Western mission in the two-thirds world. It must be recalled that nineteenth- and twentieth-century European missionaries who went to Africa and other Indigenous communities often saw their cultures and religions as inferior to their own. African religious practices, particularly their rituals, bore the full brunt of missionary denunciation from European missionaries. Since among Africans economic, political, social, and moral life are intertwined with religious life, almost every aspect of the life of African peoples was criticized and, in some cases, denounced by missionaries who called these African beliefs "superstition" and "demonic." Missionary teaching, which was highly influenced by Enlightenment ideas, emphasized the discontinuity between the African past and its present. Geoffrey Parrinder is on target when he says:

> The old attitude of missionaries was destructive; the indigenous religion was not studied; it was not thought to have any divine revelations or inspiration, and little effort was made to use any part of it as basis for fuller teaching. But it is not necessary that the old religion both taught some truths and produced some spiritual values and living.[21]

This has led to the marginalization of African agency and creativity and to the portrayal of African Christianity as a passive recipient of Western influence. In similar ways, through slavery and racism, the humanity and spirituality—religious beliefs and practices—of African slaves and their descendants have been demeaned. Until now, scholars of world Christianity have generally discriminated between the West and the rest of the world. Elsewhere, I have argued that world Christianity will need to use more interdisciplinary approaches and methods for research in order to address the many complex cultural, political, and social justice issues intertwined with religious belief and practice.[22]

Though Peter J. Paris is primarily an ethicist, his scholarship in the spirituality and the religious institutions of African and African Americans

---

21. Cited in Edusa-Eyison, "Kwesi Dickson," 98–99.
22. Biney, "World Christianity and the Evasion of Social Justice Issues," 117.

provides something important for the study of world Christianity. First, through his work world Christianity scholars can appreciate how the African and African diasporic religious experience can contribute to a more holistic understanding of global Christian thought and practice. Second, Paris's emphasis on community-centric ethics provides world Christianity with a robust paradigm for cultivating a sense of shared responsibility and interconnectedness. His work is a clarion call for Christian communities to immerse themselves in dialogue and learning across various cultural and theological traditions. Such engagement is vital in navigating the plurality within the Christian faith, allowing for a deeper appreciation and respect for the diversity that characterizes the global Christian community.

Furthermore, the acknowledgment and integration of African theology and ethics into the broader canvas of world Christianity, as advocated by Paris, will be instrumental in crafting a more inclusive and representative theological discourse. It will not only facilitate a richer understanding of the Christian faith but also engenders a space where the voices and experiences of the marginalized and underrepresented can be heard and valued.

CONCLUSION

In the chapter, I have explored Peter J. Paris's scholarship, particularly his attempt to find a common moral discourse between African peoples. This pursuit for a unified moral discourse among African peoples provides a pivotal lens through which we can understand the mechanisms required to strengthen the bonds within marginalized communities while offering invaluable insights for the study of world Christianity. His emphasis on communal values, solidarity, and shared responsibility serves not only as a beacon for oppressed and marginalized groups but also as a guiding ethos for fostering a more inclusive and socially engaged form of Christianity worldwide. In essence, "Strengthening the Ties That Bind" through the lens of Peter J. Paris's scholarly oeuvre calls for the imperative rethinking and realignment of Christian ethics and theology toward a framework that is inherently inclusive, socially responsive, and reflective of the diverse expressions of Christian faith around the globe. His profound engagement with African ethical thought does not merely offer theoretical insights but beckons practical applications that can revolutionize the ways in which Christian communities interact, worship, and engage with the broader society, particularly in relation to marginalized and oppressed groups. By understanding and appreciating the theological insights and ethical propositions from African perspectives, world Christianity can navigate the challenges of the modern world with a richer and more varied toolkit.

BIBLIOGRAPHY

Biney, Moses O. "World Christianity and the Evasion of Social Justice Issues: A Focus on Pentecostalism in West Africa." In *Alterity and the Evasion of Justice: Explorations of the "Other" in World Christianity*, edited by Raimundo C. Barreto and Deanna Ferree Womack, 5:97–118. Minneapolis: Fortress, 2023.

Edusa-Eyison, Joseph M. Y. "Kwesi Dickson, the Bible and African Life and Thought in Dialogue." In *African Theology in the 21st Century: The Contribution of the Pioneers*, edited by Bénézet Bujo, 2:93–123. Nairobi: Paulines Publications Africa, 2003.

Paris, Peter J. *Black Religious Leaders: Conflict in Unity*. 2nd ed. Louisville, KY: Westminster John Knox, 1991.

———, ed. *Religion and Poverty: Pan-African Perspectives*. Durham: Duke University Press, 2009.

———. *The Social Teaching of the Black Churches*. Philadelphia: Fortress, 1985.

———. *The Spirituality of African Peoples: The Search for a Common Moral Discourse*. Minneapolis: Fortress, 1995.

———. "Values and Experiences That All Africans Share." Kwaku Boakye Memorial Lecture, First Presbyterian Church, New Jersey, February 17, 2008.

———. *Virtues and Values: The African and African American Experience*. Facets. Minneapolis: Fortress, 2004.

Pinn, Anthony B. "Maps of Meaning: Black Bodies and African Spirituality as African Diaspora Trope." In *Ethics That Matters: African, Caribbean, and African American Sources*, edited by Marcia Riggs and James Samuel Logan, 11–22. Minneapolis: Fortress, 2012.

Raboteau, Albert J. *Slave Religion: The "Invisible Institution" in the Antebellum South*. Oxford: Oxford University Press, 2004.

Riggs, Marcia, and James Samuel Logan, eds. *Ethics That Matters: African, Caribbean, and African American Sources*. Minneapolis: Fortress, 2012.

Chapter 7

Mapping African Christianities Within Religious Maps of the Universe[1]

Afe Adogame

CHINUA ACHEBE'S SYMBOLISM OF a masquerade becomes a useful starting point for mapping African Christianities. He suggests that in order to describe a dancing masquerade, you have to move with it. According to Achebe:

> I believe in the complexity of the human story and that there's no way you can tell that story in one way and say, this is it. Always there will be someone who can tell it differently depending on where they are standing; the same person telling the story will tell it differently. I think of that masquerade in Igbo festivals that dance in the public arena. The Igbo people say: If you want to see it well, you must not stand in one place. The masquerade is moving through this big arena. Dancing. If you're rooted to a spot, you miss a lot of the grace. So, you keep moving, and this is the way I think the world's stories, and the story of Christianity should be told—from many different perspectives.[2]

---

1. An earlier version of this chapter appeared in the *Princeton Seminary Bulletin*. Originally presented as part of inaugural lecture at Miller's Chapel, Princeton Theological Seminary, April 28, 2016.

2. Brooks, "Chinua Achebe."

The late poet and novelist Chinua Achebe's premier novel, *Things Fall Apart*, has drawn local-global attention and received worldwide acclaim and recognition, having been translated into at least fifty languages.[3] It has also sold more than eight million copies. This perhaps makes Achebe the most translated African writer of all time, and *Things Fall Apart* is considered to be the book that launched the modern canon of African literature.[4] As Donna Urschel puts it, "the author gave Africa its first authentic voice."[5] While *Things Fall Apart* undoubtedly represents the book that parachuted Achebe to a global literary icon, he nevertheless wrote *No Longer at Ease*; *A Man of the People*; *Chike and the River*; *Arrow of God*; and *Anthills of the Savannah*[6] as well as short stories, poetry, essays, criticism and political commentary, and children's books.

In *Things Fall Apart*, Achebe best describes the robust culture and complexities of Igbo society in Nigeria, articulating an insider's sense of the African experience, and the book is the greatest work of literature to come out of Africa.[7] The author's original intention was to counter the depiction of Black Africa in Joyce Cary's *Mister Johnson*[8] and other related biased European colonial and Eurocentric discourses on and about Africa. One also calls to mind Achebe's infamous critique, "An Image of Africa: Racism in Conrad's Heart of Darkness,"[9] that accused the novel of stinking xenophobia.[10] In July 1989, Chinua Achebe visited Iwalewa Haus and the University of Bayreuth as a guest lecturer of the "Sonderforschungsbereich." The text of the conversation took place between Chinua Achebe and Ulli Beier was entitled "The world Is a Dancing Masquerade: A Conversation Between Chinua Achebe and Ulli Beier."[11] This description of the world in terms of a dancing masquerade is very illuminating.

More than six decades after *Things Fall Apart* was published, it continues to elicit literary, cultural, religious, historical, anthropological, economic, and political imports and reverberations locally, but also globally. Achebe's unique appropriation of the English language is evidenced in its

3. Achebe, *Things Fall Apart*.
4. Urschel, "Achebe's Impact."
5. Urschel, "Achebe's Impact."
6. See Achebe, *No Longer at Ease*; *Man of the People*; *Chike and the River*; *Arrow of God*; *Anthills of the Savannah*.
7. Quoted in Urschel, "Achebe's Impact."
8. Cary, *Mister Johnson*.
9. Conrad, *Heart of Darkness*.
10. See Achebe "Image of Africa."
11. Achebe and Beier, "World Is a Dancing Masquerade."

vernacularization, invoking Igbo language, imagery, and cultural idioms, as well as Nigerian proverbs, metaphors, and rhythmic speech.[12] It is against this backdrop that I picked a concept from this religio-cultural reservoir to draw a road map for my essay. While masquerade as a typical phenomenon is used in representing and invoking African cultural and Indigenous values, metaphorically I find it useful beyond its aesthetic, artistic significance to represent the dynamism and fluidity of African Christianities as a "faith on the move."

INTERROGATING THE COMPLEXITY OF AFRICAN CHRISTIANITY

The story of African Christianity is one of faith in motion. This mobility depicts dynamism and innovation; it portrays creativity and relevance. The texture and stature of the faith can be described as a buffet of Christianity in Africa and African Christianity. One cannot fully understand Africa without its diaspora, and neither can we understand the African diaspora in isolation. This is more so as the African Union (AU) now characterizes the African diaspora as the sixth region of Africa.[13] This nexus has religious, cultural, political, economic, social, and strategic import that cannot be undermined. Thus, a pictorial image of a masquerade with multiple colors depicts the different shades of Christianity in Africa and African Christianity in the diaspora. This is why I talk about African Christianities, in a sociological rather than a theological sense, to capture the unity in diversity and the different colors of Christianity in Africa and its diaspora.

Christians in America and Europe are often surprised to learn that the largest Christian continent is Africa. There are more Christians in Africa (some 520 million) than in the United States, Canada, and Mexico combined (380 million). Estimates are that in 1900 Africa had around 10 million Christians, but by 1945 there were about 30 million Christians in Africa. In 2008, Africa had around 500 million Christians, which was around 47 percent of the continent's population.[14] Put another way, in 1900, only 2

---

12. See Gikandi, "Chinua Achebe and the Invention of African Culture."

13. The Executive Council of the AU considers the African diaspora as consisting of "peoples of African descent who live outside the African continent, irrespective of their citizenship and nationality and who are willing to contribute to the development of the continent and the building of the African Union." African Union, "Diaspora Division." The other five regions of the AU are Western, Eastern, Northern, Central, and Southern Africa. See also African Union official website: http://au.int; and African Union, "Signing of Memorandum of Understanding."

14. Ranger, *Evangelical Christianity and Democracy in Africa*, x. See details in Johnson and Zurlo, "World Christian Database."

percent of the world's Christians lived in Africa.[15] In 2005, nearly 20 percent of the world's Christians lived there. What triggered this rapid demographic shift? It does not seem to be driven by missionary or colonial impulses,[16] but by local African agency. Indeed, once the European colonial and missionary entrepreneurs left Africa, Christianity grew fantastically: "Africa's most dramatic Christian growth . . . occurred after decolonization."[17] This is especially the case with Protestant/Independent churches, where growth rates are staggering. In the 1960s, there were already over six thousand independent Christian denominations, all born in the twentieth century.[18] It is perhaps counterintuitive that once Western colonial and ecclesial powers receded from the African continent, Christianity received a new lease on life. However, the evidence seems to illustrate that Christianity's greatest gains in sub-Saharan Africa occurred during and after the independence era—the 1950s and 1960s onward.[19]

Christians in America and Europe are even more surprised to learn that Africans are no longer merely on the receiving end of missionary work and church planting from the countries of the Global North but are also sending clergy and missionaries to Europe and North America. These clergy and missionaries are not limited to the Christian traditions (Roman Catholicism, Anglicanism, Methodism, Presbyterianism, etc.) that performed the missionary work in Africa originally. There are a significant number of Christian traditions and denominations that have arisen in Africa—traditions independently started by Africans for Africans—that have sent missionaries and church planters of their own to Europe, the United States, and other countries of the Global North. I shall return to this phenomenon. How can we possibly capture this vast richness and perhaps also contradictions in African Christianity in light of globalization? Is it at all possible for an individual scholar to comprehend this religious fervor? How do we conjecture the religious phenomenon by laying any claims to inter-subjectivity and or objectivity?

Africa is one continent with several worlds, covering an area of around thirty million square kilometers, one-fifth of the earth's land mass, and has more than fifty countries. Africa is vast in both geography and people. There are approximately one billion people in Africa today speaking around two

---

15. See Daughrity, *Changing World of Christianity*, 193.
16. Daughrity, "Assessing Christianity in Africa's Transforming Context," 51.
17. Ranger, *Evangelical Christianity and Democracy in Africa*, x.
18. Barrett, *Schism and Renewal in Africa*.
19. Daughrity, "Assessing Christianity in Africa's Transforming Context," 51.

thousand languages.[20] The over nine hundred million people of Africa have evolved as a cultural milieu, which is a study in contrast and has several dimensions. Africa is a vast continent characterized by complex cultural, religious, and linguistic varieties, as well as diverse historical experiences.[21] It is home to innumerable ethnic and social groupings, some representing very large populations consisting of millions of people, while others are smaller groups of a few thousand. All of these ethnic groups have cultures which are different but represent the mosaic of cultural diversity of Africa. Sub-Saharan Africa, also labeled as Africa south of the Sahara or tropical Africa, represents countries of predominantly Black Indigenous population that are not often considered within the geographical ambit of North Africa. There are, perhaps, no clear-cut defined geographical boundaries between North and sub-Saharan Africa regions owing to discontinuous and blurred breaking points between national boundaries, ecologies, and ethnicities. Nevertheless, the sub-Saharan Africa context seems to have produced the most profound religious vitality, with interaction of the various Indigenous religions with Christianity, Islam, and other Eastern and Western-related religious movements producing new religious constellations that have attracted more scholarly attention than anywhere else on the continent. North Africa has witnessed a longer, more ingrained history and imprint of Islam in a way that renders its interlocking with the Indigenous religion less visible. The Islamic onslaught on the former Christian strongholds in North Africa has largely stripped it of much contemporary significance as a context for Christianity.

I find statistics sometimes useful, although I am not a stout believer and would not totally rely on global statistics on religions, statistics of Christianity in Africa, nor of the other religions such as Islam and the Indigenous religions. The politicization of census on religious and ethnic grounds has resulted in unreliable religio-ethnic demographic data in several African countries.[22] The official population statistics are often manipulated for political, economic, and religious ends. This partly explains why the religion indices are completely excluded from some recent national census. In many parts of Africa, there are no credible censuses or in some cases the actual counting of members does not exist. Second, some churches actually do not take attendance nor have an adequate record of membership. This is also because membership is in many cases fluid and hardly stagnant. People

---

20. Daughrity, "Assessing Christianity in Africa's Transforming Context," 51.

21. Adogame, "Religion in Sub-Saharan Africa," 527.

22. Adogame, "Politicization of Religion and the Religionization of Politics in Nigeria," 137–53.

are engaged constantly in shopping the spiritual marketplace. Third, many people maintain multiple religious affiliations or memberships in combining multiple intra-faith traditions or even inter-faith allegiance, i.e., Christianity and Indigenous religions, consciously and unconsciously.

All of these features further complicate how aspects of the congregationalism discourse make sense within African religious sensibilities. The example of the taxi driver who had stickers and concrete object indicators of Christianity, Islam, and the Indigenous religions will suffice here. During a research trip to Lagos, Nigeria in the summer of 1995, I boarded a taxi and was soon attracted to the windshield and bumper stickers and inscriptions such as "Jesus is the Way, the truth and the life," "Jesus is Lord," "Allah is the Greatest," "Smile Allah loves you," or "Nigerian by birth, Saved by the Grace of God." My curiosity led to further revelations as I found a charm and amulet tied beneath the car's steering wheel. This eclectic religious aesthetics led me to pose a question of whether he was a Christian, Muslim, or adherent of the Indigenous religion. His rhetorical response, "Why did you ask?" led to my further probing. When I pointed out the religious insignias to him, he immediately responded: "*Aaahh* my brother, it is better to hold on to the three faiths just in case one fails, then the other will work." Such reasoning, controversial as it may be, can be better understood against the backdrop of local religious sensibilities and appropriations that are contextual in nature.

Another problem of reliable statistics is in locating African Christianity within global statistics of Christianity. The meaning, texture, and scope of church membership have changed considerably. Church membership in many parts of Africa would require regular attendance at church services and programs, paying church dues, offering, tithes, while also carrying out such rites of passage as water baptism, confirmation, and baptism of the Spirit. In other contexts such as in Europe and the United States, the prerequisite for membership can be a bit more complex. For instance, Grace Davie best illuminates the phenomenon in the United Kingdom in what she refers to as "precarious religion" in "believing without belonging" and "belonging without believing."[23] How these dichotomies are factored into global statistics of Christianity is an indication of the power dynamics inherent in global Christianity and the politicization of religious statistics. Who gets to decide on numbers? Who decides who is Christian or not; or who is Christian enough or less? What is authentic or genuine Christianity, and what is its counterfeit or fake semblance? Which Christianity is syncretistic, and which is not?

---

23. Davie, *Religion in Britain Since 1945*.

With the politicization of statistics of Christians in Europe and North America, one cannot but wonder where the Christians are (as contrasted with huge statistics of Christian population) against the backdrop of dwindling church membership, empty pews, the closing of churches, the drop in clergy/priesthood numbers, the museumization of church buildings and in circumstances in which church buildings are desacralized, sold and converted to bookshops, brothels, restaurants, pubs, bed and breakfasts, or even converted into yoga centers or mosques. Or could one suggest that despite the new phenomenon of "precarious Christianity," perhaps ancestors and saints have continued to be counted among the living?

Such hegemonic discourses obscure the rich flavor and flowerings of Christianity just as it reifies its homogeneity as opposed to its heterogeneity. Such power dynamics seem to caricature the dynamic nature of Christianity as a faith that transcends geographical, racial, social, ethnic, cultural, class dichotomies; a faith that can germinate and survive in both conducive and unfavorable conditions; one that responds to both local and global stimuli; one that has the potential to speak all languages either mundane or esoteric. It is also a faith that can survive in oral and written cultures; one that is resilient but transforms and changes in historical perspectives. It is against this backdrop that the interdisciplinary field of world Christianity now attempts to interrogate these complex questions such as "Whose religion is Christianity?"[24] or "How is the Christian faith recognized in all cultural contexts and milieus?" or "What is the public role or social relevance of the church in a constantly changing global society marked by secularizing and globalizing trends?"

This enigma of statistics raises another critique regarding how church growth is measured. Could it be that we should transcend statistics (numbers) and also look at the public role and social location of Christianity? How is African Christianity interrogating political, economic, social, cultural, and strategic issues of the day? How are churches and Christians responding to HIV and AIDS pandemics; the Ebola crisis; gay priesthood and same-sex marriage; poverty; religious conflicts/violence; global terrorism such as Boko Haram, Al-Shabaab; new forms of economic apartheid in South Africa; Afrophobia (racism of Africans against Africans); unsustainable economies; rigged democratic structures; unwarranted migrations and refugees to Europe and loss of young bodies; child and sexual trafficking; child abductions like the Chibok girls in northern Nigeria; new slavery or slave trade; social abuses within and outside the church, i.e., child abuse by priests, defrauding of members through false hopes of prosperity,

---

24. Sanneh, *Whose Religion Is Christianity?*, 3.

brainwashing, church leaders' corruption and abuse of office, endorsement of despotic and autocratic political leadership, the marginalization of women? In what ways can we unpack church institutions as employers; to what extent does the church continue to serve as the moral conscience of society; how does the church community engage in building social, cultural and spiritual capital; supporting sustainable development and democratic governance?

CONCEPTUALIZING AFRICAN RELIGIONS AND GLOBALIZATION

The perception of religion as a phenomenon completely separate from culture is not a suitable reflection of the embedded nature of "religion" in African cultures.[25] Religion is variously conceptualized as a spiritual, epistemological, and philosophical phenomenon. Beyond the typical focus on religion as a coterie of belief and ritual patterns, the treatment of religion as an epistemological phenomenon further helps to shed new light on studies of African cultures and societies. Religion viewed in this way allows for a deeper understanding of the complex interaction between Africans and non-Africans, an encounter sometimes based on incompatible worldviews. As a category of analysis to the study of culture and society, religion is, therefore, quintessential to our understanding of African cultures in a global context. A proper grasp of the texture, shape, and complexity of the different religious traditions improves our understanding of Africa and its religious culture in conditions of globality. This points to the significance of religion in contextualizing Africa in ongoing globalization processes.

The purview of African religions transcends the continent and goes into the African diaspora.[26] Contemporary "African religion" is itself a product of globalization, for it is less a single tradition than a sociological context in which the elements of a variety of Indigenous religious experiences are combined with Islam and Christianity. All three of these dimensions—Indigenous religion, Africanized Islam, and Africanized Christianity—are part of the interactive, globalized African religious experience.[27] The interface of religious cultures of sub-Saharan Africa with globalization needs to be set against the backdrop of the interlocking relationship and mutual enhancement of the triple religious heritage rather than any unilateral

25. Adogame, "Religion in Sub-Saharan Africa," 528.
26. Adogame, "Practitioners of Indigenous Religions in Africa and the African Diaspora," 75–100.
27. Olupona, "African Religion," 78.

perspective. In other words, we will understand the growth and transformation of Indigenous religion, Islam, or Christianity better when we consider them within the locus of mutual religious interaction, competition, and influence.[28] These constellations have also produced new religious movements that are far from being identical with the triple religious heritage. Such new movements have appropriated symbols and employed religious imagery from one or the other religious traditions, giving it a novel interpretation and producing a new kind of religious creativity.[29] The institutional stature, demographic mobility, and public visibility of these religious traditions in Africa and the African diaspora have shot them into global religious maps of the universe.

The spread of Christianity and Islam saw the introduction of new religious ideas and practices into Indigenous religions. The encounter transformed Indigenous religious thought and practice but did not supplant it; Indigenous religions preserved some of their beliefs and ritual practices but also adjusted to the new socio-cultural milieu. As a result of social and cultural change, some Indigenous beliefs and rituals were either dropped or modified due to the impingement of European and Arab cultures, Christianity and Islam. The change also led to the revivification and revitalization of other aspects of the Indigenous religion and culture. In many cases, Christianity and Islam became domesticated on the African soil. The contact produced new religious movements, with some appropriating Indigenous symbols and giving them a new twist. African religion is itself a product of globalization as, in its widest sense it now refers also to creativities within this triple religious heritage. These initiatives attest to the continuity of African worldviews and ritual cosmos in the midst of worldwide socio-cultural change. Sub-Saharan Africa has served as a significant theater for the dramatization of Christianity and Islam, especially in the twentieth century.

The impingement of Christianity and Islam led, on the one hand, to the denigration of Indigenous religions, culminating in their rejection and abandonment by some Indigenous peoples. On the other hand, the encounter served as a catalyst for innovation and creativity, thus portraying them as versions of African modernity. The Christianization and Islamization processes in the African context can be clearly understood in their different phases of growth and development. A brief historical trajectory of Christianity in Africa will suffice here.

---

28. Adogame, "Religion in Sub-Saharan Africa," 528.
29. Adogame, "Religion in Sub-Saharan Africa," 529.

PERIODIZATION IN MAPPING CHRISTIANITY IN AFRICA AND AFRICAN CHRISTIANITIES

To effectively map the broad history of Christianity in Africa and African Christianity, periodization is essential. The history of Christianity in Africa and African Christianity must be conspicuously located within the *longue durée* of Christian history rather than perceived as a historical "volcano." Before I highlight the different phases of history, it is important to remark that the historiography of African religions and spiritualities provides a significant template for understanding and deconstructing Christianity in Africa and African Christianity within global academic studies.[30] The historical trajectory of the study of religions (Christianity) in Africa has evolved through several phases, each involving different purposes and points of view. Jan Platvoet categorizes these overlapping epochs paradigmatically, as "Africa as object," when its religions were studied virtually exclusively by scholars and other observers from outside Africa; and as "Africa as subject," when the religions of Africa had begun to be studied also, and increasingly mainly, by African scholars.[31] Travelogues, the missionary and the colonial historiography, of the late eighteenth and the early nineteenth centuries, pioneered the study of and writing about the religions of Africa. The earliest phase was supplanted by armchair ethnographers and evolutionary anthropologists who propounded theories on the origin and evolution of human culture following evolutionary paradigms. With the decline of evolutionary theory and the advent of social anthropology, systematic fieldwork studies of African societies took root in the late nineteenth century. The 1950s and 1960s marked the era of integrated and consolidated research on the religions of Africa, the transition from "Africa as object" to "Africa as subject." The African story (agency) about and on Christianity only started to be told from this last phase of its history (the 1950s and 1960s), in a way that challenges but also further enriches the stories told for and about them and their religions, cultures, ways of thinking and doing things.

The growth and development of old and new forms of Christianity in Africa in the academic, public, and "insiders"-"outsiders" discourses they engender are laced with interpretational powers that are often conflicting in nature. Thus, this historiography is burdened, on one level, by competing claims for the power of interpretation between African and non-African scholars, the different academic/scholarly approaches and historical phases aimed at defining, explaining, interpreting, and (de-)legitimizing African

---

30. Adogame, "Calling a Trickster Deity a 'Bad,'" 1813–26.
31. Platvoet and Olupona, *Study of Religions in Africa*.

religious beliefs and ritual systems. In the intellectual enterprise highlighted above, it is important to mention that European (Western) scholars dominated and continue to dominate this endeavor, namely the academic study of Christianity in Africa and African Christianity. In the process, these scholars imported their methodologies and brought their worldviews and epistemologies to bear on the African context. In fact, the academic study of religion in Africa has its roots outside the continent, just as the very category of religion itself has a European history. Make no mistake, Western and non-African scholars have contributed significantly to our understanding of African religions generally, and African Christianities in particular. But they have also, at times, paved the way into its obscurity and public misunderstanding. Having provided some hint of the historical trajectory of the study of Christianity in Africa and African Christianity as evolving through several phases, I shall now turn to viewing Christianity in Africa and African Christianity like a dancing masquerade.

I do not pretend I am able to tell the story of the development of Christianity in over two thousand years and Africa's role and impact within the limited space I have for this lecture. Such an attempt would be overambitious and difficult to imagine, let alone achieve. Therefore, I shall paint with large strokes and will therefore isolate five broad, but hardly mutually exclusive, phases that will help us navigate this robust history. Most importantly, I will demonstrate, through my work, how and to what extent the demographic stature and texture of African Christianities could have broad implications for international politics, intercultural relations, and world religions. Also, I explore how Christianity, the world's largest religion, is becoming more associated with Africa than with the West, and how this development is gradually shaping our understanding of world Christianity.[32]

Phase 1

Contrary to popular imagination, Africa did not know Christianity through European missionaries. In other words, Africa and Africans have been integral to the emergence and development of Christianity long before the introduction of European Christianity that accompanied the early Portuguese explorations and, later, the imperial and colonial experiments. Thus, Africa is the heartland of early as well as contemporary Christianity. Indeed Africa contains some of the oldest forms of Christianity on earth.[33] The earliest known presence of Christianity in Africa is located in late antiquity, the

32. Daughrity, "Assessing Christianity in Africa's Transforming Context," 50.
33. Daughrity, "Assessing Christianity in Africa's Transforming Context," 50.

period from the first century onward when North Africa was visibly vocal in the development of the Christian tradition.[34]

Early African Christianity has deep roots in Ethiopian Judaism. As Daughrity demonstrated:

> There was significant Ethiopian-Jewish contact many centuries before Jesus, documented in the King Solomon-Queen of Sheba relationship from 1 Kings 10. Presumably, the Ethiopian-Jewish relationship continued and expanded since Africa played a key role in several New Testament passages. For example, Jesus spent time living as a refugee in Egypt according to Matthew 2:13–14. Simon of Cyrene—modern-day Libya—was forced by the Romans to carry Jesus' cross for him when he became too weak to do it himself (Matt. 27:32). Thus, it was an African who first took up a cross and followed Jesus, up the hill to Golgotha. In Acts 2, on Pentecost Sunday, we read of Libyans and Egyptians at the birth of Christianity. In Acts 8, an Ethiopian eunuch, "an important official in charge of all the treasury of Candace, queen of the Ethiopians" had gone to Jerusalem to worship. Africans were among the first to preach the gospel to non-Jews. For example, Acts 11:19 discusses evangelists from Cyrene preaching to Greeks in Antioch. The apostle Paul was probably ordained for ministry by a group that included Africans (Acts 13:1–4). One of the great evangelists of the New Testament was Apollos, a native of Alexandria (Acts 18:24). Church tradition states that Mark evangelized Egypt in the 40s and became the first Pope of the Coptic Orthodox Church. . . . One of the earliest Christian states on earth was Axum, in Ethiopia. Still today Ethiopia is a proudly Christian country that remained isolated from Christendom for centuries.[35]

From Athanasius and Anthony to Augustine, Africa helped to spawn the largest religion in human history. Thus, African Christianity has come full circle. For the first several centuries of Christian faith, Africa was the hub. Africa's extra-canonical pedigree is impressive.[36] Saint Anthony the Great, the father of monasticism, was Egyptian. Several African church fathers defined the Christian faith as we understand it today: Athanasius, Clement of Alexandria, Origen, Cyprian, and Tertullian. Athanasius was probably the leading theologian in the Trinitarian controversies as well as in the determination of the biblical canon. Athanasius's home city, Alexandria,

---

34. Adogame, "Religion in Sub-Saharan Africa," 535.
35. Daughrity, "Assessing Christianity in Africa's Transforming Context," 53.
36. Daughrity, "Assessing Christianity in Africa's Transforming Context," 50.

was well known as "the leading academic center of the ancient world."[37] Indeed, Alexandria and Carthage (Tunisia) were pivotal in shaping the earliest medieval Western universities. And perhaps the most important theologian in Christian history, Augustine (354–430 CE), was an African Berber from Algeria. It is indeed an irony of history that contexts (such as Egypt, Libya, Tunisia) that marked the birthing and hotbeds of early Christianity have now turned to be the heartlands of Islam.

Christianity had been firmly rooted in North Africa by the wake of the fourth century.[38] One inherent weakness of the church however was its superficiality, a Latinized brand of Christianity that was devoid of features of an African church.[39] It failed to be a missionary church and to penetrate the life of the Indigenous peoples, with the exception of Coptic Christianity. The church later traversed hard times in their encounter with an Islamic onslaught. In the seventh and eighth centuries, Islam grew quickly and African Christians became a minority voice.

The impact of this was the inability of Christianity to gain inroads into the Muslim population. Though the church left behind some footprints in places such as Egypt and Nubia (Ethiopia), the resilience of the church in North Africa was, to a large extent, insignificant. A myriad of factors contributed to its deterioration and subsequent demise during the eighth century. The situation has changed again in the latter centuries; it is projected that by the year 2030, Africa will surpass Latin America as having more Christians than any other continental block. With Africa's fertility rate—the highest in the world—African Christianity is on pace to continue its impressive growth trajectory.[40]

Phase 2

Following this debut of Christianity in Africa was the second Christianization phase, which occurred several centuries later in sub-Saharan Africa.[41] The late fifteenth and sixteenth centuries witnessed the activities of Portuguese Catholics in some African societies as the Congo Kingdom and Zambezi Valley in Central Africa; Warri and Benin Kingdoms (Niger Delta area) of the West African Coast; and the hitherto unpopulated islands of

---

37. Daughrity, "Assessing Christianity in Africa's Transforming Context," 53.
38. Sawyer and Youssef, "Early Christianity in North Africa," 41–65.
39. Adogame, "Religion in Sub-Saharan Africa," 536.
40. Daughrity, "Assessing Christianity in Africa's Transforming Context," 50.
41. Adogame, "Religion in Sub-Saharan Africa," 536. See also Kalu, *African Christianity*.

Cape Verde and São Tomé. As missionary enterprises to Africa appeared unattractive to the Reformation churches before the Evangelical revival, the Catholic missionaries from Portugal were alone in the task of introducing a few African societies and converting the "natives" to Christianity. Even then, they constructed their incursion on the narrative of looking for Prester John, the Christian king of Ethiopia. Aside from this religious activity, the Portuguese were not unmindful of the economic (i.e., trade in slaves) and political gains inherent in this venture. Church and state worked hand in hand to realize these possibilities. Wherever the Portuguese flag was pitched, the Jesuits and other missionaries were on its trail and established missions.

Protestantism had a strong foothold in Africa before 1800 at the Cape, where the Dutch formed a settlement, and in 1685, the Huguenots started to enter the colony.[42] Quite a number of the slaves were baptized, and in 1683 a regulation was passed which declared that all baptized slaves should be free. Organized missionary activity is thus over two-and-a-quarter-centuries old in sub-Saharan Africa. In 1737, Georg Schmidt of the Moravian Brethren came to South Africa, and the latter half of the eighteenth century witnessed the beginning of British missions in Africa. The late eighteenth century and onward witnessed a remarkable proliferation of Protestant missionary societies, many of which later became profoundly interested in the business of "spreading the gospel" to the African shores. Some of the Protestant missionaries of the eighteenth century, like their Catholic predecessors, have been caught fulfilling the role of trading in slaves or collaborating with the traders in the business. However, apart from the Evangelical revival in Europe, the full effect of the slave trade had come into the limelight (the anti-slavery movement). The majority of Africans carried overseas into slavery were by the late eighteenth-century core or nominal Christians. Many found Christianity a unifying and strengthening force, and it played strategic roles in the anti-slavery campaigns, as well as in the latter propagation of Christianity to their fellow Africans. Granville Sharp was one of the most determined protagonists of African freedom in London. When some of them were later resettled in Africa, Sierra Leone (the Creoles and Americo-Liberians), it was the freed African slaves who spearheaded the task of evangelization to their original homes. Local (African) agency represents the arrowhead for Christian growth and mobility in sub-Saharan Africa, thus paving the way for Indigenous Christianity to take root. Notable among them were Samuel Ajayi Crowther, who led the Yoruba Christians and became the first African bishop in the Anglican Church. Kimpa Vita (also known as Dona Beatriz)

---

42. Adogame, "Religion in Sub-Saharan Africa," 536.

spawned an Indigenous movement in the Kongo (1684–1706). Baptized by Italian Capuchin missionaries, she was later burned at the stake as a witch at only twenty-two years of age. Vita inspired scores of people who were sent as slaves to Brazil and South Carolina. From the late 1780s, Protestant Christianity would impinge upon Africa in a new and far more dynamic way.

The modern phase of missionary enterprise in Africa began with the foundation of the Baptist Missionary Society (BMS) in 1792, the London Missionary Society (LMS) in 1795, and the Church Missionary Society (CMS) in 1799. The process continued with the establishment of the British and Foreign Bible Society (BFBS) in 1804, the American Board of Commissioners for Foreign Missions (ABCFM) in 1810, the Leeds Methodist Missionary Society (LMMS) in 1813, the Basel Mission in 1815 and many others several years later. While most of these new Protestant mission societies differed considerably in their forms of organization, they were overwhelmingly Evangelical in character. However, the missionary concerns of these bodies were not limited to the African continent, but international in scope, with each society mapping and developing a particular regional focus for actual mission work. At their inception, the Evangelical missions demonstrated a high level of mutual cooperation. The story, however, turned sour in the mission field, where there often existed an element of rivalry between some mission bodies. It is important to note that these decades of missionary endeavor produced only a small number of African converts.[43]

Between 1880 and 1920, the heyday of imperialism, there was a dramatic expansion in the number of missionaries at work in Africa. The Berlin Conference exacerbated the scramble and partition of Africa by European imperial powers by formalizing it. Missionaries in the field often supported the imperial ambitions of their compatriots, resulting in mission and imperialism being understood by many as "two sides of the same coin." The missionizing task became synonymous with the transplantation of Western civilization. The implication of this development was that African converts were taught to repudiate African cultures in their entirety and assume a new status of, for instance, a "Europeanized African." This was the quandary that lay at the very core of the missionary enterprise. The question was: To what extent should an African adopt the Western civilization? To what extent should s/he abandon African cultures in order to embrace the "white man's faith"? It was the attempt at reconciling these inherent contradictions within mission Christianity that welled up a new phase of Indigenous Christianity in Africa. Thus, the expansion of Christianity that took place

---

43. Adogame, "Religion in Sub-Saharan Africa," 537.

in the twentieth century was largely through the handiwork of local African agency (evangelists).

Phase 3

The West African Coast was the first home and Indigenous breeding ground for the mission churches in the nineteenth century, just as it fulfilled the same function for the Indigenous African churches in the twentieth century.[44] African Indigenous or independent churches can be understood as three levels of development. The first and earliest level refers to those groups of churches that severed from the existing mission churches owing to a number of irreconcilable issues. They flourished mainly in South Africa (Ethiopian churches) and West Africa (African churches) in the nineteenth century. They emerged out of similar circumstances such as rigid white (European) missionary control and domination, discrimination against local African agency, dispute over resources, a general feeling of marginalization among educated Africans, and apartheid (mainly in the South African context). Some of the churches which seceded from the historic churches in Nigeria were the United Native African Church (1891) and African Church-Bethel (1901) from the Anglican; the United African Methodist Church (1917) from the Methodist Church. These African churches of Nigeria had their counterparts in other parts of Africa. A branch of the African Methodist Episcopal Church-Zion (1898), the Nationalist Baptist Church (1898), and the Nigritian Church (1907) were founded on the Gold Coast (now Ghana). One notable feature of these churches was that in spite of the change in the mantle of church leadership, they were still tied to the apron strings of the mission churches in their liturgical and hierarchical structures. Some of them still depended largely on the parent churches for financial resources. Let me now turn to what I consider the most recent phases of Christianity in sub-Saharan Africa.

Phase 4

Africa's encounter with European mission Christianity also gave birth to African Indigenous churches (AICs) from the late twentieth century onward.[45] Thus, the 1920s and 1930s witnessed the second wave of new be-

---

44. Adogame, "Religion in Sub-Saharan Africa," 538.

45. Adogame, "Religion in Sub-Saharan Africa," 538. See also Adogame and Jafta, "Zionists, Aladura and Roho," 271–87.

ginnings within Christian independency. John Mbiti described AICs as "an African opportunity to mess up Christianity in their own way."[46] These groups emerged under the initiative of African leaders and prophets outside the immediate context of mission churches. They include the Zionists in South Africa, the Aladura in Nigeria, the Roho/Arathi in East Africa, the Spirit or Spiritist movements in Ghana. They are also variously referred to as prophet-healing churches. The most dramatic aspect of twentieth-century Christianity in South, East, and West Africa was the growth of prophetic churches. These categories share basic characteristics in their worldview, which helped to create a rather African brand of Christianity. The centrality of the Bible, prayer, healing, prophecy, visions and dreams, elaborate rituals, flexible mode of worship and un-stereotyped liturgy, and a charismatic leader (i.e., prophet or prophetess) are some of the basic features of these churches. They embrace a functional theology and their pragmatic approach to life and existential problems had endeared them to many Africans. Though they utterly condemn and reject the traditional religion as "fetish" and "demonic," their belief systems and ritual structures appear to have affinities with the Indigenous cosmology. That is why they derive much of their membership not only from within the mainline churches, but also from other Christian as well as non-Christian groups (Islam and Indigenous religion).

In spite of the affinities that abound among the prophetic churches, it is important to note that each has its own religious dynamic. There are differences in specific doctrines and details of ritual acts and performance, just as in their histories of emergence. Their patterns of emergence are twofold. The first are those that emerged from or had their nucleus as "prayer bands" or "fellowship groups" within the mainline church but later severed their links to form an independent group. In Nigeria, the Garrick Braide Movement was the earliest of movements in this category. As early as 1916, it broke away from the Niger Delta Pastorate Church. Other churches that fall under this category include the Cherubim and Seraphim (1925), the Church of the Lord—Aladura (1930), the Christ Apostolic Church (1930). There is also the Musama Disco Christo Church (1922) in Ghana, the Nazarite Baptist Church (called Nazarites or ama-Nazaretha) founded by Isaiah Shembe (1911) in South Africa.

The second category refers to those groups that did not emerge in conscious schism from an existing mainline church. They were founded through the visionary experience of a charismatic figure and independently

---

46. Quoted in Davies and Conway, *World Christianity in the Twentieth Century*, 118.

of any existing mission church. Typical examples are the Celestial Church of Christ founded by Samuel Bilewu Oschoffa (1947) in the Benin Republic and Nigeria, the Harrist Churches by William Wade Harris (1922) in Liberia, and the Kimbanguist Churches by Simon Kimbangu (1921) from the Congo. Most of the Indigenous churches of both categories belong to a continental ecumenical movement referred to as the "Organisation of African Instituted Churches" (OAIC), while not many AICs were accepted into the World Council of Churches (WCC). The non-recognition and non-acceptance of several AICs into global ecumenical bodies such as the WCC raises a crucial question about power dynamics and the politics of religious (Christian) identity. European mission churches, other brands of Christianity and a cross-section of the public discriminated against the AICs on grounds that they were too African or not Christian enough, thus complicating the politics of religious but also cultural identity.

Phase 5

The most recent development within African Christianity is the emergence and increasing proliferation of Pentecostal (Charismatic)/Evangelical churches especially from the 1950s, 1960s, and onward.[47] For instance, the past two decades in Nigeria have witnessed a huge proliferation of new Pentecostal churches. In an attempt to forge ecumenical links and cooperation among themselves and with other churches, the majority of the churches have now come under an umbrella called "Pentecostal Fellowship of Nigeria" (PFN). There are two waves of Pentecostal movements, the Indigenous Pentecostal groups, such as the Redeemed Christian Church of God, the Deeper Life Bible Church, Church of God Mission International, Winners Chapel, Rhema Bible Church, Christ Chapel, Zoe Ministries, Latter Rain Assembly, and the Household of God Fellowship; and the Pentecostal groups and organizations such as the Four Square Gospel Church, the Full Gospel Businessmen Fellowship International, Campus Crusade for Christ, Youth with a Mission, and Christ for All Nations, which exist as branches or missions of Pentecostal churches and organizations outside Africa. The earlier is largely independent and hardly relies on any external assistance, while many groups in the latter rely greatly on funds, literature, and sometimes even personnel from their mission headquarters.

The earlier has also embarked on mission activities by planting branches in United States, Canada, Europe, and other parts of the world. One underlying feature of the Pentecostal churches is the emphasis on the

---

47. Adogame, "Religion in Sub-Saharan Africa," 540 and following.

need for a specific conversion experience, spiritual rebirth (born-again-ism), and the manifestation of charismatic gifts such as speaking in tongues (glossolalia). Some are more or less "holiness movements," interested in religious experience rather than rituals. There are those noted for the kind of "prosperity gospel" they preach.

This is becoming very popular, especially among Nigerians and (white) South Africans. The "gospel of prosperity" teaches that God is a rich God and intends his followers to prosper in all their endeavors in life. It promises a miraculous escape from poverty, unemployment, ill health, and lack of promotion. One "short-cut" way to riches is thus by tithing and giving to the poor and less privileged. Some of these groups have assimilated some ideas and features originating from American Pentecostalism. On the other hand, their commitment to the gospel of prosperity fits in well with the values of the African traditional culture, where elaborate religious rituals are engaged to ensure prosperity, health, and protection against malevolent forces. That is why Christian groups such as the Pentecostal churches, the Aladura, or prophetic churches, which seek to address these day-to-day, existential problems, will continue to expand in contemporary Africa.

The AICs and the Pentecostal/Charismatic churches have shaped African Christianity through their increasing involvement in the public sphere, especially in their political and social roles. In this vein, I have explored how African Christian communities, as strategic actors and benefactors in Africa and its diaspora, are involved in processes of religious, social, and cultural capital engineering.[48] This is partly achieved through strengthening and establishing relationships, norms, and values as a means toward realizing a new state of social inclusion/exclusion, but also through networks that mediate access to the host cultural context, new opportunities, resources, and information.

African Christian communities contribute enormous bridging, bonding, and linking social capital, but also confront barriers to development and civic engagement. Their spaces of worship are not simply religious places, they are also spaces of socialization where business, politics, education, music, home country and food cultures, even gossips are engaged and negotiated. Such spaces often transcend socio-ethnic, race, class, gender, and intergenerational boundaries. People meet others from different backgrounds, they share activities and build trust in one another, albeit temporarily. African-led churches facilitate bridge building and links building with others, thus generating local-global networking trends and new forms of association and engendering trust in shared community initiatives. Their

---

48. Adogame, *African Christian Diaspora*, 101–22.

landscapes of worship can also be a source of conflict among members, between the leadership and the followers, and between these religious communities and their neighborhoods.

THE PUBLIC FACE OF AFRICAN CHRISTIANITIES

Generally speaking, hardly any attention has yet been devoted to the unique role that African Christianities may play in building and generating social, cultural, and spiritual (religious) capital. More attention needs to be given to the dynamics of African Christianities in generating social, cultural, and spiritual capital so as to illuminate pathways in which the economy and quality of capital formation are relevant to African Christian communities in Africa, but also in the United States and Europe.[49]

No longer just a passive recipient of Western missionaries, Africa is today a major player in world Christianity.[50] Two of the six general secretaries of the World Council of Churches (established in 1948) were African: Samuel Kobia of Kenya and Philip Potter—of African descent but from the West Indies. Another important African ecumenist was Akanu Ibiam, a medical missionary from Nigeria who became a political leader and one of the presidents of the World Council of Churches. Additionally, two of the nine General Assemblies of the World Council of Churches were held in Africa: in Kenya (1975) and in Zimbabwe (1998). The African diaspora is huge and is changing world Christian demographics.[51] Examples of these impacts are plentiful. For example, John Sentamu (archbishop of York)—the Anglican Church's second-highest official—is from Uganda. The Anglican Communion is witnessing a shift in leverage as Africans are clearly taking the reins of leadership in that denomination.[52] Unmistakably, the future of the Anglican Church is African. There are more Anglicans in Nigeria than in England. It is estimated that there are over 40 million Anglicans on the African continent. Africa claims approximately 55 percent of the global Anglican Communion, and that percentage is certain to rise.[53] Perhaps the most important aspect of African Christianity is that it represents the turning over of a new leaf in world Christianity. While Christianity in the West declines, in Africa it grows in numbers, in strength, and in energy.[54]

49. Adogame, *African Christian Diaspora*, 108.
50. Daughrity, "Assessing Christianity in Africa's Transforming Context," 55.
51. Daughrity, "Assessing Christianity in Africa's Transforming Context," 55.
52. Daughrity, "Assessing Christianity in Africa's Transforming Context," 55.
53. Pew Research Center, "Global Anglicanism at a Crossroads."
54. Daughrity, "Assessing Christianity in Africa's Transforming Context," 55–56.

Mission-related churches in Africa have also acted in ways that put them on the global map.[55] For example, the popularity of the faith-healing ministry of the Zambian Catholic Archbishop Emmanuel Milingo provoked anxiety at the Vatican and has social and theological implications for the Catholic Church globally because it demonstrates one of the ways in which contextualization and enculturation processes have taken place within African Catholicism. The anti-gay stance of the Anglican Church of Nigeria (the largest Anglican community outside of England) on the ordination of homosexual bishops by the main Anglican body—as well as the blessing of same-sex unions in the United Kingdom, United States, and Canada—has drawn local and global attention. While the West has largely criticized this stance as fundamentalist, the West has also taken a fundamentalist posture in not lending an ear to understanding the reasons for the vehement opposition.

It is likely that Christianity will be more identified with Africa than with any other place in the world. And the reverberations are already being felt.[56] For centuries the Christian narrative has been told primarily from a European perspective. However, African narrators are now settling in, and African narrators have several significant implications for telling the story of Christianity. Scholars of Christianity are taking note of these changes, even if they are not widely known. In my own travels and research, it is clear that not only is African Christianity rising, but the African diaspora is making great gains in the West as well, impacting what has up to now been considered a Western religion.

Moreover, Daughrity aptly notes how Africans are impacting the way Christians read the Bible.[57] Many Westerners studied F. C. Bauer, Rudolf Bultmann, Thomas Altizer, and Paul Tillich, yet the future of biblical interpretation may not necessarily include those names. Africans offer a different set of biblical interpreters, who come to very different conclusions than the commentators of the last two hundred years in the West, the so-called "Enlightenment." Furthermore, African Christians bring confidence and come to Christianity from a very different cultural perspective.[58] Daughrity remarks that an African-infused Christianity holds many possibilities.[59] World Christianity waits in expectation for what new things will be revealed. No one knows precisely how African leadership will shape world

---

55. Adogame, "Religion in Sub-Saharan Africa," 546.
56. Daughrity, "Assessing Christianity in Africa's Transforming Context," 56–57.
57. Daughrity, "Assessing Christianity in Africa's Transforming Context," 56.
58. Daughrity, "Assessing Christianity in Africa's Transforming Context," 56.
59. Daughrity, "Assessing Christianity in Africa's Transforming Context," 57.

Christianity, but what is known is that changes are coming. He was perhaps right in observing that since Christians in the Western world still have a disproportionate amount of the world's wealth, they will likely find themselves further partnering with African Christians and African institutions, a partnership that has existed for some time but will likely increase.[60] This may come from contributing in terms of international research fellowships; it may mean theological institutions offering full fellowships that enable Africans to study at Western schools. A rising cross-pollination process is taking place that will benefit both Africa and the West. And there is a good argument to be made that Western Christians should consider taking their tuition money to African institutions and place themselves under the tutelage of African theologians and scholars. Otherwise, the relationship will continue to be one-way, perpetuating the paternalism of the past.[61] In other words, the answer will not always be to bring Africans to the West. Perhaps a better alternative is encouraging Westerners to adapt to the African educational context. He concludes that this interplay would be dynamic and certainly more authentic for Westerners wanting to know more about how and why African Christianity is growing.[62]

Ethiopianism became a clarion call for generations of Africans and diaspora Africans to take pride in their Christian roots and confront the stereotypes that had held them back.[63] Sanneh's pioneering work on how Christianity translates into new cultures has impacted the field of world Christianity like no other. His thesis is that no single people group owns Christianity; thus, it is incorrect to consider it a Western faith.[64] Daughrity again notes that African Christianity presents a series of contrasts. Christianity is ancient in the continent yet its explosion is recent. It will be fascinating to observe how Christianity continues to shape Africa, but perhaps more importantly, how world Christianity is shaped by Africa.[65]

The global stature of African Christianity is largely indicative of significant, contemporary shifts in the religious center of gravity of Christianity from the Northern to the Southern Hemisphere. Demographic considerations, the flavor and texture of contemporary African Christianity confirm this trend. Nevertheless, a consideration of this religious development in

60. Daughrity, "Assessing Christianity in Africa's Transforming Context," 57–58.
61. Daughrity, "Assessing Christianity in Africa's Transforming Context," 57–58.
62. Daughrity, "Assessing Christianity in Africa's Transforming Context," 57–58.
63. Daughrity, "Assessing Christianity in Africa's Transforming Context," 57–59. See also Kalu, "Ethiopianism in African Christianity," 227–43.
64. Daughrity, "Assessing Christianity in Africa's Transforming Context," 59. See Sanneh, *Translating the Message*.
65. Daughrity, "Assessing Christianity in Africa's Transforming Context," 60.

Africa must be seen in terms of its relation and links with the global context, but also in how and to what extent it interrogates and negotiates wider external influences and global forces. In addition, the ways in which the African Christian diaspora is contributing to the enrichment, diversification, and plurality of new geo-cultural and religious spaces becomes more and more expedient.

My work has explored the connection between religious expression and society, particularly focusing on expressions of African Christianity and Indigenous religious movements in Africa, as well as the interaction of those religious expressions with the phenomena of migration, globalization and social change. I have attempted in my research initiatives to contribute important understandings of how Christian movements that began in Africa have been transplanted into communities of African migrants in Europe and the Americas, and have helped those communities express their identity in their new context. My first monograph on the Celestial Church of Christ (CCC)[66] interrogated and emphasized local agency in the contestation and negotiation of religio-cultural identities. The book had its focus on one of the most popular, widespread Indigenous religious initiative in West Africa, the Celestial Church of Christ. This study examined the incipience, contemporary growth and development of the church, especially the period following the demise of the founder.

The book chronicled the routinization of charisma and the institutionalization of the faith and its practices, and places those developments in the context of the religious, cultural, and historical practices of West Africa at the time of the church's founding. The work explored as well how the church has embraced and developed through the challenges of globalization. In describing, analyzing, and interpreting their belief pattern and ritual structure, the study demonstrated how and to what extent the CCC situates traditional religio-cultural matrix within the context and continuum of African Christianity. I highlighted the unique aspects of the CCC as a particular church, while also establishing the church's identity as a synthesis of existing beliefs and traditions in dialogue with its adherents and their changing environment. I concluded that while the church maintains their identity as a Christian church sui generis, they have also created a synthesis of belief-ritual forms as a new rationalization, a new ordering of their religious cosmos.

This body of work on the CCC has been critical for scholars engaging with the broader implications of African Indigenous churches (AICs) and their role in world Christianity. Many churches such as the CCC were born in the tumultuous post-war era as African countries declared their political

---

66. Adogame, *Celestial Church of Christ*.

independence, and established churches had to confront their being identified as agents of the colonial powers. AICs represent a powerful witness that the Christian message resonates in Africa. I have attempted to bring scholarly attention to the unique ways in which the Christian message and praxis have become part of West Africans' expression of their identity as African Christians.

Another aspect of identity (re)construction that was central in my work bears on women and gender.[67] In demographic terms, women dominate mission-related churches, AICs and Pentecostal/Charismatic churches, although their role in leadership is somewhat negligible. Commentators have adduced patriarchy and marginalization as accounting for the inconspicuous leadership role in churches but also the charged debate about female ordination. Contrary to popular perception of Africa as essentially made up of patrilocal societies and patriarchal cultures, there are visibly matrilocal/matriarchal societies and cultures. While I do not deny how and to what extent patriarchal structures have impacted Christianity, I think the point is sometimes overstated.

In my work I contend that women exercise crucial ritual functions and occupy significant religious roles within many Indigenous religious worlds prior to the debut of missionary Christianity. I argue that missionary Christianity hijacked these roles and stripped women of most of their ritual functions by privileging the strand of Pauline injunctions that were disadvantageous to women. Female religious actors, particularly within the AICs and Pentecostal/Charismatic Christianity, are partly staging a comeback, assuming hitherto "traditional" roles and ritual functions, which colonialism and mission Christianity had largely stripped from them.

Women are assuming increasing roles as resource managers, decision makers, and captains of religious industries. Other women have become church founders, leaders, and visible religious functionaries on both sides of the Atlantic. The resurgence and public visibility of female leaders and ritual roles within African religiosity in the new diaspora and on the continent must be located in historical, socio-cultural precedents. Thus, the leadership and ritual role reversal witnessed in some new forms of African Christianity within the continent and beyond needs to be historically and contextually understood. By democratizing certain roles and responsibilities, women are increasingly incorporated into ecclesial administrative and liturgical structures in ways that mission churches before them failed to do. Let me

---

67. Adogame, *African Christian Diaspora*, 123–44. See also Adogame, "'I Am Married to Jesus!,'" 129–49.

now turn to what I consider as the most recent phases of Christianity in sub-Saharan Africa.

The research coming into fruition in my most recent publications, such as studies of transnationalism, contribute to the public understanding of contemporary society in the United States, United Kingdom, and European Union, and of perceptions of Africa and the global community. This is relevant to how people understand the world as a global village and how governments make policies, for instance, on immigration. One major emphasis through my interdisciplinary research and output is developing methodologies and techniques appropriate for studying non-Western Christianity, the new African Christian diaspora, and Indigenous African religious phenomena generally.

My second monograph, *The African Christian Diaspora*, was based on extensive religious ethnography among African Christian communities in Europe, the United States, and Africa in the last seventeen years.[68] The book maps and describes the incipience and consolidation of new brands of African Christianities in the diaspora, demonstrating how African Christianities negotiate and assimilate notions of the global while maintaining their local identities. I contend that the historical and cultural significance of African Christianity is partly discerned in their plurality and multivocality both in Africa and the African diaspora. The relevance of African Christian communities is not only located in the unique expression of African Christianity they exhibit; they also constitute international ministries and groups that have implications on a global scale. The last few decades have witnessed a rapid proliferation of African-led Christian communities, particularly in North America and Europe, thus resulting in the remapping of old religious landscapes. These have helped in the reconfiguration of Christianity in the United States and have contributed to the increasing religious diversification of host American societies. The salience of Christianity has been assisted by African-led churches where secularizing trends within Christianity are prevalent. Thus, African Christian communities in America should no longer be considered as outposts of Africa in an alien continent but as institutions that are part of American life. The impact and import of the "exportation" of African-led churches, driven by a vision of winning converts, is that it offers a unique opportunity to analyze its impact at local levels. The transnational linkages between African Christian communities in the countries of origin (Africa) and the "host" societies, such as the United States, are assuming increasing importance for African immigrants. The links and networks that are established and maintained between

---

68. Adogame, *African Christian Diaspora*.

these contexts are of immense religious, cultural, economic, political, and social importance. This suggests how African Christianities can be understood within processes of religious transnationalism. This development is a remarkable change and marks a historic moment in the relations between Africa, North America, and Europe.

AFRICAN CHRISTIANITIES AND REVERSE MISSION

African-led churches have increasingly taken to proselytizing in North America and Europe, viewing the regions as "new abodes" and promising "mission fields."[69] There are also groups existing as branches of mother churches headquartered in Africa; and others founded by African migrants in the diaspora. Examples include the Redeemed Christian Church of God (RCCG), with headquarters in Nigeria, and the Kingsway International Christian Center in East London. Both have a huge African membership with few non-Africans. The Embassy of the Blessed Kingdom of God for All Nations in Kiev, Ukraine, is a typical example of an African-led church with a majority non-African membership. Such African religions are significant within the framework of globalization, owing to the unique expression of African Christianity they exhibit—a feature that could be described as their self-assertion and preservation of religious identity. They are also important because they increasingly constitute international ministries that have implications on a global scale. As part of an increasing phenomenon of what they term "mission reversed" or "remissionization of Christianity to a secularized West," these African churches have systematically set out to evangelize the world. Notions of globalization and globality are appropriated as theological and ideological constructs, and thus feature prominently in their mission statements and strategies, as well as sermon rhetoric—although these notions are used and understood differently. It is common to find churches defining themselves as "global churches" and their mission as "global tasks."

Reverse Mission: Europe as a Prodigal Continent?

The religious ethnography that took me from Germany to Nigeria in the summer of 1996 led to a striking and unprecedented finding, an advert captioned "Europe: A Prodigal Continent! . . . Europe: A Mission Field in Need

---

69. Adogame, *African Christian Diaspora*, 169–89. See also Adogame et al., *Christianity in Africa and the African Diaspora*.

of Church Attention" adorning the Missions Office notice board of RCCG's International headquarters in Lagos, Nigeria.[70] It proclaimed: "Why has Europe's spiritual light grown dim? A mission force of years ago, becoming another missionary field at the moment!" It is not uncommon now that Christians from the two-thirds world often employ similar narratives of representation giving the impression of a "Christian" Europe as "the dark continent of Europe" or "a dead and secularized Europe." Although it has been said that Europe is an exception in this regard, however, such traces of secularization are evident in North America as well. Controversial and puzzling as such assertions may be, they cast our minds and gaze to a new, emerging global religious phenomenon.

"Reverse mission" or "reverse flow of mission" is an increasingly common buzz phrase in academia, mission circles, media, and among Christians from the two-thirds world. The (un-)conscious missionary strategy and zeal by churches in Africa, Asia, and Latin America of (re-)evangelizing the West is a relatively recent one. This enterprise, according to them, was aimed at re-Christianizing Europe and North America. The rationale for reverse mission is often anchored on claims of divine commission to "spread the gospel," the perceived secularization of the West, the abysmal fall in church attendance and dwindling membership, desacralization of church buildings, liberalization, and issues of moral decadence.

It is so far unclear whether "reverse mission" is simply operating as mere rhetoric, and/or what shape, structure, and dynamic will emerge through this process in the long run. It will suffice at this point to underscore public ignorance and ecclesial conspiracy that has left unnoticed this emerging mission trend, partly characterized by church proliferation in the South and its expansion from there to the Northern Hemisphere and elsewhere. Nonetheless, reverse mission as "rhetoric" or "an evolving process" is of crucial religious, social, political, economic, and missiological import for the West and world Christianity, as the non-Western world was hitherto at the receiving end of missions till the late twentieth century. The emergence of the "global South" as the new center of gravity of Christianity provides the watershed for the reversal and/or multidirectionality of missions.

Reverse Mission: The Antinomy of Mission?

The moratorium discourse and its fall-outs and the very concept and process of reverse mission or reverse missionaries have been documented by scholars—scholars of religion, social scientists, historians, missiologists,

---

70. Adogame, *African Christian Diaspora*, 169.

theologians, and other related works—and an interesting cross-section of the media, although sometimes attributing a variety of meanings and perspectives. It needs to be demonstrated further how reverse mission as a concept and process can be used as an analytical, descriptive tool. Adogame and Spickard identify reverse missions, South-South religious trade, and transnational organization theory as interrelated approaches aimed at breaking the stereotype that places the North Atlantic at the center of the religious universe.[71] Each of these approaches illustrates a kind of religious action that may include the West but which does not privilege it. Adogame and Shankar have taken this argument further.[72] They demonstrate how the comparative dynamics of religious expansion illuminates, for instance, the complex models of Christian expansion in different geo-historical epochs.

The emerging phenomenon of reverse mission has attracted media attention. For instance, *The New York Times* story captioned "Mission from Africa" describes the mission task of the pastor of the RCCG Chapel of Restoration in the Bronx, New York, and who coordinates the church's missionary activities in North America:

> Pastor Daniel Ajayi-Adeniran is coming for your soul. It doesn't matter if you are black or white, rich or poor, speak English or Spanish or Cantonese. He is on a mission to save you from eternal damnation. He realizes you may be skeptical, put off by his exotic name—he's from Nigeria—or confused by his accent, the way he stretches his vowels and trills his R's, giving his sermons a certain chain-saw rhythm. He suspects you may have some unfortunate preconceptions about Nigerians. But he is not deterred. He believes the Holy Spirit is working through him—aided by the awesome earthly power of demographics.[73]

The story continued, "The Redeemed Church offers a case study of the crosscurrents that are drawing Christianity southward. Its leader and guiding force, Pastor Enoch Adeboye, sums up the church's history this way: 'Made in heaven, assembled in Nigeria, exported to the world . . . .' Today the process is reversing itself."[74] Also, *The Chicago Tribune* with its front-page headline "Africans now missionaries to U.S." signposts the RCCG as the Nigeria-based Pentecostal church that is spreading its evangelistic form of Christianity to America. It noted, "For years American missionaries brought Christianity to Africa. Now African Christians say they want to export their

---

71. Adogame and Spickard, *Religion Crossing Boundaries*.
72. Adogame and Shankar, *Religion On the Move*.
73. See Rice, "Mission from Africa."
74. Rice, "Mission from Africa."

own brand of ecstatic worship and moral discipline to the United States, a country they believe has lost its fervor."[75] *The Christian Century*, a Christian magazine, carried a story "African missionaries to the U.S." and reports:

> For generations, Christian missionaries from the U.S. journeyed to Africa to teach their religion. Now, however, amid a burgeoning of Christianity in Africa, churches there are sending thousands of missionaries overseas to preach the Christian message in their own unique style. And many of those missionaries are coming to the U.S. "We have been blessed by the U.S. and now we want to give back to them through the gospel of Christ," said Badeg Bekele, pastor of Emmanuel Ethiopian Church in Los Angeles . . . . African ministries are springing up in America because "the church in Africa is on fire, while the church in America is, for the most part, losing its zeal," said Pastor Ivey Williams of a congregation in Tallahassee, Florida, established by the Nigerian-based Redeemed Christian Church of God. Williams is the first African American pastor of an RCCG church.[76]

The Herald also captures this trend with the storyline: "Out of Africa: now the missionaries head for Scotland" and notes that, "For centuries, the church sent missionaries to Africa to spread the word of God—now it needs them back."[77] In a reversal of the stream of Scots who pioneered their way across the continent, one church has turned to ministers from South Africa to stem the shortage of staff at home. In a recent development in March 2012, the BBC 2 TV series *Reverse Missionaries* epitomizes the stark reality of the enduring processes of reverse mission. In their introduction to the series, the producers note: "Nineteenth-century Britain was a golden age for Christian missionaries, who took the word of God around the globe to countries in which that religion remains and is now thriving. In a reverse of those great missionary journeys, idealistic modern-day missionaries travel to Britain to discover the historical roots of their faith and try to pursue their own missionary agenda in 21st-century Britain, trying to breathe new life into churches with declining attendance."[78] This documentary chronicled, under three episodes of one hour each, new missionaries from the two-thirds world—Jamaica, Malawi and India—to the United Kingdom.

---

75. Lieblich and McCann, "Africans Now Missionaries to U.S.," 1.
76. See *Christian Century*, "African Missionaries to the US."
77. See Bannerman, "Out of Africa."
78. See BBC Two, "Reverse Missionaries."

These academic interpretations and media perceptions of the reverse mission dynamics or reverse missionaries can hardly be thought of as a historical accident or occurring as sporadic events. What circumstances have enabled the reverse mission that has dramatically shifted the center of world Christianity to the two-thirds world? Andrew Walls best explores the complex dynamics of Christian mission by first historicizing it, and then balancing a broad, theoretical view of missions with more intensive discussions of specific missions.[79] Walls offers a panoramic view of the modern flux of the missionary movement and Christianity in general, emphasizing the recession of the church in Europe and North America and its expansion everywhere else.[80] Walls contends that the next phase of the missionary movement must incorporate sending and receiving.

A historiography of reverse mission must respond to the antecedents and precedents of reverse mission process. The discourse on moratorium and reverse mission requires a historical backdrop especially as a backlash against decolonization. The history of the decolonization process in Africa is an intricate one that implicates all spheres of life. Ogbu Kalu best captures this complex interplay by mapping African Christianity between the World Wars and decolonization.[81] Decolonization exposed the differing agendas of the colonial government and missionaries; differences on the goals and curricula of education and cultural policies betrayed the ideological cleavages and competing visions between missions and colonial government. Africans were sensitive to missionary unwillingness to afford them higher training, ordain an adequate number of Indigenous priests, devolve power, or overtly support nationalism.

Rivalry suffused the missionary enterprise as each denomination sought to imprint its own version. The main thrust of the missionary policy of indigenization was passive revolution to maintain influence using Indigenous personnel and resources. People increasingly found the missionary version of indigenization to be unsatisfactory and restrictive. By the 1960s, most former European colonies in Africa underwent decolonization and became independent, although decolonization did not imply a radical change of Africa's colonial socio-economic structure.

Missionaries' responses to nationalism varied according to individual whims, official or denominational policies, and regional contexts. Vast changes in the political climate of the decade forced enormous changes in

---

79. Walls, *Missionary Movement in Christian History*; and Walls, *Cross-Cultural Process in Christian History*.

80. Walls, *Missionary Movement in Christian History*, 257.

81. See Kalu, *African Pentecostalism*; and Kalu, *African Christianity*.

the religious landscape. The impact of decolonization on church groups varied: based on the size and ecclesiastical organization; the vertical spread and social quality of adherents; the inherited pattern of colonial relationship; and the theological emphasis and international relations.

The call for a moratorium was a more strident and different form of indigenization project. The moratorium exposed the character of Africa's relationship with the West—extraversion was in-built in the pattern of African relationship with the West as an essential ingredient to maintain "eternal juniority." It reflected African impatience with the nature, pace, and results of mission-initiated indigenization. Africans suspected a hidden agenda to embroil them in cosmetic change while the same people retained real power.

When the WCC General Assembly met in Nairobi in 1975, the choice of venue was as significant as the speech of the pope in Kampala in 1969. The themes that emerged indicated a new mood that accepted African Christian maturity in ways hardly planned by the missionaries. Some Protestant missions took the opportunity to abandon missionary engagement. In some cases, it led to the emergence of short-term missionaries. Thus, the moratorium and African liberation struggles influenced the shifts in the strategy for decolonizing the African churches. But who is this revolutionary figure who single-handedly stirred controversy within global mission circles, turning the paternalistic trend of Christian mission on its head? Where did he derive the inspiration and guts to throw such a challenging blow at an unsuspecting mission audience?

JOHN GATU, FROM COLONIAL SOLDIER TO MORATORIUM CRUSADER

John Gatu, the man whose spark ignited the moratorium debate, has been described as "a great leader, mediator, pastor, preacher, counselor, speaker, poet, writer and ecumenist."[82] Gatu initiated the call during a visit to Milwaukee, Wisconsin, in February 1971. He embarrassed his ecumenical hosts by declaring that he had not come to beg for money or personnel, but to request that missionary aid in money and personnel should cease for at least five years so that African Christians can learn how to catch fish instead of relying on gratis fish from European mission boards. The stark call by Gatu for "a moratorium on missions and missionaries from the West" put missions at a crossroad. In fact, the Reformed Church of America, sponsors of the Milwaukee "Mission Festival 71" meeting, would probably not have

---

82. Adogame, *African Christian Diaspora*, 177. See also Gatu, *Joyfully Christian*.

invited him to speak during the event, if they had any inkling that his speech was going to be so controversial to the extent of stirring up and turning the parameters of mission praxis on its head.

The moratorium call came under heavy criticism based on the mere fact that it emanated from the so-called Third World, the context that had been the primary mission field for many years. There were wide-ranging responses of mission bodies to the moratorium debate through seminars, conferences, and in the pages of journals. This call, which took a revolutionary stance, generated heated conversation, rebuttals and criticism from various quarters, particularly from the Western world. The criticisms of the moratorium were theological, ecclesiastical, and logistical in nature. As Kalu explained, it was argued that a moratorium was theologically unacceptable because of the Pauline imagery of *soma* that we are one body and one part cannot prevent the other from performing a mandatory task.[83] Ecclesiastically, it was dangerous to become a national church. This threatened catholicity; the pilgrim and the Indigenous principles must be held in tension. Logistically, it would be impossible to dismantle the mission structures that had built up over a century. Then, there was the gut reaction of those who presumed that the Africans were ungrateful after years of missionary sacrifices.

The moratorium debate in the early 1970s evoked consternation among the white missionary agencies that dismissed it as preposterous. Ironically, their rebuttals provided the impetus for an African Pentecostal missionary enterprise. Within a few decades, they achieved the goals that the mainline churches failed to consolidate.[84] Legacies of the moratorium discourse as eulogized by Gatu and his contemporaries are still fresh and resilient within world mission circles. In fact, Gatu has remained very consistent, positive and vehement about the urgency for self-sufficiency and self-reliance of the church in Africa.

Although the moratorium failed to produce a formal radical and systemic halt to the influx of Western missionaries and mission resources to Africa, it nevertheless raised a question that resulted in self-reflection and structural adjustment by Western missionaries and of their mission resources. It served as an eye-opener for many about the new, changing dynamics of mission and religious expansion in which Africans were looking not only inward for self-reliance but outwardly with a mission mandate to evangelize what they now refer to as "the dark continent of Europe," "the prodigal continent," or "the dead West." Several Third World Christian

---

83. Kalu, *African Pentecostalism*, 276.

84. Kalu, *African Pentecostalism*, 290.

leaders supported this suggestion because they believed that it would break the circle of dependency on the Western churches and create room for self-development. Alongside their African counterparts, some Asian and Latin American church leaders echoed this sentiment. The moratorium also produced a new consciousness about dependence and strategies for self-reliance that has challenged definitions of mission but also altered the unidirectional nature of missions that characterized earlier conceptions.

In 1973, his moratorium proposal took center stage during heated debates on "partnership in mission" by the Commission on World Mission and Evangelism of the Bangkok Assembly of the WCC. In the following year, it became a recurring topic at the All Africa Conference of Churches Third Assembly at Lusaka, Zambia. This empowerment of the Third World churches brought significant changes in mission practices as issues of cooperation and partnership were promoted as new mission strategies at the International Congress on World Evangelization, Lausanne, Switzerland in July 1974 and in subsequent congresses. Third World Christians participated in these congresses and held additional continental and regional conferences, which provided global challenges and opportunities. The Lausanne Covenant gave a qualified endorsement to the moratorium call: "A reduction of foreign missionaries and money in an evangelized country may sometimes be necessary to facilitate the national church's growth in self-reliance and to release resources for unevangelized areas."[85]

In 1975, the WCC Fifth Assembly at Nairobi continued to echo the moratorium call. The terms of the debate moved from discussing a possible moratorium to understanding mission as the joint privilege and responsibility of churches in all six continents.[86] A deal for a "mission partnership" had been brokered; this helped Western mission bodies to save face. Mission "partners" became a leverage to deconstruct the inherent ecclesiastical paternalism that characterized the missionary enterprise. Thus, the initiative that entailed sending African missionaries abroad came partly against the backdrop of the moratorium call to awaken "two-thirds world" peoples to their responsibility, creating new goals and formulating a viable evangelism strategy toward Europe.[87]

The Lutheran World Federation had experimented with "reverse flow," in which African ministers were posted to German congregations where they were mostly treated with cold civility. In the early 1980s, Tanzanian Lutheran pastors were sponsored to serve in various parishes in Germany.

---

85. Stott, *Lausanne Covenant*, 59.
86. Scherer, *Missionary, Go Home!*, 273.
87. Kalu, "Church, Mission and Moratorium," 365–74.

The reverse-mission agenda is growing very popular among new African-led churches, with pastors and missionaries commissioned to head already existing branches or establish new ones in the diaspora. The growth of missionary endeavors from Africa and other parts of the non-Western world has gained momentum in the 1990s, in a way that challenges Christianity in the West but also world Christianity.

By the 1990s, many churches had progressed to define their missions as witnessing communities to the Western churches and societies, which were waning numerically and spiritually. In the closing decade of the twentieth century, reverse missions became more recognized and gradually gained ascendancy due to economic decline and political conflicts, which intensified the migration of Africans, Asians, and Latin Americans to the West. Confronted by the secularization of the Western society and the decline of church attendance and public piety, these migrants took up a revivalist agenda. At the same time, these immigrant Christians looked at the Western churches as being in a state of apostasy and in a spiritual wilderness that needed re-evangelization.

As Ojo highlights, the founding of the Third World Missions Association (TWMA), in Portland, Oregon, in May 1989 as a forum for mission-sending agencies in Africa, Asia, and Latin America to enhance their capacities to undertake extensive missionary endeavors brought in an institutional perspective and transformed non-Western world missions into a global force in world Christianity.[88] In fact, the closure of some Arab countries to Western missionaries and the acceptance and success of African and Asian missionaries working among Arabs also proved quite significant in this process of reverse missions. Likewise, the AD 2000 and Beyond Movement, a global effort of world evangelization, directed by Third World Christian leaders, provided additional involvement and networking for evangelization and cross-cultural missions. By the mid-1990s, non-Western churches were beginning to achieve some degree of success in their missionary efforts, though they were largely using non-conventional missionaries. Many African churches have been evangelizing among whites and non-African immigrants since the mid-1980s. While migration continued to provide missionary mobilization, African Christian communities were able to realize their strength within world Christianity and perceive their missionary activities from a global perspective.

---

88. Ojo, "Reverse Mission," 380–82.

CONCLUSION

The implications of reverse mission for world Christianity are not difficult to see. First, reverse mission has brought a major shift in mission understanding and provided better sensibilities to and appreciation of the multicultural nature of Christianity in the twenty-first century. Second, new definitions of mission are emerging in which traditional "mission fields" now form "mission bases" of renewed efforts to re-evangelize Europe and North America. Missions changed from unilateral to multilateral, itinerant missionaries increased, short-term missions emerged, and missions moved from cultural transplantation to contextualization. Third, as churches in the West, and particularly in Europe, are declining in number and in missionary significance, the impact of non-Western missions looms large in the revivification of Christianity in the US and Europe. Fourth, this trend helps in the deconstruction and demystification of ecclesiastical paternalism that characterized global Christianity.

Lastly, the proliferation of priests/missionaries from the two-thirds world may help fill a spiritual/administrative vacuum caused by the dearth of American and European clergy. Andrew Walls's remark "Europe needs immigrants but does not want them"[89] sums up European attitudes toward immigrants in Europe. How different is it in the case of the United States? Nonetheless, this reverse trend in missions now offers the "old heartlands of Christianity" a model for renewal, transformation, and change.

BIBLIOGRAPHY

Achebe, Chinua. *Anthills of the Savannah*. Oxford: Heinemann, 1987.
———. *Arrow of God*. Oxford: Heinemann, 1969.
———. *Chike and the River*. Cape Town: Cambridge University Press, 1966.
———. "An Image of Africa: Racism in Conrad's 'Heart of Darkness.'" *Massachusetts Review* 57.1 (n.d.) 14–27.
———. *A Man of the People*. Oxford: Heinemann, 1966.
———. *No Longer at Ease*. Oxford: Heinemann, 1960.
———. *Things Fall Apart*. New York: Anchor, 1994.
Achebe, Chinua, and Ulli Beier. "The World Is a Dancing Masquerade: A Conversation Between Chinua Achebe and Ulli Beier." *Southerly* 63.2 (2003) 163–77.
Adogame, Afe. *The African Christian Diaspora: New Currents and Emerging Trends in World Christianity*. London: Bloomsbury, 2013.
———. "Calling a Trickster Deity a 'Bad' Name in Order to Hang It? Deconstructing Indigenous African Epistemologies Within Global Religious Maps of the Universe." In *The Changing World Religion Map: Sacred Places, Identities, Practices and Politics*, edited by Stanley D. Brunn, 1813–26. Springer, 2015.

89. Walls, "Mission and Migration," 10.

———. *Celestial Church of Christ: The Politics of Cultural Identity in a West African Prophetic Charismatic Movement*. Vol. 115. Frankfurt am Main: Peter Lang, 1999.

———. "'I Am Married to Jesus!' The Feminization of New African Diasporic Religiosity." *Archives de Sciences Sociales des Religions* 53.143 (2008) 129–49.

———. "Mapping African Christianities Within Religious Maps of the Universe." *Princeton Seminary Bulletin* 33 (2016) 39–65.

———. "The Politicization of Religion and the Religionization of Politics in Nigeria." In *Religion, History, and Politics in Nigeria: Essays in Honor of Ogbu U. Kalu*, edited by Chima Jacob Korieh and G. Ugo Nwokeji, 137–53. Lanham, MD: University Press of America, 2004.

———. "Practitioners of Indigenous Religions in Africa and the African Diaspora." In *Religions in Focus: New Approaches to Tradition and Contemporary Practices*, edited by Graham Harvey, 75–100. London: Equinox, 2009.

———. "Religion in Sub-Saharan Africa." In *Religion, Globalization and Culture*, edited by Peter Beyer and Lori G. Beaman, 527–48. International Studies in Religion and Society. Leiden: Brill, 2007.

Adogame, Afe, and Lizo Jafta. "Zionists, Aladura and Roho: African Instituted Churches." In *African Christianity: An African Story*, edited by Ogbu Kalu, 271–87. Perspectives on Christianity 3. Trenton, NJ: Africa World Press, 2007.

Adogame, Afe, and Shobana Shankar. *Religion On the Move: New Dynamics of Religious Expansion in a Globalizing World*. Vol. 15. Leiden: Brill, 2013.

Adogame, Afe, and James V. Spickard, eds. *Religion Crossing Boundaries: Transnational Religious and Social Dynamics in Africa and the New African Diaspora*. Leiden: Brill, 2010.

Adogame, Afe, et al., eds. *Christianity in Africa and the African Diaspora: The Appropriation of a Scattered Heritage*. London: Continuum, 2008.

African Union. "Signing of Memorandum of Understanding Between the African Union Commission and the African Diaspora Forum." Press Release No. 05/27th AU Summit, July 10, 2016. http://au.int/sites/default/files/pressreleases/31088-pr-pr_05-_signing_of_memorandum_of_understanding_between_the_african_union_.pdf

———. "The Diaspora Division." N.d. https://au.int/diaspora-division.

———. "Home." N.d. https://au.int/.

Bannerman, Lucy. "Out of Africa: Now the Missionaries Head for Scotland." *Herald*, Jan. 28, 2006.

Barrett, David B. *Schism and Renewal in Africa: An Analysis of Six Thousand Contemporary Religious Movements*. London: Oxford University Press, 1968.

BBC Two. "Reverse Missionaries." https://www.bbc.co.uk/programmes/b01dmzcz/episodes/guide.

Brooks, Jerome. "Chinua Achebe, The Art of Fiction: No. 139." *The Paris Review* 133 (Winter 1994). https://www.theparisreview.org/interviews/1720/the-art-of-fiction-no-139-chinua-achebe.

Cary, Joyce. *Mister Johnson*. New York: Time, 1962.

Christian Century. "African Missionaries to the U.S." Aug. 13, 1997.

Conrad, Joseph. *Heart of Darkness*. New York: Penguin, 1995.

Daughrity, Dyron B. "Assessing Christianity in Africa's Transforming Context." *Hekima Review* 52 (2015) 50–61.

———. *The Changing World of Christianity: The Global History of a Borderless Religion*. New York: Peter Lang, 2010.

Davie, Grace. *Religion in Britain Since 1945: Believing Without Belonging*. Oxford: Blackwell, 1994.

Davies, Noel A., and Martin Conway. *World Christianity in the Twentieth Century*. SCM Core Text. London: SCM Press, 2008.

Gatu, John. *Joyfully Christian: Truly African*. Nairobi: Acton, 2006.

Gikandi, Simon. "Chinua Achebe and the Invention of African Culture." *Research in African Literatures* 32.3 (2001) 3–8.

Johnson, Todd M., and Gina A. Zurlo. "World Christian Database." Leiden: Brill, 2007. https://brill.com/view/db/wcdo.

Kalu, Ogbu, ed. *African Christianity: An African Story*. Perspectives on Christianity 3. Trenton, NJ: Africa World Press, 2007.

———. *African Pentecostalism: An Introduction*. Oxford: Oxford University Press, 2008.

———. "Church, Mission, and Moratorium." In *The History of Christianity in West Africa*, edited by Ogbu Kalu, 365–74. London: Longman, 1980.

———. "Ethiopianism in African Christianity." In *African Christianity: An African Story*, edited by Ogbu Kalu, 227–43. Perspectives on Christianity 3. Trenton, NJ: Africa World Press, 2007.

Lieblich, Julia, and Tom McCann. "Africans Now Missionaries to U.S." *Chicago Tribune*, June 2002. https://www.chicagotribune.com/2002/06/21/africans-now-missionaries-to-us/.

Ojo, Matthew. "Reverse Mission." In *Encyclopedia of Mission and Missionaries*, edited by Jon Bonk, 380–82. Routledge Encyclopedias of Religion and Society. New York: Routledge, 2007.

Olupona, Jacob K. "African Religion." In *Global Religions: An Introduction*, edited by Mark Juergensmeyer, 78–86. Oxford: Oxford University Press, 2003.

Pew Research Center. "Global Anglicanism at a Crossroads." June 19, 2008. https://www.pewresearch.org/religion/2008/06/19/global-anglicanism-at-a-crossroads/.

Platvoet, Johannes Gerhardus, and Jacob K. Olupona, eds. *The Study of Religions in Africa—Past, Present and Prospects*. Religions of Africa 1. Cambridge: Roots and Branches, 1996.

Ranger, Terence O., ed. *Evangelical Christianity and Democracy in Africa*. Evangelical Christianity and Democracy in the Global South. Oxford: Oxford University Press, 2008.

Rice, Andrew. "Mission from Africa." *New York Times*, Apr. 8, 2009. https://www.nytimes.com/2009/04/12/magazine/12churches-t.html.

Sanneh, Lamin. *Translating the Message: The Missionary Impact on Culture*. 2nd ed. Maryknoll: Orbis, 2008.

———. *Whose Religion Is Christianity? The Gospel Beyond the West*. Grand Rapids: Eerdmans, 2003.

Sawyer, Kenneth, and Youhanna Youssef. "Early Christianity in North Africa." In *African Christianity: An African Story*, edited by Ogbu Kalu, 41–65. Perspectives on Christianity 3. Trenton, NJ: Africa World Press, 2007.

Scherer, James. *Missionary, Go Home! A Reappraisal of the Christian World Mission*. Upper Saddle River, NJ: Prentice Hall, 1964.

Stott, John. *The Lausanne Covenant*. The Lausanne Movement, 2009. https://lausanne.org/wp-content/uploads/2021/10/Lausanne-Covenant-%E2%80%93-Pages.pdf.

Urschel, Donna. "Achebe's Impact: Author Gave Africa Its 'First Authentic Voice.'" *Library of Congress Information Bulletin* 67.12 (2008).

Walls, Andrew F. *The Cross-Cultural Process in Christian History: Studies in the Transmission and Appropriation of Faith*. Maryknoll: Orbis, 2002.

———. "Mission and Migration: The Diaspora Factor in Christian History." *Journal of African Christian Thought* 5.2 (Dec. 2002) 3–11.

———. *The Missionary Movement in Christian History: Studies in the Transmission of Faith*. Maryknoll: Orbis, 1996.

Chapter 8

Friendship, Love, and Justice as a Path to Christian Social Responsibility

Luiz Nascimento

CHRISTIAN THINKERS SUCH AS Saint Augustine and Thomas Aquinas have created a long tradition of Christian reflection on morality that relies deeply on the heritage of classical thought coming down from Plato and Aristotle. Classic *eudaimonia* has inspired Christian thinkers in the search for the moral good, and for what would ultimately stand as the teleology of human life. In this paper I am set to explore how the tradition of happiness and friendship, in dialogue with the Niebuhr's theory of responsibility, can inform Christian moral decision making.

The first section of this paper will comprise a descriptive exploration of *eudaimonia* in which I will draw mostly on the Platonic and Aristotelian traditions. I will be discussing how classic philosophers engaged the idea of friendship and love as the path to the cultivation of virtues and also how that tradition influenced the thought of Christian thinkers throughout the history of Christianity. As it is not possible to engage the discussion of all the tradition of Christian thought of friendship and love, I will focus most exclusively on three Christian thinkers who have influenced the formation of contemporary Christian scholarship: Augustine, Thomas Aquinas, and Søren Kierkegaard. A second section of this paper will be dedicated to exploring how a Christian perspective of human friendship with God can connect to the thought of twentieth-century Christian thinkers Reinhold and H. Richard Niebuhr, with special emphasis on H. Richard Niebuhr's theory of responsibility. The final portion of the present work will raise the claim that considering the Christian tradition of friendship, love, and justice, Niebuhr's idea of Christian responsibility and the interconnectedness of all creation, the liberationist "preferential option for the poor" is a sound manifestation of love in the pursuit of the common good.

CHRISTIAN THINKERS AND *EUDAIMONIA*

Eudaimonia is commonly translated as "happiness," but the Greek term would find a more appropriate translation as "human flourishing"; *eudaimonia* should not be confounded with the present concept of happiness prevalent in contemporary Western society. If properly understood, eudaimonism conceptualizes happiness in a fashion that is not limited to the ideas of power, wealth, prestige, honor, or physical pleasure. While discussing how Aquinas sees the wrong turns humans take on happiness, Paul Wadell says that as "seekers of happiness, we move through life in search of whatever we think will fulfill and complete us, something so exquisitely good that once we possess it there is nothing left for us to desire."[1] Wadell claims that we are often more mistaken than astute about our search for happiness and that we are typically confounded as to what would constitute true happiness. According to Wadell, Augustine would respond to our present society's craze for power, wealth, prestige, fame, and pleasure of all sorts by saying that true happiness can be found in none of the aforementioned values because those values are not capable of bringing humans to excel in their potential for goodness. Wealth, prestige, fame, and pleasure cannot surpass human life and its limits. Wadell reminds us that human beings need a good that surpasses the human condition of limitedness.[2]

If the Christian traditional thought that sprang out of the encounter between Christian morality and the classical notion of *eudaimonia* is correct about human flourishing as depending on a source of happiness that surpasses human existence, then in what manner can contemporary Christians learn about happiness from the legacy of classical philosophy? How can Plato and Aristotle help us find a proper pedagogy of happiness? Can true Christian happiness and human flourishing be achieved individually, or does it require a communal approach to our epistemology of happiness and virtue?

---

1. Wadell, *Happiness and the Christian Moral Life*, 14.
2. Wadell, *Happiness and the Christian Moral Life*, 13–14.

Aristotle's *Nicomachean Ethics* discusses the problem of the ends and goods in human virtue. He starts his arguments on happiness by saying that "every craft and every line of inquiry, and likewise every action and decision, seems to seek some good."[3] For Aristotle, every free man and woman shares the aims of finding the good that will cause the most satisfaction and bring them to the acme of human potentiality. However, perception of what constitutes this good is diverse, and Aristotle claims that one needs to be cultivated in a nurturing environment, for only when given the proper models of virtuous life can any human being develop the political virtues necessary to become a happy and whole human being. Aristotle highlights the importance of finding what constitutes the highest of all goods[4] in political life as the way to direct our desires toward proper objects of love that can help us achieve the good that surpasses the life of gratification, which he opposes to what he describes as "a life for grazing animals."[5] Both Plato and Aristotle think of the moral life as a quest for excellence in human potential. In that vein, moral virtues are interpreted as the elements that should be cultivated in human character in order to equip the individual with the moral qualities necessary to achieve their excellent moral life.

Aristotle states that happiness is the choicest and worthiest of all goods because it is an end in itself. All human actions are intended to produce the good of happiness, or in Aristotle's own words: "Happiness, then, is apparently something complete and self-sufficient, since it is the end of the things achievable in action."[6] Using the allegory of the Olympic contest, Aristotle argues that a happy life is the prize won by those who succeed in the moral life, by those who act correctly and well. But he also argues that happiness needs external goods, as well, for one cannot do fine actions if one lacks the necessary resources.[7] Therefore, is happiness the result of good fortune or should we identify it as a particular virtue? It seems that happiness is neither a mere outcome of good fortune nor a virtue with which one is born. If moral virtues and a well-lived life are the result of a cultivated experience in life, then it needs to be understood as a communal construction, as something that is learned in contact, interaction, and shared experience with others. Friendship constitutes a crucial element in the cultivation of virtue.

Plato and Aristotle explore the theme of friendship and love in their reflections. In his *Symposium*, Plato and his companions discuss the nature

---

3. Aristotle, *Nicomachean Ethics* 1.1, §1.
4. Aristotle, *Nicomachean Ethics* 1.2, §§1–7.
5. Aristotle, *Nicomachean Ethics* 1.5, §3.
6. Aristotle, *Nicomachean Ethics* 1.7, §8.
7. Aristotle, *Nicomachean Ethics* 1.8, §§8–15.

of friendship and love. The terms *lover* and *beloved* are used constantly to describe the nature of the friendly relationship. In his speech, Phaedrus declares that Eros was the cause of the greatest things, and he says that:

> Those who intend to live beautifully must be led through the whole of life by what neither kinship nor honor nor wealth nor aught else can instill so beautifully as Eros. What do I mean by this? Shame for things ugly, ambition for things beautiful; for without these, neither city nor private person can do great and beautiful deeds. . . . For a man in love would surely not let himself be seen by his beloved, beyond all others, deserting his post or throwing down his arms; he would choose to die many times before that. And again, as to deserting his beloved or not helping him in danger—no one is so bad that Eros would not inspire him to virtue so as to be equal to him who is by nature best. What Homer said is absolutely true, that god "breathes valor" into certain of the heroes, a thing that Eros provides to lovers from his own resources.[8]

In Phaedrus's defense of erotic love as the means to inspire the search for happiness through the cultivation of virtue, he illustrates the virtue of erotic love in that lovers are the only ones who would be willing to die for others, and he uses the story of Alcestis, daughter of Pelias, saving her husband as an example of how one in love can be moved to surpass the limits of care for his or her own life in order to save their beloved.

Diotima also describes Eros as the wish for happiness. In their dialogue about Eros, Diotima and Socrates discuss the nature of Eros and whether the desire for the good is a common trait of all humankind. Diotima asserts:

> All men are pregnant in respect to both the body and the soul, Socrates, she said, and when they reach a certain age, our nature desires to beget. It cannot beget in ugliness, but only in beauty. The intercourse of man and woman is begetting. This is a divine thing, and pregnancy and procreation are an immortal element in the mortal living creature. It is impossible for birth to take place in what is discordant. But ugliness is in discord with all that is divine, and beauty is concordant.[9]

In their dialogue, Socrates and Diotima identify the desire to reach and possess the good for themselves as an innate characteristic of all human beings. If that is true, why is it that not all human beings become lovers of good and virtue? Diotima claims that it is necessary that the young have a

8. Plato, *Symposium*, 178–179b.
9. Plato, *Symposium*, 206c.

good guide to lead him or her in search of love, in search of the good. She suggests that there is a ladder of love, or a progressive scale nearness to the perfect love and good, beginning by identification with one beautiful body, then extending this identification of beauty in a single body to all beautiful bodies, and then transcending the limits of physical beauty to find beauty in the souls. That would finally enable the one who is being initiated in the search of the good to appreciate beauty and good in those whose souls have a beauty that the body lacks. Diotima synthesizes her approach to teaching the love of beauty in the search for the good with the following words:

> This is the right way to proceed in matters of love, or to be led by another—beginning from these beautiful things here, to ascend ever upward for the sake of that, the Beautiful, as though using the steps of a ladder, from one to two, and from two to all beautiful bodies, and beautiful bodies to beautiful practices, and from practices to beautiful studies, and studies one arrives in the end at that study which is nothing other than the study of that, the Beautiful itself, and one know in the end, by itself, what it is to be beautiful.[10]

Letting oneself be guided is an essential part of the Platonic pedagogy of virtue. One will need good examples and experience to become what one is to be: a virtuous person. Virtue, then, is not simply a matter of disposition to the good, but external forces are at play in the process of acquiring virtue. Factors such as being born into a good family, having educational opportunities, living in times of peace, and having an organized society around will also play important roles in the acquisition of virtues and, consequently, in finding happiness. Aristotle and Plato associate happiness with the proper direction of our passions toward something that is a good in its own right, not merely a useful good,[11] and that is complete without qualification, something self-sufficient.[12]

Both Plato and Aristotle see friendship as the context within which the learning of virtue takes place, as Aristotle says: "Virtue, then, is of two sorts, virtue of thought and virtue of character. Virtue of thought arises and grows mostly from teaching; that is why it needs experience and time. Virtue of character [i.e., of ethos] results from habit [ethos]."[13] Virtues, then, are to be learned, practiced, and acquired as one does other habits. However, friendship was not taken to be one monolithic entity; it was rather considered to

---

10. Plato, *Symposium*, 211c.
11. Aristotle, *Nicomachean Ethics* 1.6, §9.
12. Aristotle, *Nicomachean Ethics* 1.7, §5 and 8.
13. Aristotle, *Nicomachean Ethics* 2.1, §1–2.

take different forms as the object of the relationship was brought to mind. According to Aristotle, friendship could take three basic forms: friendship of utility, friendship of pleasure, and friendship of virtue. What determines the nature of the relationship is the type of object of love, and "each object of love has a corresponding type of mutual loving, combined with awareness of it."[14] But friendship is not a relationship that develops in the vacuum; it takes place in diverse contexts that inform the nature of the exchanges between the partners or friends. The nature of the shared object of love may permit the friendship to last a lifetime or to be, otherwise, short lived because the object of love is no longer shared like in the friendship of utility and pleasure, for "these friendships as well as [the friends] are coincidental, since the loved one is loved not insofar as he is who he is, but insofar as he provides some good or pleasure."[15]

Aristotle discusses the problems involved in the different sorts of friendship within the family, the city, friendship among equals and those involving some level of inequality, as well as the problem of selfishness, benevolence, and self-sacrifice in friendship. As he does his assessment of the diverse types of friendship, he explores the possible conflicts between those same types. The reason I decided to spend some time in this present article on a description of friendship in Aristotle is the fact that he highlights the importance of reciprocity in friendship. Reciprocity is an important notion in Christian historical thought, and much effort has been done throughout the history of Christian scholarship to reconcile this Christian principle with the demands of the hostile world that surrounds us. How does this philosophical discussion of friendship relate to the Christian understanding of love and justice? How does friendship play out in the Christian striving to cultivate virtue through the practices of discipleship? How has the eudaimonist tradition informed the Christian thinkers?

It is by no coincidence that Thomas Aquinas opens his discussion of charity in the *Secunda Secundae Partis* of his *Summa Theologica* by asking the question of whether charity is friendship. Aquinas quotes 1 Cor 1:9, "God is faithful: by whom you are called unto the fellowship of His Son," and Aquinas proceeds by saying that the love, which is based on this communion, that with his Son, is what constitutes charity. Aquinas says that "charity is the friendship of man to God."[16] Aquinas's definition of charity makes it clear that he understands charity to be a type of love that is proper of the Christian community, for it is not a mere manifestation of goodwill

---

14. Aristotle, *Nicomachean Ethics* 7.3, §1.
15. Aristotle, *Nicomachean Ethics* 7.3, §2.
16. Aquinas, *Summa Theologica*, II-II, q. 23.

toward others, but rather it is a loving relationship between the Christian and God.

VIRTUES AND THE MORAL CHOICE

I understand the encounter between the eudaimonist tradition and the Christian idea of friendship to take place in the interstitial space of human relation with other beings in the created world. And I draw this idea from the theory of responsibility of H. Richard Niebuhr.[17] The interconnectedness of all beings, whether animated or inanimated, springs out of the awareness that humans and the whole of the created world are interdependent. Under these circumstances, the idea of neighborliness takes up a broader range of inclusivity. The neighbor is no longer identified solely in the individuals who surround us, but our neighborliness extends to the entire created world, which we are called to care for.

The ethics of responsibility proposed by H. Richard Niebuhr places special emphasis on the kind of person one becomes because of one's moral choices. The moral virtues that one holds make the difference in this case. The development of this sort of morality relies on the internalization of a set of moral values, thus surpassing the mere obedience to the laws of a society or the achievement of one's own goals. Robin Lovin says that this kind of morality takes time and self-discipline to be developed because moral virtues are to be embodied in oneself and will no longer come as the result of obedience to a law or covenant.[18] Lovin's thought agrees with the philosophers aforementioned in this article, for whom the moral life was to be acquired and practiced. One was to become skilled in moral virtues through the instruction of good teachers and models.

However, Reinhold Niebuhr's Marxist inspired Christian realism brings to light the conflicts between individual morality, social justice, and power relations. His view of humanity and society is challenging as he describes and analyzes how perverted our social structures are and addresses the impossibility of egalitarian power relations.[19] He contends that power

---

17. H. R. Niebuhr, *Responsible Self*, 79.
18. Lovin, *Christian Ethics*.
19. At the time he wrote *Moral Man and Immoral Society*, Reinhold Niebuhr had a clear inclination to a socialist philosophy that was informed by Marxist thought. Later in his career, Niebuhr became more of a post-Marxist in his social critique and ethics. Robin Lovin claims that Reinhold Niebuhr was actually the first thinker of his generation to introduce the hermeneutics of suspicion to the discourse of American religious social ethics. Lovin quotes Juan Luis Segundo saying that, regarding Marxism, what attracted Niebuhr most was its mythical component, rather than the Marxist "rational

tends to bring along the notion of domination over others. Thus, political and social justice will come out of the empowerment of the lesser groups to balance power relations.[20] This idea reflects the protestant tradition of the total or partial deprivation of the human being, whereas it opposes the Catholic traditional emphasis on the essential goodness of human nature due to the presence of the *imago Dei* in humanity.[21] Reinhold Niebuhr does not believe that the struggle for empowerment will ever result in egalitarianism, but it may contribute to reducing the disenfranchisement of minorities in the social order. Reinhold Niebuhr comes close to his brother's thought when he says that perfect justice can only be achieved by the moral imagination of the individual that interacts with and comprehends the needs of others because this idea reflects H. Richard Niebuhr's theory of the responsible self, whose strong emphasis on relationality helped me understand more clearly the importance of individual moral choices to society as a whole. Even though most of our decisions are made in the intimacy of our private lives, they are all interrelated to what Leonardo Boff would describe as the web of life.[22] The "*I-Thou-God*" relational scheme that H. Richard Niebuhr proposes clarifies the relational nature of individual and collective human life.[23] Our responses are made in anticipation of how the others will react to us, and the action to which we responded was itself the result of the expectations the self from whom that action originally came already had as to how we would respond. Every self responds to the selves around them, as they interact with one another. And this is just to take into consideration the web of relations going on horizontally. However, we cannot ignore that all those selves are also related to the Ultimate Being. One might pose the challenge that not every human being takes the existence of God as a reality, but in that case, I understand that Niebuhr refers to the system of beliefs one carries. Then even in the case of atheists, they will act and react according to their belief in the inexistence of a god. Their atheism will play an active

---

account of economic relationships and historical change." Lovin, *Christian Ethics*, 7, 86, 88.

20. Niebuhr, *Moral Man and Immoral Society*, 113–41.

21. Curran, *Catholic Moral Tradition Today*, 38–39. In his discussion of the problem of sin and the different emphasis placed on the sinful nature of humanity between Protestant and Catholic traditions, Curran expresses his understanding that, at times, the Protestant tradition has overemphasized the depravity of humankind after the fall. In contrast, Catholic thinkers have downplayed its importance and maintained a position of belief in the fundamental goodness of humankind even after the fall.

22. See Boff, *Despertar da Águia*. Boff's latest works have taken up the theme of ecological awareness and engaged the perspective and ethic of relationality and interdependence of all forms of life.

23. Niebuhr, *Responsible Self*, 72.

role in the framework that shapes their worldview and provides elements that inform and help them make their decisions. The Christian will engage others from the perspective of the image of God that is projected over his or her neighbor by the compresence of God in their relationship.

The web of relations comprises a sequence of *trialogues*, not dialogues, because on the horizontal level, every self responds to the other selves around them, but each of them also responds to the reality that transcends their own existence, whether they believe there is a God or not.[24] Isolationism finds no place in this scheme, for even when one chooses not to respond, the denial itself is a response which will impinge on others who will react, in response. In such a context, friendship, love, and justice come hand in hand with one another, and the very nature of the relationship requires that temporal injustices be addressed and corrected, even though we know we will never have perfect balance of justice and perfect happiness for all in our present social order.

The challenge in Niebuhr's theory of the responsiveness of the self is to find the fitting response. Moral decisions are made in time and historical context, which Niebuhr calls time-fullness. Past and present are *compresent* in us when we make decisions and bring together our past, present, and expectations about the future.[25] The resources on which one relies to reach the fitting response spring out of one's personal history as well as from a set of beliefs and culture shared with the community. This means that our responses will derive from our synthesis of those personal and collective memories that inform and form our perception of reality around us. The varying contexts within which one lives in response to others will set the frameworks for relational life, and thus, a different response will fit each relational context. Here we touch again Lovin's notion that the law or rules can structure the moral life, but they cannot live that moral life for us.[26]

---

24. For H. Richard Niebuhr, one should not think of dialogic relationships, but rather, of triangular conversations in which one responds to other-selves horizontally while also responding to the Ultimate Being, or in Augustinian terms, one would be responding to the ultimate good, that is God.

25. In Niebuhr's theory of the responsible self, God is a compresence to whom both the self and the others respond; and God relates to all the creation. There is a compresence of the Ultimate Being everywhere and in everything. When one responds to the other selves, one is doing that as a response to the Ultimate Being also present in that relationship.

26. Lovin, *Christian Ethics*, 57.

FRIENDSHIP, JUSTICE, AND NEIGHBORLINESS

As I see it, context does not refer strictly to space and time. It also involves who the responsible self is as a person. Whether one is a woman or a man, rich or poor, Euro-American, African American, or Brazilian makes important distinctions to one's *Sitz im Leben* and thus to one's responsiveness. Christian love and charity will need to be lived with eyes wide open to temporal dissimilarities.

For that reason, I appreciate the instruments of feminist and womanist reflection. The contributions of feminist and womanist ethical thought bring to light the reality of a multitude of micro histories *compresent* in the fiber of our social tissue. For this reason, it has proven particularly disturbing to realize that sometimes I talk to colleagues from European schools and often am surprised at the Eurocentric views of theology they still espouse. They tend to see theology as one single, monolithic block of thought to be learned, bought, and applied to every context where Christianity has come. The idea of diversity does not sound attractive in that environment; on the contrary, it is understood as a threat to the establishment of mainstream theological thought. I contend that no conscientious theological ethics can be developed devoid of the creative and challenging encounter with diversity found among and within human societies. Any attempt to extend one's ethics as the ultimate answer to all ethical questions would be flawed by its own ethnocentrism.

I do not expect that any pluralistic ethics capable of answering all the questions may ever come out of theo-ethical enquiry. Hence, I appreciate it when Toinette M. Eugene expresses the idea that it is particularity and not universality that will provide the opportunity of being heard, expressing reciprocity and mutuality among womanist, feminist, and mujerista theologians and ethicists; and I would extend the same proposition to other minorities as well.[27] We often find ourselves subdued by the temptation of being the voice of the oppressed, but in fact it takes a hybrid of intellectual pride, academic arrogance, and naïveté for one to see oneself as such. And our academic discussion cannot give a voice to the politically powerless, either. Academic reflection can possibly and hopefully be translated into praxis when we renounce our academic monologue and engage in honest and open dialogue with those in the grassroots of society; then they will have a voice of their own. This is a lesson I believe I can learn from intellectual leaders of the civil rights movement in the USA, like Martin Luther King Jr., and the theologians of liberation in Latin America. As organic intellectuals,

---

27. Eugene et al., *Appropriation and Reciprocity*, 93.

they engaged the causes after being challenged by circumstances and the voices they heard around. Only then did they articulate their responses to those problems by joining and organizing the movements. It all did not spring out, solely, of their studies of dogmatic theology or philosophical ethics, but indeed from their sensitiveness to the movements coming from the basis of societal pyramid, from the questions and struggles that challenged them as they encountered and reflected with their communities of faith. That is what we learn when we read thinkers like Carlos Mesters, Rubem Alves, Ivone Gebara, and José Severino Croatto, just to mention some of the Latin American theologians who managed to translate their experiences of engagement with the people in the grassroots movements into their scholarly production. Of course, questions may be raised as to the efficacy of this form of intellectual engagement. Nevertheless, that represents an effort to produce knowledge that is translatable into the everyday lives of people. Christian ethics is about Christians living in society. One among many other present-day examples of social activism that has its roots in the soil of Christian experience is that of the Harvard scholar Paul Farmer, whose work has been making a difference in people's lives in poverty-stricken areas of Haiti.[28]

It is in this sort of relation that attempts to reflect on the horizontal level of life, as well as the vertical relationship one has with the higher order of goods, God, the Ultimate Being, or whatever other name one may give to the ultimate source of happiness, that Kierkegaard says, "You should let the mouth speak out the abundance of the heart; you should not be ashamed of your feelings and even less of honestly giving each one his due. But one should not love in words and platitudes, and neither should one recognize love by them."[29] Our friendship with God is to be translated into love of neighbors through acts of justice that recognize and grant each one their due.

Christian discipleship is to prepare the followers of Christ to understand that charity, or Christian love, cannot be blind to temporal structures that oppress others. Christians are to witness their faith by letting their faith interact with and change the world around them. Kierkegaard is misinterpreted when he addresses the problem of love of neighbor and temporal dissimilarities.[30] When Kierkegaard says that "Christianity, in contrast, aided by the shortcut of eternity, is immediately at the goal: it allows all the dissimilarities to stand but teaches the equality of eternity. It teaches that

---

28. See Farmer, *Pathologies of Power*.
29. Kierkegaard, *Works of Love*, 12.
30. Kierkegaard, *Works of Love*, 77–78.

everyone is to *lift himself up above* earthly dissimilarity,"[31] Kierkegaard is thinking of a sort of equality that surpasses all temporal and earthly dissimilarities, not because he takes the assumption that dissimilarities and injustices are unimportant, but rather because Christian charity and love of neighbor are to be extended to all human beings, or yet, as H. Richard Niebuhr would say, our attitudes of neighborliness are to reach out to the entire created world as participants in the compresence of God.

PREFERENTIAL OPTION FOR THE POOR AND CHRISTIAN LOVE OF NEIGHBOR

Inspired by the Niebuhr brothers' thought and in conversation with the historical tradition of Christian reflection on friendship, love, and justice, I understand that our Christian friendship with God compels us to act out of love on behalf of fellow human beings as a response to God's grace acting in us through the presence of the Holy Spirit. Our potential for happiness, even if imperfect, can only be realized in our encounters with others.

> Love's hidden life is in the innermost being, unfathomable, and then in turn is in an unfathomable connectedness with all existence. Just as the quiet lake originates deep down in hidden springs no eye has seen, so also does a person's love originate even more deeply in God's love. If there were no gushing spring at the bottom, if God were not love, then there would be neither the little lake nor a human being's love.[32]

One of the basic conceptions in H. Richard Niebuhr's ethical thought is the idea of response or responsibility as a movement of the being in reaction to its interpretation of the causes of suffering. Suffering is defined by Niebuhr as the frustration of our movements toward self-realization or toward the actualization of our potentialities. As the focus of my present analysis is the concrete reality of poverty, I will take the assumption that poverty is a social barrier which impedes the movement of millions of people toward the realization of their potentialities, thus causing suffering. As I see it, poverty is not a natural phenomenon that impinges on people's lives regardless of our decisions and actions, rather it is the result of the model of society we have created, it is a consequence of the way we respond to the reality that surrounds us. When one realizes the compresent nature of the ultimate Being in all our actions and relations, one will understand this statement

---

31. Kierkegaard, *Works of Love*, 72.
32. Kierkegaard, *Works of Love*, 9–10.

of H. Richard Niebuhr: "Responsibility affirms: God is acting in all actions upon you. So, respond to all actions upon you as to respond to his action."[33] This idea reminds me of one of Jesus' statements about solidarity:

> For I was hungry and you gave me something to eat, I was thirsty and you gave me something to drink, I was a stranger and you invited me in, I needed clothes and you clothed me, I was sick and you looked after me, I was in prison and you came to visit me. Then the righteous will answer him, "Lord, when did we see you hungry and feed you, or thirsty and give you something to drink? When did we see you a stranger and invite you in, or needing clothes and clothe you? When did we see you sick or in prison and go to visit you?" The King will reply, "I tell you the truth, whatever you did for one of the least of these brothers of mine, you did for me." (Matt 25:35–40 NIV)

Reflecting on poverty from the perspective of Niebuhr's theory of responsibility will require that one considers the notion of solidarity and assume that this is exactly what Jesus meant when he affirmed that our actions to others are, in fact, actions toward him. As Christians understand Jesus as the incarnation of God's Word, as Godself coming into the world and living the life of an ordinary human who was liable to the same suffering as any other human being, then this means that as Christians, we must look into our relations with fellow humans and also with the rest of creation in light of the compresence of God. The Christian response to whatever happens in the interim of their existence in time and space is a response to the action and compresence of Godself.

Considering this, I contend that the moral agency of the church cannot be limited to the preaching of the message of salvation in Jesus Christ, while millions of lives are lost to the power of human created structures of oppression such as poverty. I understand that in a country like Brazil, where data from the survey of social indicators released by the Instituto Brasileiro de Geografia e Estatística[34] showed that, despite the improvement in housing and better sewage systems, infant mortality rate in one of the northeastern poorest states was still at 51.9 percent, as compared to the state of Rio Grande do Sul which had a much lower infant mortality rate of 13.9 percent, the church of Christ needs to understand that their mission of

---

33. Niebuhr, *Responsible Self*, 126.

34. The Instituto Brasileiro de Geografia e Estatística (IBGE) is Brazil's official agency for social statistics. They are the institution in charge of periodic demographic census.

spreading the good news of the gospel requires a more effective ministry in promoting social justice.[35]

From the standpoint of Niebuhr's theory of responsibility, Christian moral agency must be exercised first by asking the question "What is going on?" to perceive God's action in the world around us. The Christian community needs to address the problems of human life while trying to find the fitting response to how the Supreme Being is acting in a certain situation. Of course, the answers different communities of believers will find in their geographical and historical locations will vary; however, it does not mean that communal responses affirm an absolute relativism. On the contrary, the answers will vary because the One beyond the many is placed as the value center of the Christian moral agency. Responses are relative to God; and Godself is the only absolute.

Christian responsibility comes together with the notion of accountability. Rather than understanding accountability from the more commonly opted via of legal interpretation, H. Richard Niebuhr proposes a more complex definition of accountability in his ethical reflection. For Niebuhr accountability is like a dialogue. One will be accountable for an action not in terms of whether that action is right or wrong. At this point, I find it necessary to highlight that Niebuhr's suggestion to the moral agent is not "What is my end?" or "What is my ultimate law?" Niebuhr's question intends to clarify how God is acting so that the agent's response may be fitting to God's own actions. Probably the best word to describe the sort of relation and exchange which is going on in our responses to God and the world around us is not dialogue. Indeed, it is a triangular conversation in which an "I" responds to the actions and reactions of a "Thou," while both "I" and "Thou" respond and react to the actions of the Supreme Being. H. Richard Niebuhr presents this conversation as a continuous discourse in which none of the parties involved are mere listeners or spectators. I personally understand that all the parties are actively embedded in the chain of actions and responses, and there is no moment in which the parties take turns. This is a continuous and often unconscious process. For this reason, I appreciate the idea of social solidarity which Niebuhr defines as a relationship that implies a relative continuity and consistency in the scheme of interpretations of what the self responds to. He suggests that this continuous discourse follows the pattern of "an agent's action as response to an action upon him in accordance with his interpretation of the latter action and with his expectation

---

35. IBGE, *Síntese de Indicadores Sociais*, 23.

of response to his response; and all of this is in a continuing community of agents."³⁶

It is within this community of agents that individual Christians and churches are called to act as responsible and accountable agents. I assert the idea that in such a complex and intricate setting no one can stand on neutral ground, for trying to remain neutral means to choose omission or inaction. Opting for inaction is already an action that involves reflection and decision. Thus no one can escape the responsibility and accountability that entangles all the different beings in human society and the rest of the created world in which humanity is embedded. This is why ecofeminist thinker Ivone Gebara states that "relatedness can open us up to a dimension of justice in which the life of other beings is essential to the living out of human justice. Ecojustice is the kind of justice we seek and live out when we affirm our bodies as part of the Sacred Body of the universe."³⁷

H. Richard Niebuhr's idea of responsibility, accountability, and social solidarity, along with Reinhold Niebuhr's understanding of the human incapacity to reach perfect justice due to our tendency to search for self-interest, put in dialogue with the ecofeminist quest for a holistic justice within and among the different beings in creation can all contribute to the development of human understanding and justice. These varying views need not be brought together to make a uniform block of thought, but they may inform our desire and action toward the recreation of a more harmonious world. One may wonder where I intend to lead the reader as I place the problem of poverty within the sphere of moral action of the church, and when I further put all of this in the context of an extended family of creation. My response to such a question would be that I understand poverty to be the upshot of an array of factors which cannot be understood in isolation. I propose that the moral agency of the Christian church must take a more comprehensive approach to their quest for social justice and to the realization of human potential. In this context, human potentialities cannot reach their completeness while nature and other disenfranchised human beings do not have their value recognized. This recognition cannot take place unless our relations with nature and the peoples of the world mirror the compresent nature of God in and through our actions. Yet, poverty is not a problem to be solved by politicians only, but rather it demands to be fully embraced as a moral problem that confronts and challenges the Christian church. I understand that the church of Christ was sent out into the world to become an active witness for the flourishing of life. I know that the previously mentioned

---

36. Niebuhr, *Responsible Self*, 65.
37. Gebara, *Longing for Running Water*, 87.

carries a load of utopianism, but I also am aware of the power of utopia and a certain sort of conscientious illusion to foster change, even if imperfect.

BIBLIOGRAPHY

Aquinas, Thomas. "Summa Theologica: Secunda Secundae Partis." Accessed November 5, 2007. https://www.newadvent.org/summa/3.htm.

Aristotle. *Nicomachean Ethics*. Translated by Terence Irwin. 2nd ed. Indianapolis: Hackett, 1985.

Augustine. *Confessions*. Translated by Henry Chadwick. Oxford World's Classics. Oxford: Oxford University Press, 1992.

Boff, Leonardo. *O Despertar da Águia: o Diabólico e o Simbólico na Construção da Realidade*. Petropolis: Vozes, 1998.

Carmichael, Liz. *Friendship: Interpreting Christian Love*. London: T&T Clark, 2004.

Curran, Charles E. *The Catholic Moral Tradition Today: A Synthesis*. Moral Traditions and Moral Arguments. Washington, DC: Georgetown University Press, 1999.

Eugene, Toinette M., et al. "Appropriation and Reciprocity in Womanist/Mujerista/Feminist Work." In *Feminist Theological Ethics: A Reader*, edited by Lois K. Daly, 88–117. Library of Theological Ethics. Louisville, KY: Westminster John Knox, 1994.

Farmer, Paul. *Pathologies of Power: Health, Human Rights, and the New War on the Poor*. California Series in Public Anthropology 4. Berkeley: University of California Press, 2004.

Gebara, Ivone. *Longing for Running Water: Ecofeminism and Liberation*. Minneapolis: Fortress, 1999.

Instituto Brasileiro de Geografia e Estatística (IBGE). *Síntese de Indicadores Sociais: Uma Análise Das Condições de Vida Da População Brasileira*. Rio de Janeiro: IBGE, 2007.

Kierkegaard, Søren. *Works of Love*. Vol. 16. Princeton: Princeton University Press, 1995.

Lovin, Robin W. *Christian Ethics: An Essential Guide*. Nashville: Abingdon, 2000.

Niebuhr, H. Richard. *The Responsible Self: An Essay in Christian Moral Philosophy*. Louisville, KY: Westminster John Knox, 1999.

Niebuhr, Reinhold. *Moral Man and Immoral Society: A Study in Ethics and Politics*. Louisville, KY: Westminster John Knox, 2021.

Plato. *Symposium*. Translated with introduction and notes by Alexander Nehamas and Paul Woodruff. Indianapolis: Hackett, 1989.

Wadell, Paul J. *Happiness and the Christian Moral Life: An Introduction to Christian Ethics*. 3rd ed. New York: Rowman & Littlefield, 2016.

Chapter 9

A Tribute to Peter Paris
Colleague, Teacher, Academic Statesman, Friend

Max Lynn Stackhouse

I FIRST BEGAN THIS essay as an attempt to offer critical reflections on some of the ways that the sacred texts and theological traditions of the world religions, including Christianity, have dealt with the fact that all large, complex civilizations tend to have within them minority populations who are identified by their membership in distinctive tribal, racial, national, religious, or ethnic groups as well as by their participation in the dominant society. Everyone comes from a distinct or specifically blended background. Yet, many are forced into it, and some seek to identify themselves and others as if their essential humanity and character were decisively given by that particular gene pool and as if these are fixed, timeless and definitive of identity. Profound studies of the last century, however, have established that such groups are developed over time by historical processes of political, cultural, military, and economic forces that are lived out in various social patterns, which are deeply influenced and legitimated by religious worldviews and narratives that may promote tolerance, pluralism, and accommodation for many, or they may foster intolerance, discrimination, or oppression of the minorities. These baptized forces tend to foster beliefs about the capabilities and character of persons and whole peoples, reinforcing the ever-present temptations to the arrogance of some and the self-doubt of others. The evidence, however, convincingly suggests that these groups are more like each other than they are different from each other, and when the differences are taken too seriously, they tend to reify prejudicial images and the social status of these groups, locking people into subservient roles that they are to play in the political economy. This conspiracy of social forces and ideological beliefs about heredity makes a great deal of difference as to how the relationships between those groups are structured and, thus how individuals view themselves as a member of this or that group or combination of groups, and why they are treated by others within the groups and, even more, by outsiders, in stereotyped ways. This dynamic bears in it the possibility of offering ready-made identities in the complex network of identities in pluralistic civilizations, but it simultaneously threatens to dehumanize persons in that it often saddles individuals with an identity that confines and distorts personhood and throttles the sense of freedom to make choices. It recognizes only a fragment of the person, and it loads this fragment with some mythos of meanings and limits the roles and relations, resources and rewards that such persons could have as a part of genuinely inclusive overarching civil ethos sustained by a truly universalistic religion. The issues that derive from such phenomena are critical and vast, as Peter J. Paris has recognized in his life and work. They have often shaped systems that are wrong, unjust, and not fair. But he has also argued that these dynamics can be modulated, if not entirely overcome, in the life of a person and at least partially rectified by movements for social change.

Out of his faith, experience, and study of significant movements for such change, he became intellectually and existentially engaged in constructing a compelling kind of "advocacy scholarship," one that promises to mitigate the pathological effects of this gene-pool tyranny that not only threatens to fracture the integrity of a person's identity, it also corrupts efforts to form and maintain an inclusive and equitable community grounded in a common ethic. To expose the effects of this evil and chart the prospects for more justice, he has sought to identify the religious, intellectual, social, cultural, and political-economic conditions for a post-apartheid, post-racist, post-segregationist community for an era in which all such particularities have to be seen in a broader perspective. It has been his life's work as well as a personal struggle. Rather than trying to forget particularity or to ignore race in the name of an idea of general humanity, he has focused on contributions of those persons and movements that have challenged the pathological traditions of racism and identified those themes, motifs, structures, and cultural dynamics that have challenged their civilizational pathologies. He has provided evidence that an ethic that acknowledges that the particular backgrounds of people can nearly always also find within them universal elements that foster the spiritual and material well-being of those belonging to divergent groups and inspire all who come in contact with them to join the struggle for an inclusive vision of freedom and justice in an increasingly global context. In brief, he explores various particular traditions, celebrates where they have rendered a desire to reach beyond themselves, and embraces those exemplary elements that bear the prospect of universal meaning and functional fruitfulness.

However, writing about this on an abstract level could obscure what he has convincingly shown in numerous publications. He knows that what differences there are between persons and groups cannot be attributed to "blood" or any other immutable genetic determinants or to any ontological deficit, but to particular social histories and cultural adaptations, as these are deeply shaped by religio-ethical influences—which are all malleable. Thus, the stereotypes by which people interpret their own and other people's characteristics are not archetypes but are projections formed by socio-cultural constructions and theological and moral teachings and, as such, are subject to change. In this, he is more Aristotelian than Platonic. That is, he is more concrete in his thinking than theoretical, more empirically indicative than normatively prescriptive, and more fascinated by the instructive power of descriptive analysis of particular historical developments that bear on or exemplify shared values than by the offerings of grand theory that can allegedly illumine the whole. In this regard, there seem to be a number of golden threads that run through his life and work, elemental themes that he discerns in the movements that challenge aspects of modern culture that derive from the disruptions of African traditions but which could contribute to modern complex civilization and to the formation of a more just global civil society.

Heaven knows that historic and contemporary movements to overcome the humanly damaging results of racism and stereotyping, especially as manifest in slavery, segregation and social discrimination, and the pathological effects of the psychological damage they have done, are heroic, even if they have not accomplished all that they attempted. However, Peter is aware that the damage is not indelible or permanent; it can be remedied and corrected. He knows that significant gains have been made and the gains have made a difference. At least they prove that changing the images people have about their own or other people's characteristics can bring changes in the whole social fabric and to the human psyche, especially if they are reinforced by a vibrant, articulate public witness rooted in a publicly accessible set of symbols that touches on the particulars of the cultural and social history of experience and envisions the realization of human rights, legal equality, inclusive diversity, and active coalitions. These factors are what

Peter has taught, written about, and fought for in his personal, academic, and ecclesiastical life for more than half a century.

Although I had met him earlier, I became better acquainted with Peter Paris at a gathering of younger professors of Christian theology and social ethics who came together in the early 1970s at Vanderbilt University Divinity School for a two-day consultation on the continuing impact of the German liberal theologian and historian of social ethics Ernst Troeltsch. His *The Social Teaching of the Christian Churches* had become the standard launching pad for the study of Protestant theological ethics in relation to social changes in the modern world, and the question was how we could move the church and society beyond the boundaries of that monumental effort. We were all put up for the night in the homes of various professors. I was assigned to Peter and was hosted by him and his wife, Shirley, a schoolteacher, gracious hostess, and engaged dialogue partner. We tended to agree with points made in discussion by several members of the young professorial group, such as the importance of a cultivated leadership and the indispensability of "periodization" and "typological analysis" as tools of social-historical understanding. We also agreed that ethics can become legalistic or moralistic if this does not include an analysis of the ethos in which problems occur and does not sort out and evaluate the ethical principles and purposes that are honored or violated in the ethical context. We agreed that ethics becomes abstract to the point of irrelevance if we do not have a sense of where we are in the timeline of its social development and if we do not identify and functionally evaluate the competing ideal values that underlie the responses of various parties and observers as they organize their responses to the problematic situations that need ethical attention. Then there is little chance of challenging vice or enhancing personal virtue or social righteousness.

In this connection, I vividly remember his judgment that Troeltsch needed to be supplemented by a study of the controversies, leaders, and contributions of the "Black churches" since the struggles of the Black churches against racism were the defining social ethical issue of this period. While the Black churches remained theologically within the larger family of the Christian traditions, they were formed because the church at large was ignoring the central moral and spiritual crisis of society in the twentieth century, namely the pathologies of racism. It is as if the main streams of the church had learned little about the crisis of race signaled by the Jim Crow segregation after the Civil War, by the anti-Semitism which was not overcome by the defeat of Hitler, the persistence of caste, which was not resolved by the independence of India from the British, or by the battles over apartheid in South Africa. In this regard, he argued that the Black churches have no other defining purpose than to raise and address this problem in all its settings. That observation was an early indication of what could be called the charter of his scholarly work. He later wrote several independent but related volumes that accented this theme. One was his *Black Religious Leaders in Conflict: Joseph H. Jackson, Martin Luther King, Jr., Malcolm X, Adam Clayton Powell*, which he published in 1978 and which signaled his recognition of the importance of religiously motivated ethical leadership in church and society if this crisis was to be confronted. This cluster of prominent religious and political leaders, all racial justice advocates, did not agree with each other on theological issues or, in fact, on how best to address the racist circumstances they faced, but they all represented the prophetic demand for social reform in the face of racial injustice. Another major study was *The Social Teaching of the Black Churches*, an analysis of the public stances of the various Black denominations on ethnic and racial issues, which he published in 1985 and which stressed the necessity of a community of commitment that could lend grounded institutional support for ethical change and develop articulate definitions of the problems and appropriate channels of action for the general public. He extended his research and writing on these themes in other lectures and books, including the revised *Black Religious Leaders: Conflict in Unity*, published in 1991. In all, he identified the distinctive vocation of Black Christianity as offering a prophetic word to societies that have been deeply distorted, positively sinful, and in desperate need of moral and spiritual, and thus social, reconstruction. He sought common ground on which Black leaders could stand so that they could identify some common policies. All other disputes between these figures and institutions were incidental.

 These scholarly works were not the only area in which he became a leader. I became better acquainted with him as a result of his active participation in professional organizations. Especially important were the Society of Christian Ethics, the Society for Values in Higher Education, the American Academy of Religion, and, later, the American Theological Society in the 1970s, 1980s, and 1990s. We served on various committees and held various offices in these associations. We were also both veterans of Martin Luther King's movement of the 1960s and had gained exposure to other cultures—he mostly in Africa as the "traveling secretary" of the Christian Student Movement in Nigeria and, more generally, in West Africa. I had been in India and Southeast Asia as a visiting professor at the United Theological College in Bangalore, and representative of the United Church Board for World Ministries, and coordinator of the American Committee for Indian Christian Higher Education—which gave us an international perspective on our work while teaching in seminaries in the States and abroad. Then, in the last decade of the twentieth century and the first decade of the new century, we had the chance to deepen our collaboration and friendship as colleagues at Princeton Theological Seminary.

Through these years of interaction, I saw another side of Peter's leadership. His natural gregariousness commended him to people, his constant smile and engaging humor attracted conviviality, but, more importantly, he had the ability to guide discussions of agenda, to suggest themes for annual or regional meetings, to identify promising speakers and to draw attention to quality scholarship neglected by others. This meant that he quickly became a leader in the scholarly guilds. He was thus able to get concerted attention to the issues of race in academia and to be turned to when there were debates about whom to invite to run for office, deliver the main addresses, serve on the nominating committees, and establish panels or research teams to address issues of injustice. In short, given the dynamics of the times, his issues were widely appreciated by a sizeable number of intellectual leaders of the post-World War II working scholars. Moreover, his mastery of the literature regarding racism, ethnicity, and social justice, especially as produced by Black leaders of thought, meant he was asked to recommend promising figures to search committees in ecclesiastical and academic institutions.

On the basis of these aspects of Peter's life that I knew something about, I decided to find out whether I could trace any of the golden threads that appear in his writings as well as when one thinks about his life and the issues with which he struggled personally. But there is no published biography or autobiography. I have encouraged him to write one. In the meantime, I have interviewed his charming second wife, Adrienne, whom he married after Shirley's untimely death from cancer. I also reviewed many of his writings and interviewed colleagues and former students.[1] Those who have worked with Peter were impressed by the care with which he composes his thought, the reach of resources from which he draws his ideas, and the interpretive integrity with which he develops his advocacy scholarship. I began to wonder how closely the experiences of his life were tied to his scholarly focus and activist impulses.

I turned thus to ethicist Lois Livesey who, with her husband, Lowell, now also deceased, were scholars and close friends of Peter and of his first wife, Shirley, since their graduate student days at the University of Chicago Divinity School and became friends with Adrienne later on. She agreed to

---

1. My special thanks to Cleophus LaRue Jr., a colleague and friend at Princeton Seminary. Also, to Victor Anderson, a former student and friend now teaching at Vanderbilt, and Wilmot Allen, a recent graduate now doing advanced study at American University.

help compose and edit this effort to give a glimpse of his life and pay tribute to his accomplishments. All those in the close network of his adult life loved him deeply and were willing to share anecdotes about him.

How can we portray the measure of this man in a personal way? He is not tall in stature, but he has a big presence. His trim 5'7" or so exudes an energy, a quickness of mind and motion. When he walks or talks he conveys an unobtrusive sense of confident authority and a seriousness of purpose—all well mixed with graciousness and good humor conveyed by his usual contagious smile that invites trust and engaged dialogue. I learned that he was a runner in his youth—a 100- and 220-yard "dash man" as a young athlete, undefeated in varsity meets. He also played some hockey, but his other varsity activity was the school debate team. He learned how to argue without being abrasive. He still moves and thinks with energy and maintains a schedule at a pace that would exhaust those of us who were born in the 1930s or even several decades later. It is easy to imagine that he as victor would turn to greet and graciously celebrate the effort and contribution of his competitors and teammates. For most of his life, he has been involved in group activities that invite both the development of team spirit and disciplined participation and concentrated exertion for individual achievement and excellence, which enhances the flourishing of all. That seems to have been true in his academic, church, and civic activities.

After Shirley's death, he founded a "Young Achievers" organization for underprivileged youth in her honor. This voluntary association offers the youth of Trenton, New Jersey, opportunities to discover and exercise talents that would otherwise be undeveloped and to work, indeed, to become active in entrepreneurial ventures in areas that are profitable, cooperative, and mutually encouraging. And it is borne out in the topics he takes up in writing and teaching as he traced the contributions that the peoples of African descent have made to religious, ethical, and social life, even in the face of historical forces and political ideologies that have sought to block such efforts. It also seems true of his efforts to establish and encourage excellence and virtue in his students, who can further implement an egalitarian community and just commonwealth. He started with those aspects of communal life that manifest talent, conviction, and resolve and moved relentlessly toward challenging leadership to accent those features of the culture that can be strengthened and alter the debilitating aspects of the social ethos.

I had a conversation with Peter when I was writing this tribute and I asked him some questions about his background that are not clear from printed records. What follows is my brief summary of what he said and what I have gleaned elsewhere. It seems likely that the experience of his forebears influenced this preoccupation before he knew of it consciously. He was born in Nova Scotia during the Depression, a child of parents who were themselves heirs of those waves of US slaves and freedmen who migrated to Canada during the American War of Independence. British officers had issued a proclamation stating that any slave who joined the British side would be granted freedom and land. Led by the Black Baptist preacher David George, from Savannah, Georgia, some two thousand Blacks accepted the invitation over a period of several years and were settled in and around Birch Town, in eastern Nova Scotia. Others were slaves who were taken to Canada as part of the households of white royalists, only later gaining their freedom when slavery was outlawed in the British Empire. Conditions were harsh and promises to help to get to the frontier towns developed were slow in being fulfilled. However, it is known that some of the settlers petitioned the government for relief. The records are inadequate, and the details of Peter's earlier ancestral family are lost. But some details of his later forebears are known. Some moved to New Glasgow and joined the working class of that city in 1900, and his grandparents were among those who began to record their history. In other words, Peter's farmer, worker, and craftsmen forebears were not only a product of forced migration from various parts of West Africa on slave ships to the New World, they were part of a voluntary set of migrations from "a state side" to the north in the 1770s, and later into the industrializing cities well before the underground railroad, the abolition of slavery in the British colonies (1834) or emancipation in the USA at the end of the US Civil War (1865), or the famous migration from the southern states of the USA to the northern industrial cities after World War II. Those options seemed better than what the new United States offered at the time, even if the promises were less generously fulfilled and opportune than they sounded at first. These "Canadian Blacks," as they are sometimes called still, experienced an exodus and the formation of new communities under the protection of the Crown.

These new Canadians gained support from each other and from one other source that influenced their collective status in Canada and Peter's personal development. Baptist ministers took up the cause of the migrants early and petitioned the British government for relief from the harsh conditions they faced. They also gave a sense of mission to a subject people. That prompted an offer by the British to relocate them and to establish a colony of "free Negroes" in Sierra Leone, and some twelve hundred of the Canadian Blacks accepted the opportunity to go to Freetown, motivated not only by a desire for a better life but by a missionary zeal to bring the gospel to those Africans who did not know Christ.

Peter's ancestors did not get word of the departure and missed the choice of whether to leave this continent. Still, the Baptist church leaders and especially parents such as Peter's mother encouraged those who remained behind to seek out opportunities for education, and Peter's mother became one of the most energetic advocates of preparing for the future and encouraged her young ones to get the most out of their educational opportunities. She is quoted as saying what generations of mothers have had to say as they moved into a more integrated society: "You do not only have to do good work, you have to do better than most."

Peter's father was a steelworker and a good provider while his mother managed the household. By the time Peter, the eldest of ten children, came along, scholarship aid plus the sacrifices of their parents made it possible for them to go to college or to get training for a solid profession. Racist discrimination was not legally sanctioned in Canada. Still, prejudicial cultural practice was alive and well in those early days and approved by both a highly stratified royal political order and legitimated by traditionally hierarchical Anglo-Catholic social theory. This reinforced the appreciation for the Free Church traditions that had emerged in grassroots Protestantism in the New World, particularly among the Black populations. Still, the idea of a return to Africa became part of the lore and could be seen as the first sign of what later became known as the Afro-Centric streak in the Black Christian theological development of some later theologians.[2] Thus, when Peter was later to return to Africa in several roles, it seems plausible to speculate that he could draw from the legacy of these precedents and insights to feed the religious and social struggles and developments in North America and abroad.[3] This is a story carrying overtones, not unlike those immigrant Hebrews who had sought relief from their suffering by following Joseph into Egypt and Moses out of it, empowered by the fact that they knew that they had another homeland that may require a new exodus and a new covenant beyond the enslavements of history's pharaohs and the captivities of its Babylons to which they were to be witnesses to the world's peoples.

Many of the Canadian Blacks stayed in Canada, however, and fought by persuasion for the granting of their rights through the channels of civil society, particularly through that mother of a free civil order, the independent (non-state-established) church. They formed the African United Association of the Atlantic Baptist Convention, Canada—an officially integrated body that gave recognition and legitimacy to an ethnic minority that wished to be in communion with the dominant body of believers. Still, in both the academic and church circles of Nova Scotia, a residual regard for a natural

---

2. See Paris, "Comparing the Public Theologies of James H. Cone and Martin Luther King," 218–31.

3. Paris, "Spirituality of African Peoples," 294–307.

aristocracy may have influenced Peter's inner drive to foster leaders of the talented. They would proudly affirm their African roots but refuse to be defined by race. Instead, priority was put on talent, effort, and integrity of character, which was becoming a part of the ethos that surely enveloped Peter's forebears and thus an early influence.

By the time of his secondary school education, he was exhibiting qualities that challenged the type-casting that still confined the Black minority. In the eleventh grade he entered an oratory contest, and won the prize—an event that was heralded in the newspapers as the first Black to achieve such an honor. His inspiring title was "Victorious Living." He went on to become a valedictorian of his class at the New Glasgow High School. He was admitted to Acadia University where he completed his BA and then his divinity degree with honors in 1958.

While still a student, he became involved in the first "Crossroads Africa" exchange, which took him to Nigeria in 1958, an exposure that served him well when he became more deeply involved in the Student Christian Movement (SCM), the historic ecumenical Christian movement paralleling the YMCA in ministering to Christian youth and cultivating leaders for Christian missions, church leadership, and ecumenical cooperation, all the while seeking to nurture the individual's abilities and foster international peace and social justice. He was quickly identified as a natural leader and was elected general secretary of the SCM, allowing him to attend national conferences. Indeed, when he was ordained, he was not installed as a local church pastor, as was usual for new clergy, but was called to be the general secretary of the SCM at the University of Alberta. These experiences shaped his later life in several ways. One of them is that he met Shirley, an SCM leader in Western Canada, a talented and beautiful young woman with international interests, having spent her junior year abroad in India. She became his wife in 1961 and the mother of their three children. He has an affection for his native Canada born of these experiences, and he has kept in contact with the church into which he was ordained in 1959, the university that later also awarded him an honorary doctorate, and, of course, his relatives who were proud of him and celebrated his achievements.

The next step in his career was accepting a call to become the SCM "traveling secretary" in Nigeria. So, he and his new wife moved to Africa, where he was the international representative of the SCM ministries in Nigeria, serving that ecumenical organization by visiting the chapters of the organization in the various high schools and at the two colleges and coordinating national and regional events which linked the Nigerian membership to the world federation. He held the position from 1961 to 1964. That experience and the enduring friendships he and Shirley formed engendered an abiding affection for Africa, which became a second psychological home, not least because their first child was born there.

At the end of his tour of duty, he began his advanced studies at the University of Chicago Divinity School, where he completed a PhD, giving him, as it were, a third center of identity and achievement—American academia. As he completed his doctorate, he began teaching at the Urban Studies Program of the Associated Colleges of the Mid-West in Chicago. This was during the time when "urban renewal" and "community organization" became the focus of social work, especially in the "second city" where Saul Alinsky's *Reveille for Radicals* was at the heights of its influence and Jesse Jackson, an intermittent classmate, was building his local support for what became his Rainbow Coalition. Peter, however, wanted to teach and write, so when he was invited to join the faculty at the Howard University School of Divinity in Washington, DC, one of the leading Black seminaries in the country, he accepted the invitation. He learned much about the American Black church and Southern culture, only to find out that the teaching demands on the faculty were so heavy that the opportunities for scholarly research and writing were limited. Thus, Peter accepted an appointment to Vanderbilt University Divinity School, the "Harvard of the South," one term relating to its high standards and the other relating to its dominant culture, which was still decidedly segregated. There had been an ongoing conflict there about the admission of Black students and the appointment of Black professors. Several of the leading professors resigned in protest of the discriminatory policies and called for full integration. The school had modified its policy when Peter arrived as one of the "new faces." It became a reconciling force due to his competence as an ethicist about these issues, his uncompromising resolve to support the moves that had integrated the institution, and his collegial way of working to bring about changes of attitude and culture.

During his time there, 1972–85, he also saw the rise of new issues about the role of women in the student body, in the pulpit, and on the faculty, and he eagerly joined the parallel debate. Although relatively new to the faculty and not yet tenured, Peter became one of the strongest faculty voices in the dispute—again calling for integration, this time arguing that neither race nor gender ought to be seen as a criterion for student or faculty exclusion on theological, ethical, philosophical, and biblical grounds. One can see the impact that these controversies had on Peter; and the impact he had on Vanderbilt in his essay "The African American Presence in the Divinity School."[4]

---

4. Paris, "African American Presence in the Divinity School," 234–51.

It is during these years he became a naturalized citizen and began to publish in learned journals and to compose essays that led to his early books. The focus of his research and writing was an extension of what he taught and preached. Clearly he was attempting to show that the study of the Black religious experience not only aided Black communities as they tried to face the crises that they confronted, it fostered a deeper understanding of the whole church's message for human well-being and salvation. It also empowered the Black church to join with the majority population, especially the mainline churches and the Academy, in reshaping the future of society in an ever-expanding quest for justice.

Teaching at Vanderbilt also allowed him to teach doctoral students and to direct dissertations, thus influencing the future of scholarly research—an opportunity that was expanded when he moved to Princeton. As might be expected, he attracted both African American and sympathetic white students who were interested in understanding the dynamics of racism (or similar forms of discrimination, such as sexism or classism) and in aiding the cause of justice in various areas of church, education, and society. As I saw later when we worked together at Princeton Seminary, he developed a couple of distinctive styles when directing their dissertations. He first inquired of the students as to what it was that they wanted to say. That is, he presumed that those who had come to that level of advanced learning knew the basic contours of the relevant disciplines and knew what the leading public and scholarly opinions on the major questions were. His question to the students was, "What do you want to offer to the world in this project?" He wanted to cultivate the sense that each young scholar had a contribution to make, something that he or she was called to advance. Thus, the candidate's first job was to identify and define what that was. Then came the hard intellectual work of crafting a hypothesis able to make a difference, one that could be supported by argument and evidence. Clarity on the hypothesis was critical, for most theses were based on a hypothesis that entailed a number of sub-hypotheses, and the failure to make the case for one of the legs of the main hypothesis could weaken the whole. Here, of course, the student would have to learn to consider possible objections, countervailing evidence, alternative perspectives, and resistances caused by convention, ignorance, or prejudice. Further, Peter exemplified and recommended a non-direct confrontation with opponents wherever possible. He did not compromise on the principles that he held but would seek to find a way of putting forth the arguments for them that allowed room for another way of looking at the reality at hand, one that could make the opponent willing to enter into a dialogue that might render the discovery of common ground. In short, he was developing a kind of advocacy scholarship that had a place for reconciliation. I take it that this was an intellectual correlate to the active nonviolence advocated by the two figures that emerged as his most honored heroes, Martin Luther King Jr. and Nelson Mandela.[5] It also comported with his non-absolutist and non-dogmatic vegetarianism—or, better, "fishetarianism."[6]

During his time since leaving Vanderbilt for Princeton Theological Seminary in 1985, to become the Elmer G. Homrighausen Professor of Christian Social Ethics, his leadership in academia has become more visible in still another way. He became a leader among the professors of religious studies more generally. This was true at Princeton, as I began to notice it at my first faculty meeting. When he spoke everyone listened intently. And he was honored by being elected as president of the Society of Christian Ethics (1991), the American Academy of Religion (1994), and the Society for the Study of Black Religion (2001).

BIBLIOGRAPHY

Paris, Peter J. "The African American Presence in the Divinity School." In *Vanderbilt Divinity School: Education, Contest and Change*, edited by Dale A. Johnson, 234–51. Nashville: Vanderbilt University Press, 2001.

———. "Comparing the Public Theologies of James H. Cone and Martin Luther King." In *Black Faith and Public Talk: Critical Essays on James H. Cone's Black Theology and Black Power*, edited by Dwight N. Hopkins, 218–31. Waco: Baylor University Press, 1991.

———. "Moral Exemplars in Global Community." In *God and Globalization*, edited by Max Stackhouse and Don Browning, 2:191–220. The Spirit and the Modern Authorities. Harrisburg, PA: Trinity Press International, 2001.

———. "The Spirituality of African Peoples." *Dalhousie Review* 73.3 (1993) 294–307.

---

5. Paris, "Moral Exemplars in Global Community," 191–220.

6. Prof. Paris does not eat meat but only fish.

Chapter 10

Interview with Peter Paris
Roots and Routes of an African American Scholar

Nimi Wariboko

INTRODUCTION

I conducted this interview in 2022 with Professor Peter Paris to explore his early experiences in Nigeria. After graduating from seminary, he visited Nigeria twice to serve the Student Christian Movement. His visits to Nigeria greatly influenced what he later became both as man and as scholar. This interview reveals key information about Paris that would help in the interpretation of his social ethics and theology. In 2011, I devoted an essay ("Evasion Ethics: Peter Paris Feels the Spirituals") to the interpretation of his lifelong scholarship.[1] This interview, coming more than ten years after the publication of that essay, offers glimpses to his life and era that are not accessible in his published work.

In your twenties you went to Nigeria for the first time. How did this happen?

I graduated from Acadia University School of Theology (Wolfville, Nova Scotia) with my BD (MDiv) degree in May 1958. I had accepted the position

---

1. Wariboko, "Evasion of Ethics," 215–34.

of general secretary for the Student Christian Movement (SCM) at the University of Alberta, Edmonton, beginning in September of that year. There is a bit of history behind how I came to work for the SCM.

In the summer of 1957, I directed an SCM summer study-work camp in Hamilton, Ontario, with a co-director named James Breeden, who was pursuing BD studies at Union Theological Seminary in New York City. As an undergraduate at Dartmouth College in New Hampshire, he had been active in the University Christian Movement in the United States, which, like the SCM of Canada, was affiliated with the World's Student Christian Federation with its headquarters in Geneva. Jim told me about the prospective program founded and directed by Rev. James Robinson, founder of the Church of the Master, in 1938 on Morningside Avenue in Harlem, New York City, and, later, the Operation Crossroads Africa program, which became operational in 1958. He had created a number of innovative youth and community programs in Harlem. He was a graduate of the Black Lincoln University, where he met and befriended two of Africa's pioneering leaders in the struggle against colonialism, Kwame Nkrumah and Nnamdi Azikiwe.

Robinson was an outstanding Black pastor deeply engaged in interracial and international student Christian work. He would later become an advisor and vice-chair of the US Peace Corps National Advisory Committee to President John F. Kennedy.

Robinson's international interest began when the Presbyterian Church's Board of Foreign Missions sent him on a speaking tour to European youth groups. In 1954 he visited eleven countries in Africa when he conceived the idea of taking students from America to live and work with African students. His Operation Crossroads Africa program was modeled after those in Europe that were sponsored by member organizations of the World's Student Christian Federation.

Accordingly, his plan in 1957 was to take sixty students (both Black and white) with capable senior directors to five West African countries in 1958: Sierra Leone, Liberia, Senegal, Ghana, and Nigeria. The inter-racial American groups would meet with a number of African students in those respective countries, and together, they would work on a village project during the day (e.g., building a school, a church, boring a hole for a well, or some other useful community project). In short, each group would depart, leaving behind a lasting thing of value for the village. In the process, the American and African students would get to know one another by working together during the day and studying together in the evening with a variety of local elders alongside Bible study. Dr. Robinson believed that young people did not have the same measure of racial prejudice as their elders and, hence, the future of international relations would be dependent on the present-day students who would become the world leaders in the near future. He believed that if they had experiential knowledge of and mutual regard for each other, the relationships among the nations of the world would be much better. In fact, the solution of America's race problem and Africa's colonialist problems required similar agency.

That was his dream influenced in large part by two major events: (a) the recent victory of Martin Luther King Jr.'s year-long nonviolent resistance program of desegregating the buses in Montgomery, Alabama, in 1955: a victory that would have expansive consequences throughout the South and the nation at large; (b) Ghana's independence from British colonial rule in 1957 as the first African country south of the Sahara to gain its freedom and, henceforth, a model for the rest of colonized Africa to follow. Needless to say, perhaps, Ghana's achievement was hailed by African Americans (then called Negroes or Coloreds) as a major motivator in their struggle for racial justice. Robinson's Operation Crossroads was later recognized as the principal model for President John F. Kennedy's Peace Corps.

At the end of the summer in 1957, I followed James Breeden's suggestion and applied for admission to the Crossroads program. A month or so later, I received a response stating that since the program was not open to internationals at this time, my application was denied. I was somewhat disappointed but, since it was a long shot, I centered my attention on completing my final year of study at Acadia. Yet, during that time I read Rev. Robinson's autobiography, *Road Without Turning*, and was greatly impressed by it. In fact, I thought at that time he was an ideal Christian minister: concerned about the human soul in the context of historical and political realities.

During the 1958 Lenten season, Dr. Robinson, clearly an internationally renowned speaker, was delivering a series of sermons at the St. James Methodist Church in Montreal, Canada. After telling them about his proposed Operation Crossroads Africa idea, he asked the church to join the program by sponsoring one or more students in return for hearing a report on their experience after they returned home. The church agreed to do so on the condition that at least one Canadian student be included in the group.

Upon his return to the United States, I received a letter from Dr. Robinson's office inquiring if I were still interested in joining the program. If I were interested, I would need to raise sufficient monies to travel to and from New York, get a passport, etc., by early June. Needless to say, I was excited about this extraordinary opportunity. My initial interest, however, was centered on going to Sierra Leone because of my native Nova Scotia's ancestral connection with that country, the details of which I will not describe at this point.

How did you raise the funds to travel to Nigeria? After you raised the funds did you travel straight from Canada to Nigeria?

One day, I was approached by a newly arrived professor of theology, Dr. Cherry, who had been teaching at the Southern Baptist Theological Seminary in Louisville, Kentucky. He was a very affable person, and though I never took a course from him, he had heard about my endeavor to raise money for the trip to Africa. He asked me if I had raised the necessary funds. I told him that I had raised 750 dollars and was short by 250. Without hesitation, he immediately said that he would gladly lend me the 250 dollars and that I could repay him as soon as I could after I began my work with the SCM at the University of Alberta. It was a surprising gesture of goodwill that made an enormous impression on me. As a matter of fact, I felt somewhat guilty because I had been very suspicious of him, thinking that he must be a racist since he was from the Deep South.

Flying to New York was the first time I had been on an airplane. We spent ten days in an orientation conference at Columbia University where we heard many lectures on Africa from members of the State Department and various professors. I soon learned that I was assigned to the Nigeria group. Happily Jim Breeden was also a part of that group. Needless to say, I knew very little about Nigeria and was happy to learn that it had the largest population of any other country on the continent.

We also learned that our group going to Nigeria would not have work-camp experience since the logistics for such could not be organized. Instead, we would spend the time traveling around the three regions of Nigeria (eastern, western, northern) as a way of experiencing its vast cultural, political, and religious diversity. Nigerian students in each region would join us as interpreters of their respective regions. En route to Nigeria we stopped for some days in Accra, Ghana, and stayed in the guest houses at what was then called the University College of London in Ghana (now called the University of Ghana). Much to my surprise and amazement, I heard Ghanaian students and faculty criticize Nkrumah, an experience I could not have imagined since Nkrumah was beyond reproach from my perspective at that time. In brief, the experience in West Africa was eye-opening in many ways and, from my perspective, an excellent way to gain an introduction to the scholarly elite in both Ghana and Nigeria. In Nigeria we visited such major centers as Lagos, Abeokuta, Ijebuode, Ife, Oyo, Benin, Oshogbo, Onitsha, Umuahia, Aba, Port Harcourt, Calabar, Zaria, Kaduna, Kano, and Sokoto.

You were now in Nigeria; tell us about your experience there.

We met numerous chiefs in their official residences, ate kola nuts and squash (a type of bottled orange juice) as acts of hospitality and community, and listened to the chiefs' narratives about their people's mythical origins. They said little about colonialism or about independence. Since British colonialism exercised its power indirectly from 1914 onward, the traditional status of the chiefs was, arguably, not threatened so they were able to continue their way of life unhampered by the British governance located in the major urban centers.

I soon began to see that two worlds existed side by side in West Africa: the colonialist world and those Africans who helped manage its offices on the one hand, and the traditional society that formed the substratum of the culture and remained virtually untouched by the colonialist practices. I felt drawn to know more about that substratum which was present most acutely in the Indigenous languages, names, numerous ceremonies, music, and a host of rituals governing every dimension of personal, familial, and communal life.

What other Nigerians did you meet who left deep impressions on you?

Modupe Oduyoye and Dapo Anabulu guided our tour in the western region. The two had recently graduated from the University College of London in Ibadan (now called University of Ibadan). They were both active members in the Student Christian Movement of Nigeria, which was introduced to Nigeria by Sir Francis Ibiam. He studied medicine at Edinburgh University, became a member of the Student Christian Movement there, and decided to introduce it to Nigeria upon his return in 1938. His decision to become a medical missionary surprised his Scottish mentors. Since that vocation was reserved for Europeans at that time, it was a great puzzlement to the Scots. Nonetheless, it did happen, and he became the first African missionary of the Church of Scotland.

I vividly recall Modupe who was, I think, either then or soon thereafter the secretary of the National Board of the Nigerian SCM. While cycling with him and Dapo around Ibadan, they talked to me about the SCM, thinking that we might forge a relationship of some kind between the organizations in Canada and Nigeria since I was committed to working with the former. I was deeply impressed with Modupe and Dapo, the beautiful university campus with hundreds of students in white shirts and shorts milling around.

Their quarters were amazing. In addition to their own private rooms, each student had an attendant who attended to his menial needs like cleaning, washing his clothes, running errands, etc. They were definitely the elite class in training, destined to enter some dimension of the colonial administration. Modupe was majoring in literature and hoping to be a teacher in a secondary school. Dapo wanted to be an artist. I should note that they were peers with Chinua Achebe, whose first book, *Things Fall Apart*, was published in 1958.

You were in Nigeria for only ten weeks. You went back to the country in the early 1960s. By the time you returned an important event happened in your life. What was the event?

Upon return to Canada, I traveled across Canada by train to the University of Alberta to assume my duties there. But before doing that, I attended the national conference of the Student Christian Movement, which was held annually at the time in the lovely resort town of Bala, Ontario. There, I participated in a panel discussion about international connections with student Christian work around the world: Shirley McMillen had just returned from a year's study at the Women's College in Bombay (now Mumbai); Donald Wilson had just returned from three years' work with the SCM in Chile, South America; and I had just returned from a ten-week study tour in Nigeria. I should note here that Shirley McMillen would complete her undergraduate studies at the University of Alberta two years later, and we were married in May 1961. Let me hasten to add that there were very few interracial marriages in those days. Ours was celebrated in the SCM of Canada and by our respective families and friends.

Traveling back to Toronto with Donald Wilson, who was assuming the job of world missions secretary at our national headquarters and later as secretary of the Ecumenical Assistance Program of the WSCF (World Student Christian Federation) in Geneva, I recall saying to him that if there were ever an opportunity to work for a period of time in Nigeria, I would be willing to consider it.

Much to my surprise, two years later, Don wrote to remind me of that conversation and to say that a possible opportunity to work in Nigeria had arisen. He had received a letter from Chris Groves, who had been a missionary in Nigeria under the auspices of the Church Missionary Society of the Church of England. The CMS seconded him to work with the SCM of

Nigeria, which she served as its second national traveling secretary (the first such person was an Englishman named David Head).[2]

What are some of your memorable experiences you had when you went on your "second missionary journey" to Nigeria?

We arrived in Lagos in July 1961 and were taken ninety miles east to the Ibadan Boys School where we were housed for several weeks waiting for the completion of the SCM House (a two-story house suitable for housing the traveling secretary and providing the national offices for the organization.) The SCM House was being built at 10 Awosika Avenue in the Bodija Housing Estates close to the university. Eventually, we became its first occupants and chose to live in the top flat. The management of the SCM House decided to rent the bottom flat until such time it would be used as SCM office space. Each flat contained a kitchen, a living room, three bedrooms, and a bathroom.

It took some time to get settled, which was not completed until the end of September thereabouts. All the furniture was handmade, and we spent a lot of time selecting and purchasing basic household things in the marketplace and nearby stores. We soon became aware of the difficulty of adjusting to the tropical heat. Most people rested in the afternoons from 2 to 4 p.m. We soon discovered the wisdom in following that pattern, which was followed by tea time 4 to 6 p.m. and dinner at 6:30 p.m.

I did an enormous amount of reading in those early months while waiting for the house to be completed and my traveling schedule to begin. I read a fair amount about British colonial policy as an attempt to learn about its aims and methods from its own perspective. Most importantly, I learned a lot about Governor Lugard's method of indirect colonial rule, which meant co-opting the traditional rulers (i.e., chiefs) in their endeavor and ruling without upsetting the local traditions too much.

Professor Kenneth O. Dike was then chancellor of the University College of London in Ibadan when I arrived. I recall reading his book, *Trade and Politics in the Niger Delta, 1830–1885*. It had been his dissertation and had been published in 1956. It focused a lot of attention on the cities that grew up along the coastal regions of the country to facilitate the international trade that first included slaves and later various palm oil products,

---

2. The information is from a letter from Chris to Don, letters from Modupe, the secretary of the national board of the SCM of Nigeria, and from the dean of my theological college Dr. Evans Whidden, re: Fundraising for the WSCF Ecumenical Assistance Program. These letters are in the possession of Peter Paris.

cocoa, groundnuts, and metals of various types. I also read J. Omosade Awalalu's *Yoruba Beliefs and Sacrificial Rites*; J. F. .A. Ajayi's *Christian Missions in Nigeria: The Making of a New Elite*; E. A. Adegbola's *Traditional Religion in Africa*; Geoffrey Parrinder's anthropological work which greatly inspired Idowu and others; Jomo Kenyatta's *Facing Mount Kenya*, a perceptive autobiography; additional novels by Chinua Achebe; and some plays and novels by 'Wole Soyinka, who would much later receive the Nobel Prize in Literature in 1986, which many thought should have gone to Achebe instead. Many think, however, that Achebe's creative writing suffered in the sixties and seventies because he had given much attention to the current political issues of the day.

While in Nigeria you met some of the leading public and intellectual figures. What was the experience like meeting them, scholars whom Nigerians today hold in high esteem?

Sir Francis Ibiam was the president of the national board of the SCM. He was then the governor of the eastern region. I did not meet him until I went to the east a few months later. He was a very down-to-earth type of person who actually seemed a bit uneasy living in such a palatial estate as the governor's mansion in Enugu. As he showed me the state dining room, he sat on the steps leading from the foyer to the sunken space below. He invited me to sit there with him. Earlier, when I had arrived at the gates to the compound, the guards decided that my car needed to be washed from the dust gathered from such a long trip before advancing into the compound. The contrast between the guard's demeanor and that of Sir Francis was altogether striking; the former lofty and haughty; the latter humble and amiable.

By the middle of my first year in Nigeria, Sir Francis chose to step down from the presidency of the SCM, and Dr. E. 'Bolaji Idowu, senior lecturer in the Department of Religion at University College of London in Ibadan, became his successor. Dr. Idowu was a Methodist pastor as well as an outstanding scholar. During my stay there, he completed his major work, *God in Yoruba Belief*, which I later carefully read. It made a deep impression on me by opening my eyes to the Yoruba worldview long before encountering Europeans and their version of Christianity. A smaller set of lectures on the subject were delivered at the Nigerian Broadcasting Corporation and later published, which he autographed for me.

Up until then, I had thought of African theologians as translators of European Christianity into their own respective languages. Such a viewpoint, however, gave centrality to the European understanding of the world (including the Bible), which was not a European product. Needless to say, this was a revelatory experience that changed my whole orientation to Christianity. Moreover, that change was sealed by an anecdote Dr. Idowu told me that depicted a similar revelation he had while studying in Great Britain in the early 1950s. He said that while studying in England he went to see Cecil B. DeMille's wide-screen movie production entitled *The Ten Commandments*. He said that the greatest shock of his life occurred when God spoke with an American accent to Moses at Mount Sinai. Prior to that experience, he had always thought of God speaking with an English accent. At that point, he said to himself that if God could speak with an American accent, then he can speak with a Nigerian accent. Thenceforth, he became a Nigerian in both thought and practice, shunned Western dress for the rest of his life by wearing agbadas, and dedicated his life to the study of Yoruba religious traditions.

As an ordained Methodist pastor, he soon began drawing inspiration from the oldest African Christian traditions that were shaped and practiced in the Coptic Church of Egypt and the Ethiopian Orthodox Church. Later, when he became active in effecting a union between the Methodist and Anglican communions in Nigeria, he proposed the use of the office of *patriarch* as the highest office for the new ecumenical venture, and he soon became its patriarch, an act which, incidentally, split the church instead of uniting it.

Let us go back to your reading of the books of African intellectuals. Did you continue to follow up on their scholarship after your service was concluded?

Through the seventies and eighties, I continued reading African scholars on religion though my attention was drawn increasingly to the following areas of theological interest: the rise of Black liberation theology in the United States with the publication of James H. Cone's radical thesis in his 1969 book *Black Theology and Black Power*, which was destined to have a profound effect on virtually all Black Americans bent on studying theology from the seventies up to the present. Soon, many students were drawn by Cone's work to study at Union Theological Seminary in New York, among whom were African American women. White feminist theologians were also emerging in the theological academy at that time, and by the mid-eighties, Black women launched their own unique womanist theology at Union (Delores Williams, Jacqueline Grant, and Katie G. Cannon). The womanist theologians were heavily influenced by the literary works of Alice Walker and especially her powerful novel *The Color Purple* for which she won the Pulitzer Prize for Fiction followed by the National Book Award, in 1982 and 1983 respectively. Steven Spielberg directed the acclaimed movie version of the novel. Black women rightly claimed that they had been invisible in both Black theology, which was wholly male in its composition, and feminist theology, which was wholly white in its composition. Thus, Black women were bent on telling their own story as religionists which they emphasized could not be told by either Black men or white women. I knew all of them personally: Delores Williams, Jaqueline Grant, and Katie Cannon, who had also written essays in Howard University's School of Religion *Journal of Religious Thought*.

Following the publication of James Cone's first book, the Society for the Study of Black Religion (SSBR) was formed in 1970 at Gammon Theological Seminary in Atlanta to provide an academic space for Black scholars and teachers of religion to discuss their respective research projects and to support and encourage one another in a space that was dominated by the white cultural ethos. Since most were members of the American Academy of Religion, it was thought necessary for Blacks to have their own separate space to discuss and debate issues pertaining to the subject of Black religion because many white scholars believed themselves to be scholars of Black religion.

Thus, it was thought necessary for Black scholars to work separately from whites in this venture because the sessions at the AAR were invariably dominated by white scholars whose questions and interests differed from those of Blacks. Most importantly, they did not view the SSBR as an alternative to the AAR but as a caucus bent on preparing its Black members for rigorous debate in the AAR, in which there were few Black members. Clearly, the birth of Black and womanist theologians marked a radical change in the AAR, which made a valiant attempt to do all that was needed to make the new members welcome.

Soon a Commission on the Status of Minorities in the Profession was formed by the board to advise it on all relevant policies to facilitate their work in the academy. That commission was modeled after the one that had been set up earlier on the Status of Women in the Profession.

As stated above, for several years after the birth of Black theology various African theologians spent time studying with Cone at Union even though they were bent on developing a relevant theology for their own countries on the continent. John S. Mbiti was one such scholar, whose book *African Religion and Philosophy* was much less Christian in its orientation than was Black theology. It soon became apparent from the writings from West Africa, East Africa, and South Africa that the first two were more concerned about the inculturation of religion while the latter was concerned with the political dimensions of religion. Thus, Black theology in the US appeared to be closer to the latter than those in West or East Africa.

You have an experience that is almost unique in the global academy. Early in your career you were fed by two streams of thought flowing from two continents and converging at multiple sites of theology and religious studies. You were not only in touch with the key creators of the ideas that generated the streams, but you also played important roles in inaugurating what today we would call African and African American theological traditions. How did the two streams (African and African American) of scholarship inform your scholarship?

The experience in Nigeria caused me to have a deeper appreciation of family and communal experience and to be skeptical about the Western focus on the individual and the philosophy of individualism. I should hasten to add that I found the African emphasis on the family and not the community to be more compatible with the biblical understanding of humanity than the Western emphasis on the individual.

Needless to say, it would take me a long while to determine how I could write a treatise that would demonstrate the relatedness of the religion of African Americans and the religion of Africans on the continent. Let me hasten to say that the use of the singular vis-à-vis "religion" is not intended to deny its diversity either in the Americas or on the continent. In due course, however, my book *The Spirituality of African Peoples: The Search for a Common Moral Discourse* aimed at discussing that relation between the two streams.

Acknowledging the great diversity of languages and cultural traditions among African peoples on the continent and throughout the African diaspora, I have always been concerned about what constitutes the unity of African peoples: unity that is signaled by those in the diaspora who view the continent of Africa as their "ancestral motherland or homeland." In addition to the commonality of space, race, and oppression, I searched for enduring spiritual and moral connections among the diversity of African cultures. The answer to that inquiry was discovered in the ubiquity of religion as both a guiding principle at the center of African daily life and a resource for their many various responses to the threatening conditions of suffering, poverty, and oppression, and it eventually culminated in the book I edited. It was written over a period of five years by a diverse group of religious scholars under the title *Religion and Poverty: Pan-African Perspectives*.

That book was inspired in part by the early twentieth-century Pan-African movement led by such stellar leaders as the Trinidadians Henry Sylvester Williams and George Padmore along with the American scholar and NAACP activist W. E. B. Du Bois, who carried the organizing torch for five conferences from 1920 to 1945. Most important, the Pan-African movement inspired several young African anti-colonialists, including such paradigmatic pioneering fathers of African independence as Kwame Nkrumah of Ghana, Nnamdi Azikiwe of Nigeria, and Jomo Kenyatta of Kenya. Needless to say, perhaps, their joint commitment to the task of not only unifying Africa against colonialism but also, later, funding the Organization for African Unity (OAU) with headquarters in Ethiopia embodied all the necessary symbolism for my academic work.

After spending a semester in Nigeria in 1983 doing research at the Christian Institute of Nigeria in Ibadan and another semester teaching at the Trinity Theological College in Legon, Ghana, I was able to get a major grant from the Ford Foundation to lead a multi-year Pan-African seminar over a five-year period on a subject of common interest, namely, the relation of religion and poverty. Accordingly, after a consultative seminar at Princeton Theological Seminary with selected Black religious scholars, we decided that the two subjects, religion and poverty, were common concerns of African peoples in the Caribbean, Brazil, Canada, the USA, and the African continent. Thus, a team of nineteen scholars evenly divided between men and women: six from the US, three from Jamaica, one from Brazil, two from Ghana, one from Nigeria, one from Togo, two from Kenya, one from Malawi, three from South Africa.

Your edited volume *Religion and Poverty: Pan-African Perspectives* is a book of exquisite scholarship. In it and in your other books you demonstrated your key interests and expertise in Black theology and radical social ethics. How did all these start?

I left the University of Chicago in 1970 before completing my dissertation and took a position as an instructor in ethics and society at Howard University School of Religion (now called Howard University School of Divinity). My dissertation was necessarily delayed because of a very heavy load of courses I was teaching for the first time. Yet, the experience of being in a historic Black university for the first time in my life was very rewarding largely because of close relations developed with two long-time professors,

J. DeOtis Roberts in theology and philosophy (PhD, University of Edinburgh) and Evans Crawford, dean of the Rankin Chapel and professor of homiletics (PhD, Boston University).

In 1969, James H. Cone published his first book, which shocked the theological world because he entitled it *Black Theology and Black Power*. If that were not shocking enough, he argued that God was Black. Since Howard University had a long history (1866 to the present) of being closely connected and supported by the United States government, which was far from progressive on racial matters, only two members of the faculty were cautiously supportive of the book, namely, DeOtis Roberts and Rosemary Ruether, an emerging white feminist theologian. Roberts would soon publish a response to Cone's work entitled *Liberation and Reconciliation: A Black Theology* in order to argue for the importance of reconciliation, which he thought Cone had neglected. Thereafter, a debate ensued between Cone and Roberts about that subject. Most of the faculty at the school, however, gave no attention whatsoever to this new theological discourse.

Soon I attended an organizing conference that launched the Society for the Study of Black Religion. That society provided a training space for encouraging one another to think seriously about the implications of Black theology for their particular discipline (i.e., Bible, history, ethics, pastoral care, etc.) I was greatly influenced by Gayraud Wilmore's book *The Black Church and Black Radicalism*. Because I attended its first meeting, I became a charter member of this important organization in the American religious academy. It had planned to celebrate its fiftieth anniversary in 2020, which the COVID-19 pandemic forced it to postpone.

Suffice it to say, my dissertation, revised and published as *Black Religious Leader: Conflict in Unity*, followed by *The Social Teaching of the Black Churches* were both well received in the society. I served the society as its president from 2001 to 2005. In former years, I served as president of the American Academy of Religion and the Society of Christian Ethics. Later still, I served as president of the American Theological Society.

This is an impressive, capacious career resume. What other academic honors have you received?

Over the years, I have received five honorary doctor of divinity degrees from my alma mater, Acadia University in Nova Scotia; McGill University in Montreal, Canada; Lehigh University in Bethlehem, Pennsylvania; LaFayette University in Easton, Pennsylvania; and Waynesburg University in Waynesburg, Pennsylvania. I might also add that I have been an alumnus of the year at both the University of Chicago Divinity School and Acadia University in Nova Scotia. My lecture at the former was entitled "David George, Pioneer Ancestor of Blacks in Nova Scotia and Freetown, Sierra Leone."

Lest it appears that I left my native Canada behind in my academic career, a word should be said about that matter. First of all, apart from selected clergy and a small number of male schoolteachers in the city of Halifax, Nova Scotia, there were no Black university graduates. I was the first of such from my hometown to go to university. In Nova Scotia where the largest concentration of Black Canadians lived, all the Black churches (except for one) were Baptists. They were spread out in over thirty small, racially segregated areas usually on the margins of small, predominantly white towns or in rural areas. The latter had racially segregated schools with teachers with permissive licenses until they had completed a number of courses taken during the summer at the Teachers Training College.

In my town, Blacks were allowed to go to the predominantly white schools, where the drop-out rate was high for Blacks because there seemed to be nothing else apart from manual labor for them to do after high school graduation. I did well in school and my parents encouraged me to continue. I graduated as valedictorian of my class, received a scholarship from the local Rotary club and another from the African United Baptist Association (AUBA), founded in 1853 by Black clergy to bring together all the churches throughout the province for a weekend celebration on the third weekend of August, a tradition that continues to this present day. The AUBA scholarship continued annually throughout my undergraduate and seminary education (1952–58). Consequently, I was well known throughout the province and was invited often to preach both at the AUBA and its various churches. I was honored by the invitation to speak at its one hundred and fiftieth anniversary in 2003.

Toward the end of the 1960s Blacks in Nova Scotia, encouraged by the Black Power movement in the United States, began organizing themselves for social change and a frontal attack on racial segregation. In the process of doing so they were successful in getting a major grant from the federal government for community development. They formed a provincial organization called the Black United Front. Five years later the government required an evaluation of the project by an outside observer before renewing the grant. I was asked to be the outside reviewer, which I undertook by spending several weeks in the province, visiting the various communities and writing the report. Happily, the grant was renewed.

I did a similar work for the Black Educators Association there some time later, and similarly their grant was renewed. Since those grants enabled jobs for several people in the various communities, their continuation was very important for many reasons. At one point I declined an offer to serve as the executive director of the umbrella organization, believing that my calling was to the theological academy rather than community organizing.

In the 1990s I was asked to serve as an advisor to an organizing committee at Dalhousie University in Halifax in their aim to establish a Chair in Black Canadian Studies that would serve all of Canada. After a few meetings with them the chair was finally established and has now been in existence for nearly twenty-five years. I have been invited to lecture there on several occasions.

What was it like to be the first person in your Black community to go to college? How did your education in Nova Scotia help you to understand the Black experience in Canada?

Throughout my undergraduate and seminary education, I rarely had the opportunity to see any connection between my education and my experience of growing up in a racially segregated community in Nova Scotia. Though I went to integrated schools, there were no Black teachers, and the white teachers treated Black students well only if they excelled in their academic work. Otherwise, teachers showed neither mercy nor justice. Many times I felt Black students were unjustly punished for very minor offenses that many would not consider offenses at all. Darker skinned students had the hardest time getting along with white teachers, who were always white women prone to call the male principal to administer corporal punishment on Black boys. Thus, the issue of racial injustice was omnipresent. In high school, several Blacks were praised only for their athleticism.

At my university, there were only three or four Canadian Blacks, plus a few from the Caribbean. I was bent on demonstrating that I could do anything whites could do. I joined the debating team, the light opera society, the track and field team, and eventually the Student Christian Movement, which I found very exciting because of its eagerness to debate religious questions, doctrines, the relation of science and religion, and even the relation of Christianity and Marxism. In fact, Elizabeth Adler, from East Germany, and a staff member of the WSCF visited us and delivered a lecture on the positive relations between Christianity and Marxism. The SCM staff seemed to lean politically toward democratic socialism, which I was beginning to think was more compatible with Christianity than capitalism.

Let me take you back to your Nigerian stories. Not long after you left Nigeria and returned to your native Canada, a civil war broke out in Nigeria. How was the war interpreted in Canada and America?

Yes, the Biafran war occurred after my stay in Nigeria. In fact, I had already begun PhD studies at the University of Chicago when it began. There was no one I knew at the University of Chicago who knew anything about Nigeria. Yet, many had taken sides in support of the Biafrans because news of the latter starving to death had reached America. Though uninformed about the realities of the situation, most Americans seemed to sympathize with the Biafrans, viewing them as oppressed by the Yorubas in the western region and by the Hausas in the northern region. I found myself unable to take sides during the war because I had so many good friends on both sides of the conflict. Since we had SCM units in all three regions and I had visited and befriended many of them, how could I assume one side of the war was right and the other wrong? Rather, I sympathized with all sides and viewed the war as a great tragedy because it denied all the hopes and dreams that were so dominant only a few years before, hopes and dreams for unity under Nigerian governance rather than colonialism.

While many American and Canadian churches raised monies to help the Biafrans, I felt that such help was tantamount to taking sides and, hence, I could not participate. It was not clear to me how the external world could help end the war and restore national unity and, if there had been no genuine unity before the war, to design the means for such now. It seemed obvious to me that America had so little knowledge of Nigeria that it could not be an agent for its peace. Yet, I took no great satisfaction in doing nothing and remain uncertain about what I should have done. What is the appropriate role for outsiders in another country's civil war? That remains an unanswered moral question for me.

Let me now conclude this interview with a question about your art collection. I have been to your house when you were at Princeton, New Jersey, and I was impressed by your vast collection. Do you want to mention any particular artifact from Nigeria that you have in your home in Delaware now?

I have many artifacts from Nigeria and other countries in Africa that I cherish very much, and they have been prominent decorative items in my home throughout my life. Above the fireplace in our living room is a painting depicting an artist's rendition of the castle at Elmina, Ghana, where African slaves were kept waiting for passage to the Americas. On another wall is a large framed cloth bearing the picture of a woman with a baby on her back. In our china cabinet are some pieces of pottery from the pottery factory in Enugu. I have a coffee table carved from Oroko wood by the acclaimed wood-carvers in Awka with an inscription carved on it.

I also have a chest carved out of the same wood by the same craftsmen, which I carried on top of my car across the western region in 1962. I have a bust of a man carved in the northern region out of coconut wood that I purchased from a Hausa trader in 1961. I have two ebony busts (male and female) that I purchased in Nigeria in 1958. I also purchased four masks used in Ogun festivals. They originally had the raffia attached to them to cover the body and I regret cutting it off long ago.

I have many more artifacts purchased on later trips to Africa including four framed carvings of daily scenes, which decorate the walls of our dining area. I have a framed picture of a hieroglyphics in an Egyptian tomb that I purchased at the British Museum in 1958. We usually used an African cloth for our table at Thanksgiving dinner. I have many framed art works including a carved chair from Mozambique and a carved figure of a woman that is about three feet high. I cherish all of these artifacts, which are daily reminders of my ancestral Africa. One of the saddest artifacts I have is a photo of a skeletal man, woman, and child imaging the starvation during the Nigeria-Biafran War.

BIBLIOGRAPHY

Wariboko, Nimi. "The Evasion of Ethics: Peter Paris Feels the Spirituals." *Toronto Journal of Theology* 27.2 (Sept. 2011) 215–34.

INDEX

Abia Yala, 102
Acadia University in Nova Scotia, 214–15

Achebe, Chinua, 135, 207
Things Fall Apart, 136–37, 207
Adeboye, Enoch, 162
Adegbola, E. A., 209
Adler, Elizabeth, 216
Adogame, Afe, 7, 162
aesthetics and dance, 40, 47–48, 49
African American, 5, 30
　Christianity, 43, 85. *See also* African Christianity
　civil rights movement, 85
　consciousness, 91
　moral agency, 93n13
　moral tradition, 6, 87
　response to poverty and racism, 13–14
　theologians and scholars, 119–21
　theological traditions, 212–13
　virtues, 18, 78–79
African Christianity, 7–8, 85, 91n5, 145, 156–57, 159
　Achebe's masquerade metaphor, 135–37
　Anglican Communion, 154
　Black Christian tradition, 31, 31n55
　Celestial Church of Christ (CCC), 157–58
　Christian population, 91, 137–38
　church membership definition problems, 139–42
　complexity, 137–39

diaspora. *See* African diaspora
Ethiopianism, 156
and Ethiopian Judaism, 145–45
historical phrases of, 145–53
Indigenous Churches (AICs), 150–53, 157–58
moratorium call on missions, 165–68
Pentecostal (Charismatic)/Evangelical churches, 152, 153
phases, 145–54
and reverse missionaries, 160–65
transnationalism, 159–60
and Western-centric approach, 132–33, 144–54
women in, 158–59
African diaspora, 114, 119–20
　African Union about, 137n13
　African worldview preservation in, 90–91
　common agenda, 120–21
　migration, transnationalism and, 130–32
　moral virtues as convergent values, 127–28
　religious experience, 133
　role in world Christian demographics, 154
　strengthening ties, 128–30, 133–34
　understanding of, 137
"African factor", 38–39
　body types critique, 50
　and dance as religious ritual, 42–43, 44, 46–48
　and moral philosophy, 36–37, 39

219

INDEX

African Indigenous churches (AICs), 150–53, 157–58
African-ness, 34, 35n4
  transnationalism, 130–32, 159–60. *See also* African diaspora
African Religion and Philosophy (Mbiti), 211
African theology and ethics, 133
  vs. African American theology, 77–78, 85–87
  diaspora influence, 119–20
  marginalization, 121n1
  Paris's approach, 122–24
  Paris's concepts of African morality, 125–26
  scholars of, 121–22
African Union (AU), 114, 137, 137n13
African United Association of the Atlantic Baptist Convention, Canada, 197–98
African United Baptist Association (AUBA), 215
Afro-Brazilians, 112
  African legacy, 101, 114
  African worldview preservation, 90–91
  Brazilian Black movement, 99
  Brazilian elite's response to race, 97, 98
  Brazilian religious history, 94n18
  colonial Christianity, 101–4
  history of religion in Brazil, 96–97
  and Indigenous peoples, 113–14
  Pentecostalism, 109–11
  racism, 6–7, 93–100
  religious fluidity, 111–13
  religious transformation, 105–7
Ajayi-Adeniran, Daniel, 162
Ajayi, J. F. A., 209
Aladura Church, 151, 153
Alexandria, 146–47
Alinsky, Saul, 199
All Africa Conference of Churches, 60
Althoff, Andrea, 111
Altizer, Thomas, 155
Alves, Rubem, 76, 183

American Academy of Religion (AAR), 193, 211
American Board of Commissioners for Foreign Missions (ABCFM), 149
The American Evasion of Philosophy (West), 22
American Theological Society, 193
Amerindians, 102, 102n56, 104n64, 106
Anabulu, Dapo, 206–7
ancestors in African spirituality, 126
Anderson, Allan, 91n5
Anglican Church, 154–55
Anthills of the Savannah (Achebe), 136
Anthony (Saint), 146
anti-Blackness, 43–45
anti-Semitism, 192
Aponte, Edwin David, 113
Aquinas, Thomas, 173
  definition of charity, 178–79
Arendt, Hannah, 20, 21
  influence in Paris's ethics, 23–24
  theory of power, 25
Aristotle, 20
  argument on happiness, 175, 177
  about friendship and love, 175, 176, 177–78
  influence in Paris's ethics, 21
  theory of moral virtue, 18
  theory of politics and ethics connection, 28
  about virtue, 124
Arrow of God (Achebe), 136
ashé, 37
Athanasius, 146
atheism, 180–81
Augustine of Hippo, 146, 173–74
Awalalu, J. Omosade, 209
Azikiwe, Nnamdi, 213
Aztecs Empire, 102n57

Baptist Missionary Society (BMS), 149
Barbara, Vanessa, 93
Barbosa, José Carlos, 104–5
Barbosa, Maria Jose, 97
Barreto, Raimundo C., 2, 6

Basel Mission (1815), 149
Bauer, F. C., 155
Beatriz, Dona. *See* Vita, Kimpa
Bediako, Kwame, 121n1, 122
Beier, Ulli, 136
beneficence, 127
Bergman, Majken, 62, 63
Biney, Moses, 7
Black Brazilians. *See* Afro-Brazilians
The Black Church and Black Radicalism (Wilmore), 214
Black churches in United States, 19, 21, 22–23, 24
    and racism, poverty and ecological issues, 87
    struggles against racism, 192–93
Black Educators Association, 215–16
Black Evangelical Movement, 110
Black Lives Matter (BLM), 81, 86–87
Blackness, 35, 35n4, 38, 47
Black Power movement in United States, 215
Black Religious Leaders: Conflict in Unity (Paris), 23, 26, 126, 193, 214
Black Religious Leaders: Unity in Diversity (Paris), 122–23
Black Religious Leaders in Conflict: Joseph H. Jackson, Martin Luther King, Jr., Malcolm X, Adam Clayton Powell (Paris), 193
Black theologies in United States, 74, 212
Black Theology and Black Power (Cone), 210, 214
Black United Front, 215
bodies, Black, 5, 42n30
    African epistemological traditions, 35–36
    conveyor of religious experience, 38–41
    and dance as religious ritual, 42–43, 44, 46–48
    limitations of embodied resistance, 46–51
    as *mysterium facinosum/tremendum*, 49
    ring shout, 45–47
    stereotypes about, 41
    as subtext in Paris's approach, 34–35
    values and resistance, 36–37
    violence and exploitation, 80–81
Boff, Leonardo, 80, 180, 180n22
Bordo, Susan, 40n24
Brazilian Evangelical Black Movement. *See* Movimento Negro Evangelico (MNE)
Brazilian religious landscape, 105
    Catholicism, 105–6, 108–9
    Mayan Pentecostals, 111
    Pentecostalism, 107–10, 111
    permission for hybrid faith practice, 106–7
    "theology of African roots," 110
Breeden, James, 203, 204
British and Foreign Bible Society (BFBS), 149
Bullard, Robert, 83
Bultmann, Rudolf, 155

Candomblé, 91, 107–8
Cannon, Katie G., 210, 211
capitalism, 41, 76, 84–85, 96
Carter, J. Kameron, 96
Carthage, 146
Cary, Joyce, 136
Catholicism, 180n21
    dominance in Brazil, 103–9
    in Latin America, 91–92
    social teaching in America, 17
Celestial Church of Christ (CCC), 152, 157–58
Cesar, Waldo, 113
Cherubim and Seraphim Church, 151
The Chicago Tribune, 162
Chike and the River (Achebe), 136
Christ and Culture (Richard Niebuhr), 23
Christ Apostolic Church, 151
The Christian Century, 163
Christian Missions in Nigeria (Ajayi), 209
Christian moral agency, 185–87
Christianity, 173, 174–79, 189. *See also* African Christianity; Catholicism

Christianity *(continued)*
  discipleship, 183–84
  ethics, 183
  evangelization, 112
  impingement of, 143
  integration with traditional beliefs, 126
  Jesus concept, 185
  love and charity, 182
  love of neighbor, 183, 184
  problems with religious statistics, 141
  realism by Reinhold Niebuhr, 22, 179
  role in anti-slavery campaigns, 148
  role in slavery, 101–5
  white colonial, 111
  world, 1–3, 1n1, 120, 132–33, 155–56, 169
Christian Student Movement, 193
Chuchiak, John F., 103
Church Missionary Society (CMS), 149, 207
Circle of Concerned African Women Theologians, 54
City of Joy initiative, 68–69, 69n37, 70
colonialism, 35n4, 80, 85, 101–4, 111
"The Color of Death" study, 100
The Color Purple (Walker), 210–11
communal ethics, 5, 124, 125
Cone, James H., 11, 11n1, 17, 26, 29, 76, 122, 210, 214
  on culture of domination, 76–77
  on ethics, 78
  on safe environmentalism, 87
  on white supremacy in US, 76
Congo, Republic of, 5, 54, 56, 65–66
conscientização, 95
Consultation on Black Culture and Theology in Latin America, 94n16
COVID-19 pandemic, 6, 76
Covington-Ward, Yolanda, 41
Cradling Abundance: One African Christian's Story to Empowering Women and Fighting Systemic Poverty (Mukuna), 55
Crawford, Evans, 214

Croatto, José Severino, 183
Crowther, Samuel Ajayi, 148
Cullors, Patrisse, 86
Curran, Charles E., 180n21

dance, 42–43, 51
  actual activity of body, 46–47
  aesthetics and, 40, 47–48, 49
  "flash of the spirit" concept, 48
  modalities of movement, 45
  moral-ethical values, 48–49
  religiously engaged and embodied body, 44–45
  as ring shout, 45–47
  soul in *Black* movement, 45–46
da Silva, Hernani, 109, 110–11
Daughrity, Dyron B., 146, 155, 156
Davie, Grace, 140
decolonial theories, 95–96
decolonization, 164
DeFrantz, Thomas F., 48
DeMille, Cecil B., 210
de Oliveira, Marco Davi, 109, 110
Deschryver, Christine, 69n37
Dewey, James, 22
diaspora. *See* African diaspora
Dike, Kenneth O., 209
Diotima of Mantinea, 176–77
Du Bois, W. E. B., 13, 14, 22, 213
Dumping In Dixie: Race, Class, and Environmental Quality (Bullard), 83
Dussel, Enrique, 84–85
ecowomanism, 79–81
Ecumenical Association of Third World Theologians (EATWOT), 94n16
Ecumenical Decade of Churches in Solidarity with Women, 61
Embassy of the Blessed Kingdom of God for All Nations, 160
embodiment. *See* bodies, Black
Ensler, Eve, 68
  City of Joy documentary, 69n37
  voice against sexual violence, 68
environmental racism, 6, 74–76, 87–88

Dussel's critique of global capitalism, 84–85
ecowomanism, 79–81
Flint water crisis case study, 81–83, 86
Paris's African and African American ethics, 77–78, 85–86
social structures and cultural practices, 79
and virtue of forgiveness, 78–79
ethics, 19, 28
African American context, 77–78
of care and responsibility, 125
of Christian churches, 23
epistemology-centered, 15, 16
legalistic or moralistic, 192
Paris's understanding of, 4–5, 10–19, 26–30, 38, 123, 124
presupposition, 123
scholarship in, 120
theory-centered, 15
value of social analysis in, 26
ethics of Paris, intellectual roots, 20
Arendt's influence, 23–24
Aristotle's influence, 21
King Jr.'s influence, 20–21
"labor, work, and action" schema, 24–25
liberation theology's influence, 11, 25, 26
Reinhold Niebuhr's influence, 21–22
social science method, 25–26
Tillich's influence, 21
Troeltsch's influence, 22–23
Ethiopianism, 156
Ethiopian Judaism, 145–46
eudaimonia, 75, 173, 174–75
Eugene, Toinette M., 182
evangelization
Evangelical Black Movement, 109–11
Evangelical revival, 148–49
moratorium call on, 165–68
in Latin America, 92
re-evangelization of Europe, 168–69
and slavery in Brazil, 104–5

Facing Mount Kenya (Kenyatta), 209–10
Fanon, Frantz, 36
Farley, Margaret, 31
Farmer, Paul, 183
feeling, creative role of, 12, 30
Femme, Berceau De L'abondance (FEBA), 60–62
Fernandes, Florestan, 99
Fiorenza, Elisabeth Schüssler, 80
"flash of the spirit" concept, 48
Flint water crisis, 81–82, 86
Pilarski's examination, 82–83
problem of environmental racism, 82
Flores Filho, José Honório das, 109
forbearance, 127
forgiveness, 78–79, 127–28
"free Negroes" in Sierra Leone, 196
Freire, Paulo, 95
friendship, 8, 173
Aristotle's view of, 175, 176, 177–78
Christian idea of, 178
Diotima's view of, 176–77
forms of, 178
with God, 183
Plato's view of, 175–76, 177
Socrates' view of, 176–77

Garrick Braide Movement in Nigeria, 151
Garza, Alicia, 86
Gatu, John, 165–66
Gebara, Ivone, 80, 183, 187
and ecowomanism, 80–81
liberationist theology, 81
George, David, 21, 29, 196
God and Race in American Politics (Noll), 28
God in Yoruba Belief (Idowu), 209–10
González, Justo L., 102, 105
González, Ondina E., 102, 105
"gospel of prosperity," 153
Gottschild, Brenda Dixon, 41n26, 44
definition of spirit and soul, 45
about *soul* in *Black* movement, 45–46
governance, 128
Grant, Jacqueline, 210, 211

Groves, Chris, 207
Gutiérrez, Gustavo, 94, 94n17

happiness, 174–75. *See also* eudaimonia
Harrist Churches, 152
Harris, William Wade, 152
Hartch, Todd, 91n6, 92
Hartman, Saidiya, 47
Hauerwas, Stanley, 19
Head, David, 208
The Herald, 163
Hernandez, Aline, 101
Hochschild, Adam, 54
Howard University School of Divinity, 213
Huguenots, 148
The Human Condition (Arendt), 23
human flourishing. *See* eudaimonia
Hutu-Tutsi political violence, 65

Ibiam, Akanu, 154
Ibiam, Francis, 206, 209
Idowu, Bolaji, 209–10
Ilunga Mbiya, 60
improvisation as virtue, 127
Incas Empire, 102n57
Indigenous Christianity in Africa, 149–50
Indigenous Pentecostal groups, 152–53
Indigenous religion, 142, 143
Instituto Brasileiro de Geografia e Estatística (IBGE), 185, 185n34
Islam, 139, 140, 142–43, 147
isolationism, 181
"I-Thou-God" relational scheme, 180

Jackson, Jesse, 199
Jackson, Joseph H., 29
Jouili, Jeanette S., 41
justice 128, 181

Kabila, Laurent-Désiré, 65
Kalley, Robert Reid, 110
Kalu, Ogbu, 166
Keller, Catherine, 80
Kenyatta, Jomo, 209, 213
Kierkegaard, Søren, 173, 183–84

Kimbanguist Churches, 152
Kimbangu, Simon, 152
King Leopold's Ghost (Hochschild), 54
King, Martin Luther, Jr., 17, 18, 20, 29, 31, 201
Kingsway International Christian Center, 160
Kobia, Samuel, 154

Latin America, 102–3
  early empires, 102n57
  history, 94n18
  liberation theology, 94–95
  new model of global power, 96
  poverty in, 94, 94n17
  slavery in, 101–5
Latin American Christianity, 91. *See also* Afro-Brazilians
  Catholicism, 91–92
  Hartch's description of, 91n6
  Pentecostalism, 92, 107–10, 111
  Protestantism, 92, 108–11
  scholarship on, 92–93
Lausanne Covenant, 167
Leeds Methodist Missionary Society (LMMS), 149
Leone, Sierra, 148
Levinas, Emmanuel, 85
liberation, 49, 50, 87
  Dussel's politics of, 85
  "preferential option for the poor," 184–188
  theology, 11, 25, 26, 81, 94–95, 210
Liberation and Reconciliation: A Black Theology (Cone), 214
life sacredness in African spirituality, 125–26
Livesey, Lois, 194
Livesey, Lowell, 194–95
London Missionary Society (LMS), 149
Long, Charles, 46
love, 31, 173
  Aristotle on, 175, 176, 177
  Christian love of neighbor, 183, 184
  Diotima on, 176–77
  nature of shared object of, 178
  Plato on, 175–76, 177
  Socrates on, 176–77

Lovin, Robin, 179, 179n19, 181
Lucumi, 37
Lumumba, 63
Lutheran World Federation, 167

madness, 43, 43n35
The Making of a New Elite (Ajayi), 209
Malcolm X, 29
Malone, Jacqui, 41n26, 42, 43n34
Maluleke, Tinyiko Sam, 55
Maman Monique, 55. *See also* Mukwege, Denis
  childhood role, 55, 58–60
  courageous activities, 57–58
  covenant of violence against women, 55–56
  FEBA foundation, 60–62
  self-initiation principle, 53, 56, 58, 61, 72
  studies in pedagogy, 58
Mandela, Nelson, 78, 201
A Man of the People (Achebe), 136
Martin and Malcolm and America: A Dream or a Nightmare (Cone), 26
Marx, Karl, 85
masquerade metaphor, 135–37
materiality, 34
  ashé in, 37
  modes of relationship, 39
Mayas, 102n57, 111
Mbiti, John S., 121, 121n1, 131, 151, 211
McKee, Elsie Tshimunyi, 55n7, 57
McMillen, Shirley, 192, 207
Merkel, Angela, 71
Mesters, Carlos, 183
Michigan Civil Rights Commission (MCRC), 81–82
Middle Passage, 41n26, 47, 91
Milingo, Emmanuel, 155
Mills, Dana, 44, 48
"Mission Festival 71" meeting, 165–66
Mister Johnson (Cary), 136
Mobutu, Sese Seko, 58, 59
Monique Misenga Ngoie Mukuna. *See* Maman Monique
Moral Man and Immoral Society (Reinhold Niebuhr), 179n19

moral/morality. *See also* ethics
  Christian, 186, 187
  moral agency, 93n13, 185
  moral-ethical values, 48–49
  Paris's understanding of, 19–20, 123
  virtues, 126–28
  vulgar systems of, 15
Mott, Jason, 38
Movimento Negro Evangelico (*MNE*), 109–10
Movimento Negro Evangelico da Bahia (*MONEBA*), 110
Mukuna, Monique Misenga Ngoie. *See* Maman Monique
Mukwege, Denis, 55, 63. *See also* Maman Monique
  childhood experiences, 55, 62–63
  City of Joy documentary about, 69n37
  initiatives against sexual violence, 67–69
  leadership qualities, 55–56
  medical career, 63–64
  Nobel Peace Prize for, 62, 69–70
  The Power of Women, 64–65
  role in Panzi Hospital during Second Congo War, 65–67
  self-initiation principle, 56, 64, 72
  social works in Shabunda village, 70–71
  Ubuntu philosophy, 72–73
Murad, Nadia, 62, 71
Murray, Albert, 43n34
Musama Disco Christo Church, 151
muscle memory, 40, 41n26
mutual solidarity organizations (MUSOs), 69

Nadar, Sarojini, 55
Nascimento, Luiz, 8
Nationalist Baptist Church, 150
Nazarite Baptist Church, 151
Negrão, Lísias Nogueira, 105, 106, 111, 112
neighborliness, 183, 184
Nicomachean Ethics (Aristotle), 21, 175
Niebuhr, H. Richard, 20, 174, 180

226 INDEX

Niebuhr, H. Richard *(continued)*
 on accountability, 186–87
 conceptions in ethical thought, 184
 God concept, 181n24, 184–85
 influence in Paris's ethics, 21, 23
 "*I-Thou-God*" relational scheme,
  180, 186
 on social solidarity, 185, 186, 187
Niebuhr, Reinhold, 20, 173
 hermeneutics of suspicion, 179n19
 on humanity and society, 179–80
 influence in Paris's ethics, 21, 22
Niebuhr's theory of responsibility,
  173, 174, 179–81, 184
 God's concept, 181n25
 importance of individual moral
  choices, 180
 moral virtues, 179
 poverty, 185
 responsibility of Church, 186–88
Niger Delta Pastorate Church, 151
Nigritian Church, 150
Njoroge, Nyambura J., 5
Nkrumah, Kwame, 205, 213
Noll, Mark A., 28
No Longer at Ease (Achebe), 136

Oduyoye, Mercy, 121n1, 122
Oduyoye, Modupe, 206–7
Ojo, Matthew, 168
Olupona, Jacob, 41
Omari-Tunkara, Mikelle Smith, 107
"Operation Cross-roads Africa" program, 129, 203, 204
Organisation of African Instituted
  Churches (OAIC), 152
Organization for African Unity
  (OAU), 213
Oschoffa, Samuel Bilewu, 152
the Other/"others", 35n4, 45, 84–85
"out of Africa" thesis, 91n5

Padmore, George, 213
Pan-African, 3, 53n1, 53–54, 213
Panzi Foundation, 69
Panzi Hospital, 67–70
Paris, Adrienne, 194

Paris, Peter J., 2–4, 3n7, 8, 10, 34, 74,
  90, 190. *See also The Spirituality
  of African Peoples* (Paris)
 academic honors, 214–16
 advocacy scholarship, 190, 194,
  200–201
 about African and African American ethics, 77–78, 85–86
 about African and African
  American theological traditions,
  212–13
 about African moral and spiritual
  discourse, 125–26
 about African religious scholars,
  210–12
 Aristotelian perspective, 191
 art collection, 217–18
 Black Communities connection,
  215–16
 Black theology development,
  213–14
 career, 198–99, 200, 201
 charges against, 30–31, 30–31n55
 criticism of Cone, 11–12n1, 26
 early life, 194, 195–97
 about ecowomanism, 79–80
 education and studies, 198, 199,
  215–16
 ethical methodology, 10, 12–13,
  26–29, 30
 ethics, intellectual roots, 20–26
 family background, 196–97
 on forgiveness, 78–79
 goal of theological reasoning, 75
 importance of world Christianity
  study, 132–33
 leadership qualities, 194
 lived experience of African Americans, 36–37
 marriage, 207
 migration, 130–32
 moral virtues as points of convergency, 126–28
 in Nigeria, 202–10
 Nigerian scholars, 206–7, 209–10
 Operation Crossroads Africa Program, 203–4

Pan-African scholars/ scholarship, 53n1, 53–54, 213
  on practical wisdom/approach, 79, 86–87, 127
  professional organizations membership and leadership, 193–94, 201
  scholarly approach and philosophy, 122–25
  about social ethics, 13, 14, 16
  about social science method in theology, 25–26
  spirituality, 101, 101n52, 130–32
  "Strengthening the Ties That Bind" article, 133
  Student Christian Movement involvement, 198
  teaching philosophy, 200
  transnationalism, 130–32
  "Values and Experiences That All African Peoples Share" presentation, 128–29n16, 128–30
  at Vanderbilt University Divinity School, 192, 199–200
  "Young Achievers" organization, 195
Parrinder, Geoffrey, 132, 209
Pedro II, 107
Pentecostal Fellowship of Nigeria (PFN), 152
Pentecostals/Pentecostalism, 92, 113, 158
  in Brazil, 107–10, 111
  Indigenous Pentecostal groups, 152–53
  Movimento Negro Evangelico (*MNE*), 109–11
  de Oliveira's argument, 109
  Pentecostal (Charismatic)/Evangelical churches, 152, 153
Pereira, Agostinho Jose, 110
Perez y Mena, Andres, 95
Philosophy of Liberation (Dussel), 84
Pilarski, Ahida Calderón, 82–83
Pinn, Anthony, 5, 130
Plato, 18
  friendship and love, 175–76
  happiness, 177
  moral life, 175
Platvoet, Jan, 144
political emancipation, 6, 76
Politics (Aristotle), 21
Portuguese Catholics, 147–48
possession, 25, 39, 47, 49
Potter, Philip, 154
poverty, 3, 8
  in Latin America, 94, 94n17
  liberationist "preferential option for the poor," 184–188
  Paris on, 123–24
  reality of, 184
  responsibility of Christian church, 186–88
  in United States, 13
Powell, Adam Jr., 29
The Power of Women: A Doctor's Journey of Hope and Healing (Mukwege), 55, 64–65
practical wisdom, 86–87, 127
Prandi, Reginaldo, 91, 91n4
Princeton Theological Seminary (PTS), 122n3, 128
Protestantism, 180
  in Africa, 148–49
  Free Church traditions, 197
  in Latin America, 92, 108–11
  and slavery, 104–5

Quijano, Aníbal, 96

Raboteau, Albert J., 130n18
race/racism in Brazil, 6–7, 93–94, 98–100
  "The Color of Death" study, 100
  and decolonial theories, 95–96
  elite's response to, 97, 98
  modern racial discourse analysis, 96
  myth of racial democracy, 97–98
  Unified Black Movement, 99–100
  of women, 100
racism
  Black churches fight against, 192–93
  in Brazil, 6–7, 93–100
  environmental. *See* environmental racism

racism *(continued)*
  Paris's focus on eradication of, 30–31
  systematic, 27
  UNESCO statements on race, 84
  in United States, 4, 11, 13, 14, 86
  Western imperialism and, 121
reciprocity, 126, 178, 182
Redeemed Christian Church of God (RCCG), 160
Reformed Church of America, 165
Religion and Poverty: Pan African Perspectives (Paris), 53, 123–24, 213
responsibility theory. *See* Niebuhr's theory of responsibility
Reveille for Radicals (Alinsky), 199
Reverse Missionaries TV series, 163
reverse mission, 160–65
  academic interpretations, 161–62, 164
  media attention, 162–63, 164
  missionaries' responses to nationalism, 164–65
ring shout, 45–47
ritualization of life, 43, 43n34
Road Without Turning (Robinson), 204
Robert, Dana, 2
Roberts, J. DeOtis, 214
Robinson, James, 129, 203–4
Roosevelt, Theodore, 97
Rosario Rodríguez, Rubén, 6
Ruether, Rosemary Radford, 80, 214

Sagan, Carl, 75
Sanneh, Lamin, 2
Schmidt, Georg, 148
Scott, James, 95
Secretaria de Promoção da Igualdade Racial do Estado (SEPROMI), 99–100
Segundo, Juan Luis, 179n19
self-initiation principle, 5
  Denis Mukwege, 56, 64, 72
  Maman Monique, 53, 56, 58, 61, 72
Sentamu, John, 154
SEPROMI. *See* Secretaria de Promoção da Igualdade Racial do Estado

sexual violence
  Ensler's contribution against, 68
  global fund for survivors of, 71
  Mukwege's initiatives against, 67–69
Shankar, Shobana, 162
Sharp, Granville, 148
Shaull, Richard, 113
Shembe, Isaiah, 151
Skidmore, Thomas, 98
Slave Religion: The "Invisible Institution" in the Antebellum South (Raboteau), 130n18
slavery
  Christinity role in, 101–5
  trade in Africa, 148
Smith, Mychal Denzel, 51
Snyder, Rick, 83
The Social Teaching of the Black Churches (Paris), 21–23, 26, 27, 126, 193, 214
The Social Teaching of the Christian Churches (Troeltsch), 23, 192
social welfare, 128
Society for the Study of Black Religion (SSBR), 211, 214
Society for Values in Higher Education, 193
Society of Christian Ethics, 193, 201, 214
socioeconomic reductionism, 95
Socrates, 176–77
solidarity:
  Jesus on, 185
  Niebuhr on, 185, 186, 187
  with women, 61
soul,
  in *Black* movement, 45–46
  Gottschild's definition, 45
The Souls of Black Folk (Du Bois), 14
Spickard, James V., 162
Spielberg, Steven, 211
Spillers, Hortense, 35n4
spirit/spirituality, 37, 45
  African, 3, 40, 79, 101, 112, 130–32
  as alternative to environmental racism, 77–78
  Paris on, 125–26, 101, 101n52

The Spirituality of African Peoples: The Search for a Common Moral Discourse (Paris), 18, 34–35, 123, 125, 126, 131, 212
   African factor, 37
   body-types, 49–51
   concern with moral evil and suffering, 37
   dance, 42–49
The Spirituality of African Religions (Paris), 130
spiritualization of life, 48
spirituals, 5, 30
Stackhouse, Max Lynn, 8
"Statement on Race" by UNESCO, 84
"Statement on Race and Racial Prejudice" by UNESCO, 84
Student Christian Movement (SCM), 9, 198, 203, 206, 216
   national conference, 207
   SCM House, 208
suffering, 31, 184
Summa Theologica (Aquinas), 178
survival, Zondi's statement on, 49–50
Symposium (Plato), 175–76

tabula rasa, 90
Tavarez, David, 103
The Ten Commandments (movie), 210
theology. *See also* African theology and ethics
   African American context, 77–78
   Eurocentric views of, 182
   Paris's. *See* Paris, Peter J.
   scholarship in, 120
   value of social analysis in, 26
"theology of African roots," 110
A Theology of Liberation (Gutiérrez), 94n17
theory-centered ethics, 15
Things Fall Apart (Achebe), 136–37, 207
Third World Missions Association (TWMA), 168
Thompson, Robert Farris, 48
Tillich, Paul, 20–21, 155
Tometi, Opal, 86
Townes, Emilie M., 122

Trade and Politics in the Niger Delta, 1830–1885 (Dike), 208
Traditional Religion in Africa (Adegbola), 209
transcendence, 81
translatability principle, 2
transnationalism, 130–32, 159–60. *See also* African diaspora
Troeltsch, Ernst, 20, 192
   influence in Paris's ethics, 21, 22–23
Tutu, Desmond, 121, 121n1

Ubuntu philosophy, 72–73
Ultimate Being, 180, 181n24, 181n25
Umbanda, 91, 107
UNESCO, 84
Unified Black Movement, 99–100
United African Methodist Church, 150
United Native African Church, 150
University of Chicago Divinity School, 25–26
Urschel, Donna, 136

The Vagina Monologues play (Ensler), 68
"Values and Experiences That All African Peoples Share" presentation (Paris), 128–29n16, 128–30
virtue(s), 18
   of African Americans, 18
   Aristotle's understanding of, 124
   of beneficence, 127
   of erotic love, 176
   ethics, 125
   of forbearance, 127
   of forgiveness, 78–79, 127–28
   of improvisation, 127
   justice, 128, 181
   Platonic pedagogy of, 177
   as points of convergency, 126–28
   of practical wisdom, 127
   of thought, 177–78
Vita, Kimpa, 148–49

Wadell, Paul, 174
Wakes, Nakiya, 82, 83
Walker, Alice, 210–11
Walls, Andrew F., 1–2, 164, 169

Wariboko, Nimi, 4, 8–9, 74–75
West, Cornel, 15, 22
white supremacy, 49
   Cone's statement, 76
   consequence of, 86
   in North America, 35n4
Williams, Delores, 210, 211
Williams, Henry Sylvester, 213
Wilmore, Gayraud, 214
Wilson, Donald, 207
Womack, Deanna Ferree, 2
Woman, Cradle of Abundance. *See Femme, Berceau De L'abondance (FEBA)*
women
   in African Christianity, 158–59
   Afro-Brazilian, 100
   environmental racism voices, 82, 83–84
   feminist ethical thought, 182–83
   Maman Monique's covenant of violence against, 55–56
   in Pentecostalism, 158
   solidarity with, 61
   theology at Union, 210–11
World Alliance of Reformed Churches. *See* World Communion of Reformed Churches
World Communion of Reformed Churches, 60
World Council of Churches (WCC), 60, 61, 152
   Fifth Assembly at Nairobi, 167
World Student Christian Federation (WSCF), 207

Yong, Amos, 91n5
Yoruba Beliefs and Sacrificial Rites (Awalalu), 209
"Young Achievers" organization, 195

Zondi, Mlondolozi, 49–50

www.ingramcontent.com/pod-product-compliance
Lightning Source LLC
Chambersburg PA
CBHW051639230426
43669CB00013B/2362